Vivid and Repulsive as the Truth

The Early Works of Djuna Barnes

Edited and with an Introduction by
Katharine Maller

Dover Publications, Inc., Mineola, New York

Bibliographical Note

This Dover edition, first published in 2016, is a new compilation of short works and illustrations by Djuna Barnes, reprinted from authoritative sources. Katharine Maller has made the selection and has written an Introduction and a Note on the Sources specially for this edition.

Library of Congress Cataloging-in-Publication Data

Names: Barnes, Djuna, author. | Maller, Katharine, editor, writer of
  introduction.
Title: Vivid and repulsive as the truth : the early works of Djuna Barnes /
  Djuna Barnes; edited and with an introduction by Katharine Maller.
Description: Mineola, New York : Dover Publications, 2016.
Identifiers: LCCN 2016011698 | ISBN 9780486805597 (paperback) |
  ISBN 048680559X
Subjects: | BISAC: LITERARY COLLECTIONS / General.
Classification: LCC PS3503.A614 A6 2016 | DDC 818/.5209—dc23 LC record
  available at https://lccn.loc.gov/2016011698

Manufactured in the United States by LSC Communications
80559X03   2019
www.doverpublications.com

Introduction

I FIRST CAME across Djuna Barnes quite by chance, which is the way I think she'd have preferred it. I found her through the company she kept—at the time, I was researching the culture and writing of Paris in the 1920s, particularly the lesbian literary scene. One thing led to another, and by a few pages into *The Ladies Almanack* I was so struck by her wit and art that I was determined to read everything of hers I could get my hands on. Of course, I decided this before realizing just how much Barnes wrote in her lifetime. (I'm still very much in the process of reading her oeuvre.)

This volume of output was, at least in part, spurred on by necessity. Barnes was born in 1892 to an untraditional household—she lived with her grandmother, Zadel, who was a literary giant in her own right and with whom Djuna was incredibly close; her mother, Elizabeth; her father, Wald; and her father's mistress, Fanny. Elizabeth became increasingly frustrated by her marital situation, and, in 1912, she asked her husband to choose between her and Fanny. He chose Fanny, and Elizabeth moved to the Bronx with Djuna and her other children. This move was traumatic for Djuna, not only due to the separation from Zadel, but because the family was desperately poor. It fell to Djuna to support them financially, and, beginning in 1913, she began writing and selling articles to the various papers publishing in New York.

Barnes took to journalism quickly. Her obvious talent was complemented by her blunt charisma—legend has it that she walked into the *Brooklyn Daily Eagle* offices in 1913 and said, "I can draw and write, and you'd be a fool not to hire me." Such a story seems absolutely outlandish, especially considering that she was merely twenty-one at the time, but her bravado is a constant undercurrent in her writing. It manifests itself in the ease with which she interviews some of the greatest talents of her time, in her attraction to risky news subjects (especially her stunt journalism for *The New York World*), and the frankness of her prose.

By 1915, she was earning enough money to leave her family's apartment. Her move to Washington Square immersed her in the Greenwich Village bohemian literary scene, and her writing blossomed. She found inspiration in the streets of Lower Manhattan, using them as the settings for her short fiction and the subjects of her articles, and she made the literary connections that set her career in motion. The same year she moved to the Village, Guido Bruno published her first book, *The Book of Repulsive Women*. It is in her Greenwich Village writings that we see the first echoes of the themes that would reemerge in her later significant works; namely, the grotesque nature of reality, how relationships offer respite from it, and how that respite is inconstant, temperamental, and temporary. One of the best descriptions I've read of Barnes's work came from Emily Coleman, who told Barnes: "You make horror beautiful—it is your greatest gift." That is not to say that her work is gloomy, or pessimistic. When her pieces deal with the grotesque, they rely on juxtapositions—the beautiful moments in these works shine brightly, made valuable in contrast to their opposites. And however dismal the subject matter, Barnes's wit is ever-present.

These early works are especially intriguing because they are very much of their place and time. The articles, interviews, and stories of this collection are set in a recognizable world; they are grounded in their settings, they are concrete, and they are often raw. Barnes builds a sense of space through her characters—the teens years of 1900 in New York have never felt so textured and tangible. It's a world that's long gone, but Djuna has preserved it more charmingly than a history or photo book ever could. This charm is due in part to Barnes's subjective writing style. Barnes is an active and constant presence in her journalism, and she invents much of her subjects' dialogue, imbuing it with a literary wit—*her* literary wit.

There are, of course, arguments to be made against these works. Barnes herself was loathe to see them republished and dismissed them as juvenilia because she essentially wrote them to survive. With all due respect to Barnes's wishes, I believe it would be a shame for the bulk of this work to fall into obscurity. However, being of their time includes the many unsavory views of their time: crude racism, xenophobia, and sexism. While Barnes was shockingly progressive with regard to social issues such as sexuality, in some of her articles she expressed views that, in my opinion, belong firmly in the past. I have not created a revisionist history of her work—indeed, some of the pieces included in this collection espouse views with which I'm still uncomfortable. That discomfort is important; however, some articles quote language and viewpoints that I find not only uncomfortable, but reprehensible. Rather than edit the language of these pieces, I've chosen to exclude them entirely.

In compiling this book, I strove to collect a representative sampling of these early works. I have included work from as many publications as I could access—the "note on the sources" supplement delves further into the history of these myriad publications, offering information that illuminates not only the publishing world of the early twentieth century, but also demonstrating how adaptable and prolific Barnes was as an author. In selecting an eclectic mix of journalism, fiction, and poetry, it is my hope that the reader will come away not only entertained—for these works are, above all, a pleasure to read— but with a deeper understanding of and appreciation for Djuna Barnes, the "most famous unknown author in the world."

Acknowledgments

I AM DEEPLY indebted to Douglas Messerli in the compilation of this work—as the preeminent Djuna Barnes scholar, he has laid the groundwork in bringing Barnes's work back into publication, and his bibliography of her works was an invaluable resource for this project.

I'd also like to thank John Grafton, Joann Schwendemann, Pete Lenz, Drew Ford, M.C. Waldrep, Frank Fontana, Laura and Bob Maller, and Brian Cahill Moledo for their support and encouragement.

Katharine Maller

A Note on the Sources

DJUNA BARNES'S NEW YORK is a world that no longer exists—a world of Greenwich Village bohemians and unbelievable artistic production. The publications that featured Barnes's work showcased it alongside the era's foremost modernist writers, and in doing so established her as one of their rank. As most of these publications ceased production decades ago, I compiled a list of the sources with a bit of information about each, so that you might better understand the context in which Barnes's work appeared.

All-Story Weekly (1905–1919)

All-Story Weekly was one of the many publishing ventures of Frank Munsey, who invented "pulp" magazines, which could be mass-produced on cheap pulp paper and therefore sold at a very low price. *All-Story,* also at one point titled *All-Story Cavalier Weekly,* had a bombastic and successful eleven-year run, publishing Edgar Rice Burroughs's first Tarzan stories, along with genre fiction by Rex Stout, Mary Roberts Rinehart, Abraham Merritt, and Johnston McCulley. In 1920, *All-Story* merged with another of Munsey's successful pulps, *Argosy,* which ran until 1978.

Brooklyn Daily Eagle (1841–1955)

Once the most widely circulated newspaper in the country, the *Brooklyn Daily Eagle* covered a variety of topics, from national politics to the local-color pieces that Barnes most often wrote. One of the paper's most notable features was its continued focus on Brooklyn as its own cultural entity, rather than ignoring the city-cum-borough as an extension of Manhattan—as such it played an integral part in the development of Brooklyn's unique identity. The *Eagle* successfully rebranded and renamed itself several times over the course of its history before folding in 1955 after a prolonged worker's strike.

Bruno's Weekly (1915–1916)

Short in run yet vast in impact, *Bruno's Weekly* was one of Guido Bruno's many Bohemian projects. Produced in his garret on Washington Square, the *Weekly* featured Barnes's work alongside such Modernist voices as Sadakichi Hartmann and Marianne Moore, as well as established literary giants Oscar Wilde and George Bernard Shaw. Guido Bruno supported Barnes's other endeavors as well— her book of poetry, *The Book of Repulsive Women*, was published as part of the Bruno's Chapbooks series.

The Dial (1840–1929)

There were three major iterations of *The Dial* between its 1840 launch and the release of its final issue in 1929. It was initially a Transcendentalist journal edited by Margaret Fuller, and while the concept had promise, the journal itself had no teeth. The low subscribership could not sustain the journal, and it ran out of funding in a mere four years.

The Dial was revived in 1880 as a general political magazine. Under the leadership of Francis Fisher Browne, it achieved a reputation for a high standard both in content and design, a distinction it enjoyed until Browne's death in 1913. After floundering for a few years, *The Dial* was rebranded as a literary journal. Ezra Pound edited the journal in its first three years and established it as a major voice in the literary world. Its list of contributors is vast, but some of the most noteworthy are T.S. Eliot (*The Waste Land* debuted on its pages), W. B. Yeats, William Carlos Williams, Khalil Gibran, Amy Lowell, and e.e. cummings.

Harper's Weekly (1857–1916)

Taglined "A Journal of Civilization," *Harper's Weekly* gained notoriety for its coverage of the Civil War, during which it was the most widely read publication in the country. Along with its focus on politics, it published some of the foremost illustrators of the nineteenth century, including Thomas Nast and Winslow Homer, as well as fiction by the likes of Charles Dickens, William Thackeray, and Sir Arthur Conan Doyle. After publishing its last issue in 1916, *Harper's Weekly* merged with *The Independent,* which was then purchased by *The Outlook* in 1928—both were highly political publications.

The Little Review (1914–1929)

The Little Review has a brief-yet-bombastic history; in its fifteen-year run, it became one of the most important modernist publications in both its native United States and the world. It was created during the Chicago Literary Renaissance by Margaret Anderson. With wide-ranging topics such as fiction, poetry, and philosophy, *The Little Review* immediately made an impact on the literary scene by publishing a mixture of emerging and established modernist voices, from T.S. Eliot to William Carlos Williams, to Emma Goldman.

The magazine was cemented in history when it published James Joyce's *Ulysses* in serial, for which Margaret Anderson and *The Little Review* were sued for obscenity in 1921. While they won the trial, they were forced to publish less risqué material thereafter.

Munsey's Magazine (1889–1929)

Munsey's Magazine was the foundation of Frank Munsey's print empire. Credited as the first mass-market magazine, it was established as "a magazine of the people and for the people" and featured art, editorials, news, fiction (including the newly emerging genre of speculative fiction), and poetry. At the peak of its popularity, circulation hit a whopping 700,000 copies per month. As other publications emerged that copied *Munsey's* format, the popularity of the magazine declined. In 1929, it briefly merged with *Argosy,* another Munsey pulp, before reemerging as *All-Story Love,* a romance pulp that ran until 1955.

New York Morning Telegraph Sunday Magazine (1839–1972)

Paired with a cigarette, the *New York Morning Telegraph* was referred to as "the chorus girl's breakfast"—the paper specialized in horse-racing and Broadway. It also included general reporting on the arts

and was one of the first newspapers to offer regular coverage of film
when it was emerging as an art form. Because of the *Telegraph's*
theatrical focus, many of the articles Barnes published therein were
interviews of those in the industry, though some of her most mem-
orable cultural pieces about New York and Greenwich Village were
published in the Sunday Magazine.

New York Press (1887–1916)

New York Press had a short run—it faded into relative obscurity after
it was merged with the *New York Herald* in 1916, shortly after Djuna
Barnes published her many articles with them. In addition to Barnes,
the paper published works by Stephen Crane.

The *Press* has two enduring claims to fame: it was the first to print
and popularize the term "yellow journalism," and was the first to
call a certain New York-based baseball team "Yankees."

The (New York) Sun (1833–1950)

One of the top three New York papers during its run, *The Sun* was
a "serious" newspaper that broke ground as the first publication to
report crimes and personal news—and the first newspaper to report
on a suicide. It was also the first paper to employ reporters who
sought out stories, which revolutionized the way news was collected
and reported. The paper is most famous for publishing the 1897
editorial "Yes, Virginia, There is a Santa Claus." The paper took on
several names during its run after being bought by Frank Munsey,
but it finally ceased production in 1950 after merging with *The New
York World-Telegram.*

New York Tribune (1841–1966)

In a news world saturated with sensationalism, *The New York Tribune*
sought to be an unbiased and reliable news source. It maintained this
reputation through the 1800s, when it gave a forum to writers such
as Margaret Fuller and William Henry Fry and enjoyed the largest
circulation of any New York daily paper. The *Tribune* was hugely
influential during the Civil War, going as far as to affect battlefield
decisions. The paper merged with *The New York Herald* in 1924 to
form *The New York Herald Tribune*, which continued to publish for
another forty years before folding.

New York World (1860–1931)

New York World became a phenomenal success under the direction of Joseph Pulitzer. Sensationalism became its trademark and drew in readers—the term "yellow journalism" originated in reference to *The World*'s content. Pulitzer used his paper's notoriety to bring attention to serious issues, including immigrant affairs, drawing attention to the abuses suffered by immigrants to New York in the late nineteenth century when few other papers would. *The World* was at the forefront of journalistic innovation and trends; they employed Nellie Bly, one of the first investigative journalists, and they published the first modern crossword puzzle.

Djuna Barnes's writing style adapted perfectly to the paper's intersection of the dramatic and the newsworthy, and *The World* published some of her most enduring works, including "How it Feels to be Forcibly Fed."

Pearson's Magazine (1896–1939)

Pearson's editorial slant is evident in the authors it published, from socialist political writings by Upton Sinclair and Maxim Gorky to the speculative fiction of E. Phillips Oppenheim and H. G. Wells. Perhaps most notably, it published H. G. Wells's *War of the Worlds* in serial in the late nineteenth century.

The British publication expanded to the U.S. in 1899, at first distributing identical content before taking on a separate American editorial staff with its own editorial viewpoint. At the time Barnes was published, the magazine was under the helm of Irish writer Frank Harris.

Smart Set (1900–1930)

Subtitled "The Magazine of Cleverness," *Smart Set* was established with the goal of providing high-brow literary content; each issue included a novella along with poems and other short works. It provided a forum for many up-and-coming and unknown authors, including James Joyce (publishing two stories from *Dubliners*), F. Scott Fitzgerald, Edna St. Vincent Millay, and Aldous Huxley.

Smart Set saw several influential publishers and editors—at the time that it published Djuna Barnes's poetry, H. L. Mencken was a co-editor—before being sold to William Randolph Hearst in 1924.

Under Hearst's influence, the magazine lost its literary core and began publishing more commercial and sentimental pieces. *Smart Set* declined, readership failed to revive after several rebrands, and it finally ceased publication shortly after the stock market crash of 1929.

The Trend (1911–1915)

One of the most experimental and controversial of the era's journals, *The Trend* had no strict editorial policy; it specialized in a diverse, unpredictable content, requiring only that the writing be compelling. As such, it published an array of work, from political writing to miscellany to creative pieces. Djuna Barnes published several pieces in *The Trend*, as well as creating the cover art for a 1914 issue.

The Trend published renowned writers such as Edna Kenton, Helen Hoyt, Witter Bynner, Carl Van Vechten, Wallace Stevens, and Mina Loy before running out of funding in 1915 and largely fading from the public memory.

Vanity Fair (1913–1936)

The *Vanity Fair* of Djuna Barnes's time was a different creature than the *Vanity Fair* on newsstands today, with a greater focus on literature, culture, and society. Established by Condé Nast in 1913, it enjoyed booming success under the direction of Frank Crowninshield, Robert Benchley, Dorothy Parker, and Robert E. Sherwood. Its contributor list reads like a who's who of the early twentieth century: Thomas Wolfe, Aldous Huxley, P. G. Wodehouse, T. S. Eliot and, yes, Djuna Barnes.

Vanity Fair successfully competed with *The New Yorker* through the 1920s as an influential cultural publication, but due to declining advertising revenue throughout the Great Depression, it was merged with Vogue in 1936. The magazine was revived in 1983, and the mix of the original editorial vision of astute journalism and cultural critique with the glossy photography of contemporary publishing has resulted in renewed success.

Contents

Articles and Interviews

YOU CAN TANGO—A LITTLE—
AT ARCADIA DANCE HALL

REGINALD DELANCEY—WHICH really isn't his name at all but will do as well as any other to tack onto and distinguish this young man— lolled in a soft armchair in the window of his club on Clinton Street and scanned the evening papers. He was bored. The tips of his immaculate tan shoes shone brightly as ever; the creases in his trousers were like the prow of the *Imperator* in their incisive sharpness; but his mind was as dull as a tarnished teapot. His fashionable friends had all fled town after the international polo matches, and he was left alone to sun and solitude.

Reginald yawned and glanced carelessly at a newspaper beside his chair. "A Night in Arcadia" read the black headlines glaring at him from the floor. Arcadia? He thought a moment. He remembered now: it was all about Evangeline and broken hearts and—Longfellow, of course. Then he picked up the paper; but what he read had nothing at all to do with misfortune and shattered home. It told of the recent opening and subsequent success of a new Arcadia, a modern dance hall built under the auspices of the Social Centers Corporation—a body of men and women banded together for the absolute elimination of the old-style dance hall with its flickering gaslights and furtive faces. The Arcadia is at the corner of Saratoga Avenue and Halsey Street, and on Wednesday, Thursday, Saturday, and Sunday evenings one may dance to one's feets' content. It is all quite—but hearken unto what Reggie did, and then do thou likewise.

First of all, he cut out the article about the Arcadia. Then he went home and had dinner. He was not quite certain how he ought to dress for such a place, but he finally selected a quiet, Balkan cravat and a harmless-looking suit and, armed only with a silver-handled stick, sallied forth. When he got off the Halsey Street car at

3

the Arcadia, he was agreeably surprised. There were arc lights and electrics and even a respectable automobile chugging with satisfaction before the door. Reginald paid twenty-five cents and trotted inside. He checked his hat and stick and sat down on a comfortable chair.

"My word," he said to himself, "Longfellow's Arcadia couldn't touch this."

Which was very true, at least as far as the dancing goes. The new hall, a fireproof structure 150 × 200 feet, has a dancing space of 89 × 100 feet and a promenade twenty-five feet wide. It is a one-story building, splendidly lighted, with a seating capacity of 4,500, and it is everything that a dance hall should in every way be.

When Reggie arrived, it was about 8:29, and Bill Doxie was waxing the floor, which already shone like a mirror in sunlight. Reginald, however, was not certain of just what was in store for him, so he

BY 8.29 DOXIE WAS WAXING
THE FLOOR

asked Sydney S. Cohen, a pleasant man with a welcoming sort of smile, who is secretary and treasurer of the Social Centers Corporation.

"I say, Mr. Cohen," said Reginald, "what about these dances—the turkey, the tango, and all the rest?"

"The turkey trot is absolutely taboo, along with the bunny hug," said Mr. Cohen. "But the tango may be danced in modified form; in fact, we will have a demonstration of it tonight by professional dancers. We are endeavoring to elevate the tone of dancing and to place the dance-hall business on a clean and wholesome basis. We want particularly to attract the girls from the dance halls where liquor is sold, evil acquaintances are met, and bad habits are formed. We have already opened a hall in Newark which has received the commendation of the civic authorities, and we also run one in Philadelphia. During the winter we will run dances here four nights a week and rent the hall the other three nights."

Mr. Cohen then gave Reginald a pink pamphlet containing a list of the rules for correct dancing and announcing a list of specialties, to include a "Snookey Ookum" party, a Coney Island night, a robbers two-step, and other marvelous accompaniments of a night of dance and song.

Suddenly the orchestra of eight pieces struck up a lively tune, and immediately hundreds of gaily dressed girls and happy-looking men glided onto the floor and were two-stepping with vigor and vim. But there wasn't even so much as a wiggle of the shoulders to suggest the turkey trot. Reginald found that the sight of so many swaying bodies was infectious. He looked about for an "introducer" but found none. He was just beginning to think he would have a poor time of it after all when way off in a corner he spotted Thomas Murphy, his father's office boy. Social barriers flew out of the window. Reggie almost embraced Tom, who was quite overcome by the unexpected and, in fact, quite unbelievable appearance of his employer's son.

"Don't ask any questions," said Reggie quickly. "Introduce me—that's all."

Tom grabbed him by the arm, and the two shied into a corner.

"What's your style, eh?" asked Tom.

"Anything at all, so long as she can dance. I'm not at all particular."

As a matter of fact, Reginald was very particular—that is, with girls of his own set—but now it seemed that the one great desire of his life was to get on that floor and dance. "I know just the one," said Tom. "She sells perfume and such stuff at the Paris department

THE RULES PROHIBIT
CLOSE DANCING

store on Broadway." And before Reginald knew it, he was introduced
and found himself dancing away across the floor. It was a waltz, and
Reggie did know how to waltz; also, although he kept it dark under
his shock of bushy red hair, he knew how to turkey trot and tango
and all the rest. But Phil Post, censor, stood right in the middle of
the floor. He wore a red carnation over a white vest, and although
he seemed almost asleep with a sort of beatific look of delight, his
keen eyes kept tabs on every couple. But there was little need. It was
an awfully good crowd, Reggie thought, and the dancing was far
more polite and graceful than that done on the previous evening at
a fashionable society dance by girls of Reggie's own sort.

When the music stopped, Reggie took the girl, whose name was
Delia O'Connor, to the soda fountain, where all sorts of wonderful
mixed sundaes and frappés were served by white-coated attendants.

Although it was probable they would never meet again, they sat and soda'd together.

"Where do you work?" asked Delia confidingly.

"I—I—that is—," and Reggie swallowed a huge piece of ice cream.

"I work at the Paris," said Delia, with the air of imparting a secret. "Perfume's my line. It's something fine, too. You smell the bottles day after day, and by and by you begin to think of beautiful flowers and shady paths and goldfish. And then, lately, I have been coming here at night. Before the Arcadia opened, we used to go to the hot and stuffy movie shows. But this has that beaten to a thirty-nine-cent bargain sale on a rainy Monday." She carefully stuck out one dainty foot and stretched a bit.

Reggie laughed.

"You're really dancing now," he said. "You know, the word *dance* comes from an old High German word, *danson* which means 'to stretch,' so that what you are doing now is really a sort of dance."

"Quit throwing them cashmere bouquets," said Delia, "and let's get to that two-step."

Reggie paid ten cents for the drinks and sailed forth on the waxen sea with Delia, as lightly and trippingly as two smart yachts tacking against the wind.

And so the evening wore on. Everyone had a glorious time. The Arcadia was light and cool, the music was good, and best of all, the authorities were not too critical. One might even tango a little in a tame sort of way. The whole place was pervaded with an air of refinement and good behavior (and the men who are running it intend to keep it so). At last midnight came, the lights were lowered, and the dancers departed.

"Say, Mabel," said Delia on the way home, "I met the real frangipani sort of guy tonight. Uses three-for-a-dollar words and told me all about some Dutch dance. Never once tried to get fresh, either."

"It's the Arcadia," said Mabel, knowingly. "Everyone behaves there like a kid dolled up for Anniversary Day before the ice cream is passed."

And Reginald, back in his club, resolved to go to the Paris department store on the morrow and buy a bottle of perfume, a thing he had always considered one of the seven deadly sins of manhood.

IMPRESSIONS OF "TWINGELESS TWITCHELL" AND HIS
AWE-STRICKEN AUDITORS.

"TWINGELESS TWITCHELL" AND HIS
TANTALIZING TWEEZERS

SHAKESPEARE, WHITTLER OF epigrams, no doubt said something in some of his plays about teeth. If the truth were known beyond question, it would be found that an aching tooth in many cases has had far greater effect on the world's history than the rainfall on the eve of Waterloo (which, besides annihilating Napoleon's army, gave that dear Victor Hugo an excuse for several chapters of guerrilla philosophy in *Les Miserables*). This is a modern version of the Hugo tale.

A tooth! Its first appearance is hailed with frantic delight by the young mother and the assembled relatives; but how different its end! A book might well be written on the pathos of forgotten teeth. But after all, the purpose of this simple tale is to tell how not to suffer and not to disturb an otherwise quiet Sunday by bringing back memories of hours of dental inquisition.

But before we go any further, you must be told, just as you are always told at the beginning of every short story, that Reginald Delancey—whom you may remember meeting a few weeks ago at the Arcadia Dance Hall—was very much interested in a certain young woman whose name was Ikrima, as she was born in Turkey of a Mohammedan father who with all the wisdom inspired of a twenty-four-inch beard sent her to America to be educated. (The poor little perfumery girl with whom Reggie fell in love at the Arcadia had been abruptly deserted once Reginald discovered that she used a certain cologne, which he decided was a trifle too "racy.")

On Wednesday evening Reginald and Ikrima were strolling languidly down a street on the Heights.

"How slow the city is in summer," said Ikrima in that pretty, poutish way which always appeals to the biggest sort of men.

"Do I understand that you are seeking excitement?" asked Reginald, who always spoke in complete sentences as the result of four years at Harvard. "If I am correct in divining your intent, let us proceed at once to the next street crossing, where a somewhat large assemblage of persons leads me to believe that the unusual is either happening or about to happen."

So Reggie and Ikrima walked with stately tread to the corner.

A good-natured-looking man clad in white flannels was standing on a platform built upon the back of an ordinary touring-type automobile. At his side was a white enamel dentist chair, with all the necessary appurtenances; close by stood a table with medicine bottles and instruments that shone wickedly in the light of a flickering acetylene torch that sputtered vain protests at the darkness.

"My name is Twingeless Twitchell," the little man was saying with mighty dignity. "My business is pulling teeth, and I am frank to confess I am in it for the money I can make. There are two hundred thousand paid persons in this country to tell you how to take care of your souls, but as far as I know, I am the only man who tells you how to take care of your teeth. Yet there is as much brimstone contained in an aching tooth as there is in all the hereafter put together."

Groans rise from the crowd as each one remembers a sleepless night and a swollen face. But "Twingeless Twitchell" gives them no time to think. He holds them with his glittering instruments.

"No doubt you are wondering," he thunders forth, with a splendid gesture of deprecation, "just why I stand here upon this platform tonight discussing teeth. Well, I'll tell you."

He leans forward with the air of him who is about to tell the secret of the Sphinx.

"I'm here to collar the dollars," says Twingeless Twitchell. "I don't like the tooth-carpentering business." (Shudders run through the crowd at the expression.) "I don't believe in art for art's sake, not I. I'm the man that put the *dent* in *dentist* and the e's in *teeth*. And now I'm here to prove it. I invite anyone in this vast audience to step upon the platform and have a tooth extracted without knowing it. I know how to do it, believe me. I started to study teeth at the age of ten, and I've been at it ever since."

And Twingeless Twitchell, with a modest bow, stepped back and awaited all comers. A thrill of anticipation ran through the crowd. People in the el trains twenty feet above leaned out of the windows, entranced at the sight. A taxi went chugging by and then suddenly stopped, and a fat man alighted and joined the throng. Up above on a balcony of a beer garden, a lugubrious-looking German pointed out the enthralling sight to his stolid companion. A chic French maid came tumbling forth from a nearby millinery shop, chattering volubly in her native tongue.

"It is the spirit of the arena," said Reginald learnedly. "They all want to see a human being suffer."

"Do you really think it's twingeless?" asked Ikrima, with a memory of a tooth she left in Constantinople when a little girl.

Then, on a sudden, a hush fell over the crowd. A man, collarless, red of beard and bald of hair, mounted the steps to the platform with his eyes fixed on the glaring lights, like a rabbit that has been charmed by the bead in the python's eye.

Twingeless Twitchell placed him gently in the chair and raised the torches a little higher. The unknown folded his hands resignedly over his stomach. Then the dentist took a formidable hypodermic in his hand.

"You see, ladies and gentlemen," he explained glibly, "I take this glittering instrument, filled with my specially prepared anesthetic, and do thus," and he injected a quantity into the unknown's gum. Then he grabbed the tweezers, and with all the finesse of a skilled surgeon performing for an academy of the world's best physicians, he eliminated the aching tooth.

The unknown arose with a dazed look in his eyes. Twingeless Twitchell handed him a card with his name and address printed thereon.

"Good evening," said Twitchell, escorting his first victim to the stairway. "Next!"

But Reginald and Ikrima waited to see no more. With hurried steps they left the crowd, wondering if they had actually witnessed a painless extraction.

"I say," said Reginald, after a little, "that's—that's not a bit nice. Just like washing one's linen in public and all that sort of thing."

"That may be true," said Ikrima, "but after all it reminds one that they ought to watch out and never let such a thing be necessary. I could never marry a man who didn't have a perfect set of teeth."

The following evening, Ikrima telephoned to Reginald. The butler answered the call.

"I want to speak to Mr. Delancey," said Ikrima.

"He's not at home," said the butler.

"Where did he go?"

"To the dentist," answered the butler, who was no diplomat.

But Ikrima, with very rosy cheeks, kissed the telephone mouthpiece at the other end.

VETERANS IN HARNESS, NO. 1:
POSTMAN JOSEPH H. DOWLING,
FORTY-TWO YEARS IN SERVICE

SCENE: THE POST office on the corner of Washington and Johnson Streets. The lights are low and burn a steady blue. In the dun, the forms of moving mail carriers talking in low tones together among the great bulk of the mail-bags. Upon tall stools the clerks nod over the ink bottles and the stamps, the grated window throwing patterns on the wall, the gentle murmur of a great city putting on its nightcap outside.

Enter Joseph H. Dowling, the oldest mail carrier in service, seventy-seven in April; short and gray, his official cap pulled over his head, the empty mail pouch over his shoulder. He looks around and slowly sits down, taking his cap into his hands, the mailbag—wherein an hour before a world lay undistributed—slipping down. He speaks.

"Forty-two years in service and never a sweetheart in all the blocks I've walked. Married fifty-four years, twelve years ahead of the mails," he laughs. "It spoiled a good deal of the romance of the road, but thank the mercies that she's been spared to me along with the children—the children, and the oldest is fifty-three.

"And the changes that I've seen," he goes on. "Why, I helped build the Brooklyn Bridge. I stood under the bed of the East River and bossed men—foreman with human lives under me—and Lord, how the city grew when she started. I'd go down it seemed between tea and dinner, and when I came up they had built a block."

He passes his hand over his eyes. Back in a darkened corner a letter slides noiselessly down upon the pile of the uncollected.

"I remember the time when there were no stages in Brooklyn, and no cars, and it seemed to me as though at the reckoning there would be very little complication with nothing more intricate to record than the birth and the death of a few people who never

13

dreamed of competition. And then the cars came and the elevated went up, and then I was satisfied that there was going to be a reckoning hereafter that would involve a lot of rapid calculating.

"In the beginning I used to listen to the wheels running overhead, and I said, 'At last the world has a second floor.'

"In 1871, the year I came into service, there were only forty carriers to cover Brooklyn, running routes from the East River to Stone Avenue, from Flushing Avenue to City Line, and only two deliveries a day. At this time there were not over seventy-five men in the office—officials, carriers, and all. The post office was then a wood frame building just below the Eagle Building. Out of them all only two are left who started with me, and they are still serving as clerks.

"I served alone a route that eight men cover now; my usual delivery was about twenty-five hundred pieces. I served under nine postmasters—Samuel Booth was the first. Those were hard days, and we got fourteen hours a day, till the eight-hour day came along and gave us a second excuse for going down on our knees. Still there were some blocks to the route that we would not have taken away from us about Christmas time.

"I'm a Yankee through and through, as my folks for five generations were born, as my father before me was born, in Brooklyn, and I've lived here all my life. I used to go to school back in Adams Street, studied a map that hadn't any Brooklyn on it above a few blocks. Where the fountain now stands in front of the Borough Hall, they were building a prison, and as children we used to play hide-and-seek among the incomplete cages."

He looks about him. In the dim, blue light the mail carriers, still young, are preparing to go home. He does not see them; he has gone back to the years in which their fathers lived.

"You talk of temperamental people; there's nothing so temperamental as the mailbag. You people who know nothing of it do not understand." He touches it with reverent fingers. "Here, in this, have laid letters that spoke of love and letters that held broken hearts. When I was five minutes late in my rounds, five hundred lovers held their breath and five hundred sorrows waited to be born." He shifts in his chair.

"I wonder just how many people realize how short a time it takes to see a street full of new faces. Some blocks keep the families for generations, and then again in six months you are taking mail to strangers. It seems a bit funny when you miss the photograph that used to hang just inside the hall, the photograph of the mother in the old country. You get to connecting numbers to people—like convicts it seems—and then suddenly you realize that the number that you have seen upon the ceiling as you lie awake in bed has another family attached to it, and you have to reconstruct all your thoughts to fit it.

"Well, I have just three interests in life now: the health of my family, the coming of the pension, and continuance of the widow and orphans fund. I'm president of it, and I think about that more than anything else."

The room is empty of life, but still the blue lights burn on, and the mailbags throw shadows across the floor.

He rises, his hat in his hand. "The saddest thing in life is the bringing of the black-bordered envelope." He nods. "Aye, the black envelope. And the brightest thing is my home."

He steps out into the night.

VETERANS IN HARNESS, NO. 2: CONDUCTOR "KID" CONNORS, FORTY YEARS RINGING UP FARES

SCENE: THE TRACKS along Meeker Avenue. Year: 1913. Time: 3:30, any day. (Incidental remark: It was some job getting Connors on the run.)

John Kelley, "Kid" Connors's motorman, comes along on the front deck of a trolley car, power and brake handle in hand; old, too, and "wise in his craft."

Swinging upon a strap, as his ancestors swung a thousand years ago when a wind swept through the jungle, pitched with the mincing step of his trade, the unsteady floor of a running car, is "Kid" Connors, Brooklyn's veteran conductor.

"I'm ringing up the fares," he says, "and it's many a character I've rung up on my memory. It's the cars that have made America. The swaying, swinging, six-wheel cars, the jumping, rolling, rock-a-bye, four-wheel cars, the yellow-nosed cars that poke their noses through the fog over the Brooklyn Bridge, little flaunting cars creeping along like glowworms upon a terrace vine. The cars give you humanity; in a way, you get it on the jump.

"Born in 1847, I came from County Wexford. I was young and timid then. My friends got me a place on the railroad. I did not think I would stay; that was forty-one years ago," he laughs, passing his hand across his chin. "The tracks that run around the world bind us tight; there's many a man who can thank the car for his business career. The car takes your self-consciousness out of you, it makes you unafraid, you meet everyone; the car is the universal doorstep."

The chink of coins is followed by the ring of the register; it is pacifying, this murmur of money, amid the din of heavily laden trucks and the sounds of a noisy city from streets full of color. Out of the speeding car's windows are streets full of red petticoats that bring the crimson to the puddles among the cobbles; full of drab shawls and nearly bare feet, of pleading brown hands tense with the lust of barter.

Above this the ancient land mariner hears the question: "Have you ever rung up any hearts?"

"No, there's no time for the registry of love on the cars; the cars mean work and the game of beating the clock."

The car slows up across the city in a winding line of black, carriage on carriage, following the nodding plumes of slow-stepping horses. The conductor nods toward the cortege. "He used to ride on this car every morning and evening. He got to his home in five minutes, the way I used to run. He's going home today, but he won't make the run in schedule time."

The car moves once more.

"When we started—that was in the panic of '72—we worked fourteen hours a day with twelve minutes for dinner and only made about $2.50 at that. The first car ran on Myrtle Avenue one sunny afternoon in '54. As the city grows, so the railroad grows.

"The first route I served regularly was Graham Avenue. I served nearly thirty-three years on that. For eight years now I've run Meeker." Kid Connors paused upon his strap, a heavy man with a good hold upon optimism. If no world trembled at the touch of his hand, his hand has not trembled at the knocks of the world.

"When I first started, they had some very hard rules. Oh, you had to be on time in those days. If I reported a minute late for duty, I lost my run and went to the bottom of the list, had to wait for the promotion of the man ahead, or for death or some other incident that would gradually bring me back into the order of the list. We had shorter swings, too; now we get from an hour-and-a-half to three hours swing. A swing, you know, is time off for lunch between runs. Everything changed with the coming of the transfer system, about ten years ago. Now we get paid by the hour; we get longer swings, and we can be late four times before we get dropped to the bottom of the list.

"Does life change with the years? Of course it does. Everything changes in quantity, not in quality. The people are about the same; I'm carrying a former patron's son now on the cars that I know is his son from his likeness. Nothing changes but the growth in population and the younger strata that comes in.

MICHAEL CONNORS

Bjorn Braner

"Am I content? Of course I am. I'm so happy that I don't feel that I need my picture taken; in fact, I have not had one taken in over forty years. When a man is fearless of time, he does not heed to preserve his looks against discontent."

He looks out, a smile upon his face. "I never made a night run, though that's the easiest—fewer people riding, and the dark in the city makes it seem less like a job.

"And what have I to say for the people? The people that ride on the cars are not the gruff, disagreeable-mannered beings they are reported to be. Nearly always the man will give up his seat for a woman, and if she has children and he wants to compromise on comfort of mind along with comfort of body, he takes the kid or kids upon his knee.

"Some men that railroaded with me ride in their autos now, but all I have is experience and an arm full of stars." He extends his left arm, on which gleam five golden emblems of service: the first represents twenty-five years, the others five years apiece.

"When shall I retire? Not until I cannot see, or until I lose the power in my legs. While I'm here, the cars are Kid Connors's and Kid Connors belongs to the cars."

VETERANS IN HARNESS, NO. 3:
WAITER PATRICK DUNNE, FORTY
YEARS CARRYING A TRAY

SCENE: THE SITTING room of a Brooklyn hotel. The evening is advancing, and the twilight creeps about the pink candle shades upon little tables. The dull brown of oak and the gloom of dark corners are broken where the light sparkles on the rounded sides of a cut-glass punch bowl, little sharp-edged tumblers, and groups of silver. The smoke of myriad cigars, the household cloud of civilization, blots out the ceiling.

Waiters are hurrying about with the napkins of their trade upon their arms, balancing polished trays the shape of half-circles, endeavoring to carry all the edibles on one journey.

Enter Patrick Dunne, tall, cleanshaven, well preserved, well groomed, well satisfied—welcome. He speaks.

"Oh, this is the season for business. The sense of cold outside, and then the lights burning behind lace, the odor of the roast and bay leaves and flowers can't be resisted. Summer is all very well, but winter is the time for prosperity. Tips! That's when the tips come in."

Patrick smiles and shifts his napkin along his arm.

"When did I start? Forty years ago. Born in '52, in Kings County, Ireland; stopped there twenty years, and now I have been in Kings County, New York, forty more years.

"I began as a railroad man; and winter, my delight now, was my misery then. I was too cold. So I broke into the waiter job, served six years in a private family, and since then, excepting for a short time, I have held one position.

"When a chap applies for a waiter's job, he has to start at the bottom, just like any other man, by carrying away the dirty dishes, bringing in the water and butter, and setting the tables. The waiter

20

apprentice is known as the 'bus.' I never had to begin this way because I was in the wine business in the old country, and I had a way with me that they liked.

"I used to have very long hours, but since an illness of three or four years back, I have had beautiful hours." He nods. The word "beautiful" expresses his sense of complete satisfaction. "And," he adds, "I get the same pay. Just come up from twelve to two and from four to six. The rest of the day is mine."

"How have you kept so young?"

"By going home at six."

"What do you do from two to four?"

"Keep in good company; take an interest in someone else's opinion of things—and laugh."

He moves away, coming back presently with a contented air. "There have been two or three great days in my life. If a person has to live a great day, let him live it in a dining room—a public, popular dining room. If he wants to know what a real big day is like, let him be a waiter. That's the way to realize it all.

"I remember when the Brooklyn Bridge opened. All New York came over, just to say they had ridden the rails, and they were hungry, of course. I'd hate to try to convince you how many people I served that day. It was grand. I can only think what it would have been like if there had been two bridges opened instead of one.

"I've served some very interesting people in my time—men like Henry Ward Beecher, Judge Fullerton, J. J. Hill, and all the Beecher lawyers. They were a jolly bunch, even though there was a great trial in progress.

"Dinner has a strange effect upon the world—a leveling, humanizing effect. The spirit of the dining room is one of cheerfulness, and if they are not exactly happy, the diners smile that way because everyone else is smiling. The evening is the best part of the day. A different class comes in at twelve—mostly businessmen, who are almost too busy to think and too busy to be content. But in the evening everyone laughs. Those people appreciate you better, think more of your service, are pleased with themselves, and let a little of that satisfaction run out to you. Of course, they are the hardest to please because their women are with them, and they are particular. At twelve they grab at the menu and order anything, nearly, and eat it with their mind on the stock market or on the political tangle. But in the evening their minds are on their companions, and these companions must be well fed. So they are particular; they linger longer, for they know that a whole evening is between them and the next day's work."

"Don't you ever get hungry, serving so many nice and tempting things?"

"No; I don't get a chance to get hungry. You see, I'm on good terms with the cook; that is——" Patrick hastily puts a crease down the center of the white napkin.

"And do you intend to go on serving all your life? Are you not going to retire?"

"What should I retire for? Does a man retire from his skin or his hearth? I like the job. I think it would be wise if more young men took it up as a profession and tried to do well by it as a profession and did not consider it lowering. It has many a big problem in it, and it can be done ill or well, according to the way the waiter feels about it.

"I like it. The only place I am not waiter is at home. My wife is head waiter there. I would not give up my job to anyone but my wife."

THE WILD AGUGLIA
AND HER MONKEYS

MIMI AGUGLIA HAS entered into America as spice and pepper into a good pot roast. Into the world of cutlery has come a sharper knife. Into the well-ordered life of our society a human has catapulted some hundred pounds of passionate flesh. The devil is inadequate in his absolute grandeur when Mimi sleeps.

Back behind scenes, where the blue of Herod's court lay chilly upon wilted palms that clung to dingy netting, the tropics just out of mothballs, Mimi Aguglia spoke of a temperamental world. "You have such beautiful, calm women in America; yes, and so simply gowned, and they do not have to marry because the family says so, and they do not have to stay in the house all day and wish they were born men that they might enter politics. The suffragist, ah!" The shoulders go up in a violent shrug. "The suffrage is not good for the woman; it is less good for the artist. Let the men do something, eh?" This very naively. "I have children. Off the stage I'm a good mother; on, I am, I hope, a good actress. Always I love the animals, and oh! the lion Diaz gave me—I hug him so.

"I do not want the American to think I like only tragedy. I like the comedy; but the comedy depends upon the word, and I cannot make you understand. I'm going to begin with the less subtle emotions, so!"

The long, dark eyes, with their sudden flashes of white, glinted like the sun between two sullen borderlands. With the same inscrutable calm she watched the monkeys, the company's monkeys, the company with six Aguglias on the program; the company which was entirely married and bids fair to become a Hippodrome production if multiplication continues at the present rate of speed.

Metallic Impressions

In a quarter of an hour she was due as Salome, and yet she gathered handsful, armsful, of monkeys to her, and cried over them in Italian and spoke of the good spaghetti.

Then she stood before the public, palpitating in fine, small shivers, elemental emotions and spangled net.

Slowly, with feet that curled, she came, browned and spangled, and shaking with tinsel, blue in the blue light of the court, swaying prophetically.

She took her balance on the brink of the well and offered John her soul in all the shapes that a heroically tragic woman could offer it, and was scorned. From every staccato scream, from every sudden-reached crescendo of misery, from every backward head shake and every troubled posture, in every lunge and the spasms of her dancing, she was getting her pride back. This was the epic of undulating spaghetti, turmoil of tragic chiffon, damp spurning feet. The back-thrust head, the lure and the scorn and the contempt and the desire of scarlet lips. And, then, the fight on the mat.

There wasn't much left of John to gurgle over, only the matted, tousled hair that maddened her fingers into hazy shakings, and sudden darts and halts of the greedy palm. Then the cry and the tightening of the already taut body, with head and arms and passion in the platter. The very climax of Mimi Aguglia's art of expression.

Silence, as she lies there, a figure before a head, contemplating the unresistance of resisting lips, and then the obeyed command, as twenty arms crash down upon her frail omnipotence. The overturned victory, the scream of death realized; woman-churned ether, and two straight, clutching hands dragging down sheer set jaws. The end of the oblique eyes, the soft sound of a woman's body threshing the inevitable, and—back to the monkeys again.

"I COULD NEVER BE LONELY WITHOUT A HUSBAND," SAYS LILLIAN RUSSELL

IN WALKS LILLIAN Russell.

Six bounteous ruffles gird her at the knees, white duchess laces enhance the splendor of her throat, the odor of Eastern incense lies heavy on everything. Grotesque potentates, squatting, smirk over their imprisoned rose leaves and myrrh; the switching tail of a sun god moves restlessly in the corner where long silken, dust-somber draperies shut out the light from Broadway.

I could just make her out in the dim room, sitting over there in the corner upon a wide chair like a throne, just make out the high-piled drift of gold that is her hair, the still beautiful eyes, only half-claimed from youth, the smiling mouth that has expressed all that can live within a black satin gown.

I leaned forward. I did not like to shatter the silence that was unbroken save for the spit-spitting of a chafing dish somewhere in a rear room.

The roses in the vase spilled a purple gloom upon the floor. Even then I could not have spoken, but from somewhere I caught the sound of a clock.

"All this is very mysterious and wonderful," I said, nodding toward the Eastern decorations in the room. "Do you believe, Miss Russell, that surroundings affect us?"

"More than anything," she said softly, "more than inheritance, more than inclination, more than one can really comprehend. If our vacant society would do with less gilt upon their chairs, they might donate more gold to their store of wisdom. These surroundings just tally up to the best that's in me. I am deeply contented when alone, without the sense of the hurry of the present day. I lift up a porcelain Buddha and hold him in my hand; it is peace to me, happiness. I

26

could never be lonely without a husband, but without my trinkets, my golden gods, I could find abysmal gloom."

"What, then, do you think the surroundings of a Huerta should be."

"A comprehensive circle of guns," she replied without a minute's hesitation. She leaned forward and, cupping her hands, drew into them a wilted rose. I was beginning to make more headway in the Eastern twilight that had lodged upon one floor of an apartment house in Manhattan, and I could see what she must have been twenty years ago by what she was now.

The singing of passionate notes had made her chest a little deep, so that she swayed like a great, languorous harebell. She had a home, and could not be called a housewife; she had a husband, and could not be called adoring, for more than anything else, Miss Russell has acquired poise.

I asked her about her home life.

"I am as well contented with an apartment as a home. So many times I have read that the real home cannot be found in apartments, and I know better, because I've found mine. You can be just as happy as you like in any sort of apartment, providing you have the apartment spirit. Of course the best and the most agreeable place to double up and become domestic is in a nice large house; but here, all I have to do is reach out my arm, this way, and pass James the butter, and out this way, and close the piano for the night.

"All I have to do to pass on my thoughts to my husband is to think. I don't have to speak. That makes a great difference, I can assure you. So many pleasing episodes of one's life are spoiled by shouting. You never heard of an unhappy marriage unless the neighbors have heard it first."

"But," said I, "haven't you any violent views about anything?"

"Ah, yes—the Panama Canal controversy! When I think of any other country meddling with the thing that we have suffered and worked for, I become furious. It incenses me; it puts me into a black rage. I could do war; I could fulfill the portent of a six-inch gun; I could make death telling—oh, I am passionate about this, because I know, I have been down there. To some people it is a mere ditch with a network of steel. It is a valley of shadows out of which America has come, and it is interlaced with blood and tears, and I cannot think of it without losing control.

"It has become beautiful, from a vermin-racked town. Now they are proud of their hospitals. Not a patient in them—that's a record."

"But," I inquired, "have you no violent views nearer home?"

"Not that I can recall at present, unless it is my occasional visits to the kitchen. I have to be pretty determined to get there; my cook does not like me to mess about, but I have a particular passion for mushrooms, you know. Wait, I'll give you the recipe, then you poor, deluded persons may really discover what heaven is dished up in onions.

"Put a lump of butter in a chafing dish (or a saucepan) and a slice of Spanish onion and the mushrooms minus the stem; let them simmer until all are deliciously tender and the juice has run from them—about twenty minutes should be enough—then add a cupful of cream; let this boil. After it has come to a boil, squeeze in the juice of a lemon. There you are; that's the only way in the world to cook them, and it's the only way that you will want them after you have had them that way once."

"But fancy," said I, "if you had a date that evening!"

"Oh, you're worrying about the onion. It is no longer an onion when the cream and the lemon have been added; not an onion, but an epic."

At this juncture entered a square of white linen and a ruffle, that reminder of social, as well as domestic obligations, accompanied by a freshly framed painting of a dog.

"It's French," Miss Russell commented, turning, about to scrutinize it, a yard-square stretch of canvas supporting a morsel of velvet cushion, and upon this a little irreproachable island, a mere penwiper of a long-haired dog with a plaintive look in the eyes that came of breeding.

It was one of those poodle pups who, after a long bolt upon the road of progress, has selected his mother and father so well that he has been considered a thoroughbred and therefore worthy of a yard square of canvas.

"Take it away," she said presently and returned to the conversation. "That was my only pet; he died a little while ago. I have had no pets since. I cannot bear to have caged birds and I don't care for cats, and I can't keep horses up here and I won't have another dog, so you understand the reason for the lack of other moving bodies other than myself."

"And about suffrage?"

"I was brought up on mother's milk and suffrage. Don't you know that my mother was the famous Cynthia Leonard, who ran for

Sitting Over There in the Wide Chair Like a Throne

President years ago? Ah, yes, I'm for suffrage and hope that it comes soon in my time, so that I can vote, and I'll vote good and stiffly."

"What about the modern dressing?"

"Wonderful! What more sensible than modern clothes? No binding, no nonsense, nothing extra, just sufficient and an end, just becoming and dignified, just normal and healthy and sane."

"Well, then, what about the modern dances?"

"Splendid! Much prettier and more healthful than the old-fashioned dances. I believe in them. They will not die; they are here to stay, they should stay, and they will stay. A few variations, perhaps, a few new steps, but otherwise the same, excepting the dip; that will die, it is not graceful, not interesting, not even indecent; it will die."

"Well, then, don't you think at least something is going to the dogs, Miss Russell—surely some one thing?"

"I can't think of a single thing. Let me see—with women in the world how can things go to the dogs."

"Then you firmly believe in the women?"

"I never find a single fault with a woman. I can give the men a jolly calling down at times, but my sisters, they are splendid, they have such great ideals, even if they are tied into knots by husbands; they have aspirations even if they have not as yet learned to walk on the outer side of the street."

"But the thing that's going to the dogs?" I reminded her.

"But I can't think of anything that is going to the dogs really and truly. I think that America is about all right and the rest of the time I work. When a woman is busy she hasn't time to fasten the straps about the wrists of the infamous. When one is busy cultivating roses she cannot speculate on cactus."

And then she thanked me.

"What for?" I inquired.

"For not having asked me a single question about the way I preserve my good looks. Everyone always asks that first. For a few minutes you have let me forget my face, and I want to forget it. I get very tired of it—very, very tired of it. I hate a mirror sometimes.

"What, after all, is there great in being beautiful? To be a great woman, a great person, one must have suffered, even as our women in Panama suffered, as our women have suffered in great crises. What have I done that I should be famous—nothing but powdered a bit gently the cheeks that God gave me and smoothed the hair that I was born with, laughed and proven a faultless set of teeth. Any grinning idol, well painted, can do as well, but the real women, the big women, are those who toil and never write of it, those who labor and never cry of it, those who forfeit all and never seek reward. Begin this article with the name of Lillian Russell, but end it with the name of such as was Cynthia Leonard."

Out of the purple dusk I walked, and the simple-minded porcelain Chinaman smirked at me from the piano, and the wise-mouthed sun god rolled sightless eyes toward the peacock feathers and the array of silver mugs, and the incense rolled on and up about the chair like a throne with its burden like a queen.

MY SISTERS AND I AT A
NEW YORK PRIZEFIGHT

"A LARGE PERCENTAGE of the spectators were women."

This bald statement of fact had repeatedly caught my eye and attention from the sporting pages of many newspapers.

Friends had several times asked me, "Have you noticed that, of late, women have taken to attending boxing matches?" I had not noticed it, but I wished to if it were fact.

Therefore, one night I found myself at Far Rockaway and in Brown's Athletic Club. Far Rockaway, which lies some fourteen to sixteen miles up Long Island, is scarcely more than half-an-hour's journey from the homes of Manhattan. It is within the boundaries of the city of New York and has many beautiful summer residences occupied by New York families. The clubhouse stands a few feet from the railroad, inconspicuous, dun colored, crouching.

A man leans at the ticket window with its admission prices painted in red. Women stop before him, hesitate for the fraction of a second, then, putting down the two dollars required for a ringside ticket, pass on slowly, their faces set in a smile. The man at the window does not even raise his eyebrows.

Out in a beer garden, empty chairs are leaning across tabletops on which brown pools, now run dry, trace fantastic memorials of past feasts. Beyond, through a blue mist of tobacco smoke, gleam rows of human faces, and feminine laughter rings out in a shrill, piercing scale. I, a woman, join the others and watch the women come.

They do not appear self-conscious, nor is there anything in their behavior to indicate that the situation is unusual. They look indifferently upon the raised square with its shivering, taut ropes, its limp towels and scarred brown pails, the stools in the corner, the sponge in its pool of water that widens ever and drips to the floor below. And they finger their chatelaines and speak of the boxers' build.

The men who make up the audience are opulent and portly; they smoke cigars; their hands, gesticulating, gleam with a flash of diamonds. The women are frail, slender-throated, swathed in the dainty trickery of silk and crepe.

This was the first set of three four-round bouts, with "Black" Lahn and Mike Rosen to lead off; two ten-round bouts to follow; and the last and star feature to be between Phil Bloom and "Young" Gradwell.

Across the bare ground walks the referee, the turn of his head indicating expectancy and importance. Life for him, at its most exciting, lies within the space encompassed by the ropes. Men have trodden greater fields than this but never did chest expand with more conscious pride.

And now the scene, enveloped in still-denser haze, seems to grow more and more remote. The lights appear dim, further off. You sense a long, low line of heads—those of the men hatted or with rumpled hair, those of the women elaborately coiffured, oddly incongruous. At intervals through the blue-gray of the smoke the red of a cigar tip glows brilliantly, smolders, and glows again. And from within the enclosure of the ropes a white arm flashes as its owner thrusts out one hand for the glove or submits to the scurrying rubs of zealous, eager seconds.

"A fine, clean-cut fellow," says one man behind me; and another, "Look at the muscles of his back!" But a woman says, softly, "He has fine eyes."

Then these two, whose names are scarcely heard—for their fight is a mere episode preceding an event—stand out to play their part, the simplest and most human that the evening is to see. As they grip hands, eyes measure carefully, muscle for muscle. Then, with a sudden squaring of the jaws, they start the game.

After a sudden, uneasy stir, the crowd settles down to watch. Some lean forward with hands, palms outward, thrust between their knees. Others lean back, with arm extended over another's chair. But the women who dared the ringside and the girls further back sit rigidly upright, balanced between wonder and apprehension, their faces still set in a fixed smile, as of a man beheaded while a joke still hovered in his throat.

As the worst part of death is not the dead but those that mourn, so it is not the boxer that is horrifying but the crowd that knows no mercy and seeks but sensation. Through the cry that goes up the boxers close on each other, chins thrust out, wary, watching, alert. They come to a lock, where head meets breast. They move stiffly, jerkily. Then the slap of the referee's bare hand resounds on naked flesh; they are thrust apart; then they meet again.

And each one of us, meanwhile, sits motionless, scarce permitting a breath to pass our lips.

Then, like a bird thrown helpless against the bars of a cage, one of them is hurled against the ropes. With wet, shaking limbs he strives to regain his footing. He strikes out, but his fists feel no shock of contact. His antagonist becomes a blank; his arm muscles seem numbed. But he still fights on, and to the audience his arms, moving ceaselessly and ineffectually, seem like the branches of a tree caught in the fury of the blast. A low groan escapes him as he vainly endeavors to combat this overwhelming force. Then comes an abrupt stillness. He hears the taunts of the crowd, but they do not affect him. Only a great loneliness, a sense of complete isolation, fills him as he slowly sinks to the floor.

And there stands the victor, looking around with dulled eyes. In the last few seconds he has lost touch with his surroundings; they merged for him into a swaying, struggling figure on whom he was expanding all the might of his muscles. He runs his fingers along the top of his belt and taps it gravely, as if to assure himself that he is not in a dream.

The referee is bending close to the man who is down but who still, seemingly, refuses to accept his fate. Sprawling on his knees, head bent on supporting hands, he strives for breath. The referee stoops lower, his mouth now close to the boxer's ear. He begins to count—"One, two, three"—in a voice loud and full of command, as if he would like to tell the boy to get up and try again. But the figure on the ground only sways to and fro; he is no longer a fighter but a great and bewildered pain.

"Seven, eight, nine."—the referee straightens up, and feet first, they carry the lad through the ropes to the oblivion beyond the ring. He has failed.

"God!" says one woman softly. Another, sitting wedged between brother and husband, argues hotly upon the relative merits of the fighters. A third, just behind her, who has never ceased to smile picks up the ribs of a broken fan.

You realize presently that a man dressed in white is selling ginger beer and ice-cream cones. Then there are some who can even now wish to eat!

The star bout comes at last. The glove is laced into place once more; another arm is rubbed with alcohol. Gradwell bends back for the douse of the sponge; Bloom thrusts his face out to receive the forward swish of water thrown from an adept hand. Drops of it fall on our faces like drops of rain—a boxer's baptism.

They shake hands.

All the men are aware from the beginning that Bloom has the best of it; somehow they know the things that count in the game, and their interest is proportionate to their knowledge. But the woman's interest lies not in strength but in beauty. She is on the side of the boxer who has a certain trick of the head, a certain curve of the chin, a certain line from throat to brow.

Why try to describe it? The star bout was not the one in which the human game was played. The first round was the same as the last—a listless, apathetic battling of two who seemed very tired, very weary, who climbed over the ropes in the end only a trifle more tired than they had come.

For them the battle had lost its zest. The shock of clashing bodies no longer roused the blood. It was a business, not a sport, and the human element of the first amateur bout was lacking in this more finished contest.

In the blank pause that followed the finish, a man suddenly struck a match. It illumined a face drawn, paler than it had been, with eyes more heavily lidded. The match went out, and I was left to puzzle and question.

Was it, after all, the men in the audience who had been careless and indifferent to pain? Was it the sound of a snapping fan that I had heard? Was it a woman's voice that had murmured, "He has fine eyes?" A woman's hand that had gripped my arm in the dark? A woman's breath that had ceased so suddenly?

And whose voice was it that had cried out just before the finish— "Go to it, and show us that you're men?"

HOW IT FEELS TO BE FORCIBLY FED

I HAVE BEEN forcibly fed!

In just what relation to the other incidents in my life does this one stand? For me it was an experiment. It was only tragic in my imagination. But it offered sensations sufficiently poignant to compel comprehension of certain of the day's phenomena.

The hall they took me down was long and faintly lighted. I could hear the doctor walking ahead of me, stepping as all doctors step, with that little confiding gait that horses must have returning from funerals. It is not a sad or mournful step; perhaps it suggests suppressed satisfaction.

Every now and then one of the four men that followed turned his head to look at me; a woman by the stairs gazed wonderingly—or was it contemptuously—as I passed.

They brought me into a great room. A table loomed before me; my mind sensed it pregnant with the pains of the future—it was the table whereon I must lie.

The doctor opened his bag, took out a heavy, white gown, a small white cap, a sheet, and laid them all upon the table.

Out across the city, in a flat, frail, coherent yet incoherent monotone, resounded the song of a million machines doing their bit in the universal whole. And the murmur was vital and confounding, for what was before me knew no song.

I shall be strictly professional, I assured myself. If it be an ordeal, it is familiar to my sex at this time; other women have suffered it in acute reality. Surely I have as much nerve as my English sisters? Then I held myself steady. I thought so, and I caught sight of my face in the glass. It was quite white; and I was swallowing convulsively.

And then I knew my soul stood terrified before a little yard of red rubber tubing.

The doctor was saying, "Help her upon the table."

He was tying thin, twisted tapes about his arm; he was testing his instruments. He took the loose end of the sheet and began to bind me: he wrapped it round and round me, my arms tight to my sides, wrapped it up to my throat so that I could not move. I lay in as long and unbroken lines as any corpse—unbroken, definite lines that stretched away beyond my vision, for I saw only the skylight. My eyes wandered, outcasts in a world they knew.

It was the most concentrated moment of my life.

Three of the men approached me. The fourth stood at a distance, looking at the slow, crawling hands of a watch. The three took me not unkindly, but quite without compassion, one by the head, one by the feet; one sprawled above me, holding my hands down at my hips.

All life's problems had now been reduced to one simple act—to swallow or to choke. As I lay in passive revolt, a quizzical thought wandered across my beleaguered mind: This, at least, is one picture that will never go into the family album.

Oh, this ridiculous perturbation!—I reassured myself. Yet how imagination can obsess! It is the truth that the lights of the windows— pictures of a city's skyline—the walls, the men, all went out into a great blank as the doctor leaned down. Then suddenly the dark broke into a blotch of light, as he trailed the electric bulb up and down and across my face, stopping to examine my throat to make sure I was fully capable of swallowing.

He sprayed both nostrils with a mixture of cocaine and disinfectant. As it reached my throat, it burned and burned.

There was no progress on this pilgrimage. Now I abandoned myself. I was in the valley, and it seemed years that I lay there watching the pitcher as it rose in the hand of the doctor and hung, a devilish, inhuman menace. In it was the liquid food I was to have. It was milk, but I could not tell what it was, for all things are alike when they reach the stomach by a rubber tube.

He had inserted the red tubing, with the funnel at the end, through my nose into the passages of the throat. It is utterly impossible to describe the anguish of it.

The hands above my head tightened into a vise, and like answering vises the hands at my hips and those at my feet grew rigid and secure.

Unbidden visions of remote horrors danced madly through my mind. There arose the hideous thought of being gripped in the tentacles of some monster devil fish in the depths of a tropic sea, as the liquid slowly sensed its way along innumerable endless passages that seemed to traverse my nose, my ears, the inner interstices of my throbbing head. Unsuspected nerves thrilled pain tidings that racked the area of my face and bosom. They seared along my spine. They set my heart at catapultic plunging.

An instant that was an hour, and the liquid had reached my throat. It was ice cold, and sweat as cold broke out upon my forehead.

Still my heart plunged on with the irregular, meaningless motion that sunlight reflected from a mirror casts upon a wall. A dull ache grew and spread from my shoulders into the whole area of my back and through my chest.

The pit of my stomach had lapsed long ago, had gone out into absolute vacancy. Things around began to move lethargically; the electric light to my left took a hazy step or two toward the clock, which lurched forward to meet it; the windows could not keep still. I, too, was detached and moved as the room moved. The doctor's eyes were always just before me. And I knew then that I was fainting. I struggled against surrender. It was the futile defiance of nightmare. My utter hopelessness was a pain. I was conscious only of head and feet and that spot where someone was holding me by the hips.

Still the liquid trickled irresistibly down the tubing into my throat; every drop seemed a quart, and every quart slid over and down into space. I had lapsed into a physical mechanism without power to oppose or resent the outrage to my will.

The spirit was betrayed by the body's weakness. There it is—the outraged will. If I, playacting, felt my being burning with revolt at this brutal usurpation of my own functions, how they who actually suffered the ordeal in its acutest horror must have flamed at the violation of the sanctuaries of their spirits.

I saw in my hysteria a vision of a hundred women in grim prison hospitals, bound and shrouded on tables just like this, held in the rough grip of callous warders while white-robed doctors thrust rubber tubing into the delicate interstices of their nostrils and forced into their helpless bodies the crude fuel to sustain the life they longed to sacrifice.

Science had at last, then, deprived us of the right to die.

Still the liquid trickled irresistibly down the tubing into my throat.

Was my body so inept, I asked myself, as to be incapable of further struggle? Was the will powerless to so constrict that narrow passage to the life reservoir as to dam the hated flow? The thought flashed a defiant command to supine muscles. They gripped my throat with strangling bonds. Ominous shivers shook my body.

"Be careful—you'll choke," shouted the doctor in my ear.

One could still choke, then. At least one could if the nerves did not betray.

And if one insisted on choking—what then? Would they—the callous warders and the servile doctors—ruthlessly persist, even with grim death at their elbow?

Think of the paradox: those white robes assumed for the work of prolonging life would then be no better than shrouds; the linen envelope encasing the defiant victim a winding sheet.

Limits surely there are to the subservience even of those who must sternly execute the law. At least I have never heard of a militant choking herself into eternity.

It was over. I stood up, swaying in the returning light; I had shared the greatest experience of the bravest of my sex. The torture and outrage of it burned in my mind; a dull, shapeless, wordless anger arose to my lips, but I only smiled. The doctor had removed the towel about his face. The little, red mustache upon his upper lip was drawn out in a line of pleasant understanding. He had forgotten all but the play. The four men, having finished their minor roles in one minor tragedy, were already filing out at the door.

"Isn't there any other way of tying a person up?" I asked. "That thing looks like——"

"Yes, I know," he said, gently.

THE GIRL AND THE GORILLA

A NEW SPECIES has come to town!

We thought we had a line on all the different kinds of femininity in the world, their fads, fancies, and fashions, their virtues and their indiscretions—when suddenly enters Dinah, the bushgirl.

She is neither very feminine nor very fragile, to look at. She has fashion's wide shoulder-cape of hair, but this is as far as the semblance goes, as she stands before us leaning upon bowed forearms, taut as suspense, looking out of faraway eyes upon a life called civilized.

Such is the gorilla woman, the only living captive of her race.

Looking in at her from the public's side of the bars, I perceived only a vague, gray thing with head sunk between shoulders—a bundle of unfathomable apprehensions. But when I stepped into the cage, with the keeper Engelholm on one side and Professor Robert L. Garner on the other, she stood abruptly upright and, putting out a crinkly, black, glacé-kid hand, demanded something—something to eat. Her appetite is astounding.

Keeper Fred Engelholm was a little doubtful as to the way that Dinah would receive me, I being the first woman who had come within caressing or battling distance. But Professor Garner seemed confident that Dinah would find something, however trifling, in me that would meet with her approval.

She ambled toward me with her knuckles doubled under her, a slanting bulk of body that shut out what little light the cage permitted, until she reached the chair they had set for her.

There is a queer sort of drawing-room caution about her. She has a cold sort of appraising stare that holds neither envy nor malice. The crowd that collects outside her cage she does not see, or if she does, it might as well be a row of cabbages. Apparently she does not object to cerise or black stitching upon a pair of dress gloves.

I found—for I had come to study her—that the largest and most splendidly satisfying thing in Dinah's life is herself. She would rather stand well in her own estimation than upon a social footing.

The professor, who surely ought to know, told me that she had her own way of talking. So I said to her, "Look here, Dinah, what conclusions have you come to regarding our United States?"

She took her knees into her arms with an air of long-studied calculation that would have given an analytical novelist infinite pleasure. Rocking from side to side on hairy haunches, she began to laugh—an extraordinary laughter, that disturbed the virile hair upon her breast.

Her mind was as a blank of well-arranged ignorance!

Three feet of the newest womankind in the world was making me feel—well, awkward, to say the least.

She did not trouble to answer for a while. Looked down upon, she is merely a little gray blur. Reviewed upon her own level, she is a small wildcat elevated wrecking train. If your dignity permits a competition in faces, you will be left three miles behind at the first loop of the jeering mouth; for believe me, Dinah has the most perfectly ordered set of unbalanced jokes on view of anybody in the world. Her face is the jumping-off place for humor.

Having crawled after her for some twenty minutes, I sat up and argued. I said to myself: Now we will see if, after all, the advantages of civilization do not enable me to dominate this rather unique situation.

Once again I lit out upon her with "Now then, Dinah, answer my question. What do you think of our United States? You have been here a month."

She paused, her head poised sidewise.

"Let me see"—she cupped her hand about her ear and dusted a piece of lint from her shoulders. (I freely interpret according to Professor Garner's rules.) "The first thing that really attracted my attention was the meter upon the taxi that the professor hired to bring me here to the zoo. That thing climbed exactly three-and-a-fourth times faster than a chimpanzee, four times faster than an ordinary monkey, and six times faster than a gorilla. I hated to see anything get away from control so.

"Also, I was quite grieved," she continued plaintively, "to observe that the sun has no chance in New York and that the moon is only a past memory. I couldn't make out whether it was daylight or electricity."

She took a stroll about the cage, ducking between Engelholm's legs and looking very much like the other side of a funny camera. She paused abruptly and smiled.

"There is one thing that I haven't tried yet."

"And what is that?"

"Chewing gum. Gee whiz! I would like to find out what it is in that little delicacy that keeps so many people rotatory beneath their hats. But I have been getting the most weird and winsome feed here at the zoo that ever passed my understanding: bananas, oranges, meat, and French rolls in particular."

Certainly a bushwoman has come to us who is little and quaint and gray; and you who go up to the Bronx to see her will discover that there is something terribly old about her, and yet not old at all. Her eyes alone will make you seem to remember something that has gone before. She weighs less than fifty pounds and stands about three feet high. She is immature yet and will grow as time passes. I am only wondering if I will then be as willing to hug her and have her embrace me in return as I am now.

When she puts her arms about you, it feels something like a garden hose. It is at once impersonal and condescending, and yet rather agreeable. And when she laid her head upon my knees, I was not embarrassed but only pleased that she had found something in me, as representative of the women she had come among, to make her trustful.

Of course, she had to spoil it all by gravely putting an orange peel upon her head.

She moved off at the same time, Engelholm after her, she disrespectfully making faces at him—faces so mean and comprehensive that Engelholm got riled on the instant with a kindly sort of scorn.

Outside, the crowd roared in delight as she ran easily out of reach in a side-swinging, ungainly, loping movement, Engelholm catching up a little at each turn—Germany gaining upon Africa with difficulty.

She growled ominously when, lunging forward, he caught her by the scruff of the neck and paused in full view of the crowd, wiping his forehead, holding her off like luggage from back home.

"She's so darned cussed," he remarked illuminatingly, as she tinkered with her ear. "As nice a little girl when she wants to be, and then as mean—as mean——" He searched in vain for something that would symbolize Dinah's soul and personality.

Failing, he stood and shook his head. It had just been borne in upon him that even here Kipling's remark about the female of the species holds true.

MY ADVENTURES BEING RESCUED

THE BUSINESS OF being saved was brought to my attention one day this week when few people were occupied with the all-engrossing thought of salvation.

The business of saving and being saved, like the Brooklyn Bridge, is an institution. We save money, time, breath, and occasionally words, all of which are easy and comforting compared to the saving of one's body.

It is nicer to have the city pray over you than it is to swing above a city yourself and say a few prayers on your own account in midair. It is a fearful, almost a terrible thing, to climb onto a level with the sparrows' nests.

Three times that morning I was saved, and each time I had wished it onto myself. When you get into a fix by the act and workings of providence, you are looking for salvation in the natural course of events. It is a different matter to get into danger for the express purpose of making providence practical.

Up at Sixty-seventh Street the School for Recruits was alive with its merit pupils. With exact precaution and skill, each recruit went through his morning task. The hose shot a long, heavy stream dripping and sliding down the bricks and across the windows. One man gasped as a copious and undesired bath was thrust upon him.

The blue shirts, blue trousers, belts, and caps, the formidable yet kindly faces, and kindliest of all, Chief Larkin smiling at me comfortingly—these were my stage settings and surroundings.

I had watched the man padding across the shed roof and seen him stretch out stiffly and taut, to land comfortably in a man-encircled net. I looked past the ladders, over the heads of many men and into the faces of many more, as my eyes ran along the buildings. In every window they were watching us—me—in the court below. It was the first time in my knowledge that I had earnestly desired to be sure of living ninety-nine years.

Through it all, I caught Chief Larkin's order, "Fetch the belt." I felt like the man who hears the hangman's words, "Fetch the rope."

One of the boys brought a wide belt of canvas and leather and strapped it about my waist. I followed him up a winding flight of stairs to the topmost window.

At my belt hung a full pound weight of steel loop. It swung and swayed and pulled me down. For even the iron that saves and the hands that succor have their inconveniences.

I climbed out upon the sill. I looked down.

Recruits who had been men dwindled to funny, grotesque shapes, futuristic patterns without purpose. The faces at the windows were blurred masks.

I reached across the crimson sill and swung against the sky some hundred feet or so above the city pavement.

Out on the other side of the wall the world had stopped to look on. An auto slowed down. A flock of school children and a couple of "white wings" all stood with heads upturned skyward. A man with a screaming white apron tied about a conscienceless girth, who had been cutting perishable merchandise, grinned in the glare of light shining and dancing upon his cleaver. A drowsy expectancy lay along Sixty-Eighth Street and touched the spectators with a sort of awesome wonder.

I was a "movie," flashing transient pictures upon a receptive sky.

As I dangled and sprawled against the horizon, I realized that it was no family inheritance of courage nor yet any individual bravery of the soul that kept me from becoming horribly sick. What prevented it was the perhaps ridiculous sentence that I kept repeating to myself: "There is one act that must be committed beautifully—suicide!"

Needless to state, I reached the ground quite safely.

The method of descent that I had just demonstrated to my own satisfaction and to that of others was the method used when a fire has reached such a point that a fireman cannot hope to make a safe and sane rescue. The rope is shot up to the window—a thin, strong rope—onto which is tied the thicker, stronger one on which I had descended.

Now I retraced my steps once more to try the second method, the one more commonly in use.

This time, I climbed out on the sill as before but sat and awaited the fireman coming down from the roof.

Revolving like a great undecided bird he came, crying out an order which I was prompt to obey—a command that I should put my arms about him under his own and hold tight.

I reached out, I felt myself sliding, the sill was jerked suddenly away from me. I felt his body take the wrench, felt his breath as he grunted softly. Then slowly, very slowly, we swung onward and down.

Space is a good thing into which to hurl epithets, but it's not so agreeable to swing in.

The rescuer kept whispering "Golly, golly" and making funny noises in his throat, little self-approving noises, agreeably confident. Our hearts beat as closely as those of escaping lovers in a melodrama.

Once more I reached a foothold. We swayed apart, walking tipsily upon the slack net, and then slid to the ground.

The third adventure was with the ladders, a shaky proceeding with slippery spindles underfoot. I hoisted the ladder to the window above, and I jammed its spikes into the ledge.

In this wise I went all through the business of being saved.

The world's machinery moved again as I touched the ground to stay.

The belt was unstrapped. My dress was brushed. The Chief felt my pulse and pronounced me "Game, all right!" The boys made remarks about my weight and the good old hemp, suggesting that I do the stunt every morning for exercise, also for the benefit of the free-amusement-loving public.

Wild sky-tangoing had been mine, and the memory of it I shall cherish doubly because it was the first time in my life that I knew what a coward I was.

After this I asked the Chief what was the best fire escape so far devised, and he said:

"These newfangled, fire-escaping things that have been invented from time's beginning have not proved practicable, that's why we have not adopted them. We are still awaiting the inventor who will really invent something that will not take fifteen to twenty minutes to excuse itself in. All so-far-discovered methods have proved inadequate because they operate too slowly. Therefore, we returned to the old method—the rope, the fireman, and the girl."

FASHION SHOW MAKES GIRL REGRET LIFE ISN'T ALL REDFERN AND SKITTLES

PROBABLY, HAD I a really thorough knowledge of the old masters in literature, I should discover that it had all been done before. But being charmingly and precociously ignorant, I indulge in phantasmagoria upon the mental horizon, to announce with bland and trite composure that there is something a little different happening for the world of fashions; in short, a beauty fashion show has been delivered to the public by the resourceful Keiths.

There were twenty of them, they were young, they were without doubt pretty; they all stood some five feet odd; they produced upon the spectator a sensation of orgy; they caused acute concentration, and they all so nearly approached the standard that one groaned for a flaw.

It brings one back so shockingly to earth to mention names, but it must be done. Miss May Tully started it; Sam Ash sings, ushers, and bows it in, and Audrey Munson, Selma Pittack, Peggy Hopkins, Betty Brown, Virginia Kelly, Edna Burton, Ethel Schaffner, Mary and Sadie Mullen, Kathryn Beach, Kent Jackson, Maude Mason, Kay Karey, Marjorie Demerest, Blanche King, Ivy Melzer, and Nan Foley trip it sweetly out. By the time they all have taken their positions at the sides—some standing with butterfly hands in clinging chiffon and tulle, in satin and in lace, or smiling over powdered bosoms—and by the time, we say, each creation has been drawled before your senses, languished before your longing, and hesitated upon your hopes, you feel so ultra ultra up your spine that your ninety-eight-cent near-linen waist suddenly perceives that it is passé.

With a shock you appreciate that you are not a la mode, that you do not Maison Maurice through life, that you do not negligee a la

Bonwit Teller to bed. Ah, well! Life has never been all Redfern and skittles!

And, if we may ask, what next? Yet do not answer. I fear to hear. For surely we are becoming but the models to our gowns. I ask you what temperament could dominate such things as the swirling, truculent, commanding, belligerent, docile, and arrogant charm of this thing that is laced upon the body of a girl?

It does not matter we are glad; we scent temptation in the air, and we scent the odors of invasion. The styles have got us by the throat—we laugh as they hurl us to the ground. We exult as we sink into that deep peace, gently lulled into stupefaction by the burden of duchess lace upon our minds, tulle upon our hearts, and gossamer upon our senses. We should worry if we look beautiful in captivity.

After all, life is merely a matter of succumbing becomingly. Therefore, let us root out this fear; let us lean back and be ordained.

Well, take it from you, beauty parade, the sensations are simply great! Paw up the ground! Tousle the skyline with your arrogant headgear! Flaunt the trickery of foliage with the foliage of foot-kicked hems! Life hangs upon a thread—the drawstring of a chemise, the ribbon in a petticoat.

"There are moments in a woman's life when both love and hate must be suspended." The voice is plaintive, yet full of absolute certainty. One turns sharply, and there in the shadow of the wings you observe her drawing a fine line of distinction while she draws one equally as fine with the tip of a stick of rouge upon her lips.

"What! Is there, then, something a little out of place?"

She throws her arms out wide. "Everything," she says. "The rehearsals take all one's time, and when one is young they simply must have dates——"

"Dates? Dates, did you say? Dates, you little ninny! Why, this is your supreme chance. What could you be but a chorus girl if you hadn't been picked to be a star in a beauty parade?"

"What could I have been," she demands sharply. "Why, a model, of course. That's what I am. I'm not a chorus girl at all and never have been. You've bought my face a million times upon the current magazines."

"Not that picture of a girl trying on a poke bonnet?"

"Perhaps," she retorts mysteriously, "and perhaps not. Oh dear, I know I'll be late. Don't I look beautiful?" Naive to say the least.

And upon the psychological point of this I was engrossed when the stalking, heartbreaking calves of Beau Brummell walked into my vision.

"No one has mentioned me yet," said Sam Ash with a mid-Victorian dejection. "Not a single notice about me in any way, nothing about my voice, my satin suit, my yellow vest, my lace cuffs, my peculiar type of masculine charm, my simplified manner of looking upon events that pass me by—the girls, you understand. Not a notice about my entrance, and none about my exit."

"You're all wrong, Sam. We not only noticed you, but we thought your voice was exceptional and——"

He put up his hand, "Don't say it," he whispered, smiling beneath his greasepaint and confusion. "I know it, but that is an inheritance, and I'm in no way responsible for those qualities that also put me in the blue ribbon class. Enough, enough. It's a distinction to be the only male among this swirl of perfection, and neither do they make me wear a bell upon my knee as they did in a certain convent in Paris in the days of Victor Hugo. I come, I go; I am content."

"We felt that the public still found something wanting," May Tully said, as she leaned against a dressing-room door with her pocketbook clasped to her bosom. "The fashions have been getting a pretty tight hold on the world, and when one sees which way the mind runs, it's simple enough. What could be more entertaining to the average woman than a beauty parade? Well, if you ask me, nothing. Nor is it merely the women who like to look on. Observe for yourself, look out there: is every face in ten a woman's or a man's?"

I looked and by the way disproved that fallacy about an actor's being unable to see anyone out front. A thousand heads like a field of well-ordered cabbages broke upon my vision. Holy smoke! Did I look like that to the actors? Just an anonymous head stretching on an unperceivable neck with mouth slightly ajar, and with eyelids descending—a white blur in a dark distance—a person too intelligible for the social register and too fragmentary for a pedigree, and too lacking in foliage to be descended from any very luxuriant family tree?

"I don't like it at all," I said aloud.

"What?" asked Miss Tully, whereat I turned crimson and felt like Alice in Wonderland when the white queen shouted at her.

"Do you make your observations correctly?" she continued. "Did you notice for yourself what that house out there says? Listen—hear the hand-clapping. If I'm not mistaken, fifty percent of that at least wears no. 9 gloves."

"What attracts them most?"

"The sublime teamwork of it. That's what counts—they are all thoroughbreds, these girls."

RUTH ROYE, GREATEST "NUT" IN VAUDEVILLE

THE JOY OF being pat, the gaiety of repartee, the tickle of humor, the patter of laughter, have come to Ruth Roye; but most of all, when she serves herself up, she is not *à la* this nor yet *eau de* that. She comes in ungarnished with sauces of France or giblets of England, nor is there a paper ruffle upon her corners, as upon a chop. Ruth Roye is just simple, rough-tongued ginger—the greatest "nut" in vaudeville, eccentric beyond the limits of belief unless you have seen her.

She walks bowlegged across the stage, singing, and through life she goes just as unaffectedly, though straighter.

Upon the stage she syncopates her sentences; off, she is liberal with the commas.

Upon the boards she hitches up her ruff as Old Cy his overalls; in life she is still mentally hitching up something that may be a sentence to a song or a ribbon to a hat. She gurgles behind the footlights, and she sits upon her legs and growls good-naturedly behind the curtain of her dressing room because a "gosh-darned cleaner didn't know enough to do the accordion pleats right."

She pins her hair into a little sharp knob at the back of her head; she smears her palms and her cheeks with cold cream; she drops her slippers off, and then—instead of hissing behind the panel that you cannot come in just yet because "she doesn't look presentable"—she calls out a quick, jolly "Enter," and you are face to face with her as she is to herself.

You are not a visitor, you are a second mirror.

In other words, she does not seduce you; she welcomes you. She does not lure you, she admits you. She does not place before you a finale, but a personality.

51

She might have come from the Five Towns, she might have hailed from a dairy out in Jersey, she might have been one of ten in Staten Island. She might even have been a farmer upstate. Her accent is frightfully Yankee, her smile Irish, her birth Jewish. You don't know what to make of the program of her anatomy; therefore you expect nothing, and get a lot—that you could not have expected.

She is small. Five feet will easily reach the top pin in her curls. (It's a secret, she says; she's going to get new ones soon, they are so nice to shake.) She can't weigh more than a Scotch oatcake, and she takes up no more room than a vanity case.

"I adore being provincial," she says. "I love being new-mown hay in this city of cut flowers. I like being slangy, incorrect, incautious, and impudent. It makes me happy to chase myself across the stage. I can never quite catch up to that gol-darned little streak of lightning that keeps in front of my feet and dances in my eyes. I'm proud that I'm homely in the same way that a person accepts a birthday present, without looking for the 'sterling' until the donor has departed. Of course, I'll admit that once, a long time ago, I peered into a certain mirror and, failing to find the 'sterling,' I gave up. I accepted instead the assurance that the mirror gave me 'snap,' and here I am. And I'm happy and glad to be alive, and that's about all, please, ma'am." She folded her hands in her lap, ducked her chin and surveyed me.

"Of course," she continued, "one has off days when being funny hurts." Well, it evidently wasn't this day. She combed her hair and talked about audiences.

"I love them in Chicago—"

"That's because they love you," broke in the voice of her sister, who was sitting, Hindu fashion, high up on the top of a Saratoga trunk.

"I know it; that's a good reason, all right. I was second girl and a nobody a few years ago, and I made a hit—it was simply great! I put it all down to the fact that I'm kitchen all the time. People are tired of seeing parlor."

"She has no vestibule through which you have to pass before reaching her real self," once more broke in the sister, this time changing her position for one less knee-cracking.

"Aren't they, your family, dead proud of you?"

"You bet," said the sister. "I don't know where Ruth gets the nerve. I'd die right in the middle of the stage if I had to do the fool things she does, and make the faces she makes, and take the attitudes she takes—"

"I really was shoved onto the stage," Ruth went on. "I hated it in the beginning, but, oh, gee!" she gurgled (the only simon-pure gurgle I ever heard outside of a Chambers novel). "They couldn't get me off now with a derrick."

She proceeded to get into her gown, a thing of chiffon, white satin and green velvet, moaning about the accordion pleats all the while. "That cleaner did it up so wonderfully the first time, and then he sends it like this. Do you really think it looks so bad?" She fluffed the ruffles out and turned around.

"Not in the least. Now, tell me, what laugh pleases your heart the most?"

"The laugh of the man out front. No girl's, no woman's laugh ever pleases me as much as a man's. When he laughs—good night! You have got his whole system resounding; the circles you made throwing the stone into his pond reach the bank. A woman just ripples, and I do hate ripples—they are the four hundred in the world of joy, and I hate elite enjoyment as much as I hate the high hand-shake. When a man laughs it nearly breaks me up. There is a joy loose; they feel it, they let go, and they get their enjoyment across to you, where you can grab it with both hands and feel encouraged. But a woman—Lord!" Then she laughed—a little, short, fluttering laugh, pursing up her lips. "That's the way, mere shirred mental vacuum.

"Now let's get down to brass tacks," she continued, pushing her pink-stockinged feet into white pumps. "This season is the best in history for the comedian; it ought to produce at least some half-dozen new and great funny men or women. Why? Because the war has taken something out of nearly every family. They want comedy this year as never before. The thing would drive them mad otherwise."

"Why is it that comedy goes better than tragedy?" I asked.

"Simple. People come to vaudeville houses to get what they don't get at home."

"Do you always know when you are going to get across—that is, before you start your song?"

"The minute I land on the stage with a slam, I can taste the atmosphere. And if it's the right kind it simply grabs me by the chin and pushes me into action. But if it's chock-full of bromide and has a brown flavor—oh, well, carry me off, that's all—carry me off."

"How do you try for effects?"

"I don't try. Why, I thought I had been telling you right along. If you're born funny you know your job, and I was, so why shouldn't I know mine?"

"Do you like popular music?"

"I love it."

"Better than classical?"

"Absolutely. Classical music has no message for me; popular music is a telegram. Perhaps," a little wistfully, "it's because I haven't got used to classical music."

"Don't you think, however, that the public should prefer—"

"Classical music to ragtime, and tragedy to comedy?" she interrupted. "No, the ordinary existence of a person is too classical and too tragical. Change the existence: make the bulk of life comedy and ragtime, and then I'll say let us have *Hamlet*."

"At what point, after all, does ragtime begin?"

"Where Verdi leaves off," laughing.

"I am looking for an actress who will admit or at least says that she stays up late, eats what she likes, loves whom she pleases and goes where her mind inclines."

"Here she is," she put her hand on her breast. "All but two items—"

"Don't strike them out, Ruth. I know one of them is going to be eating."

"No, you're wrong; I eat all the time, what I like and as much as I like. I go where I want to go and I stay up late because—," she pointed her finger at me as a mother to a naughty child, "—because I play in the evening and a play gets out about eleven or twelve, and I like my family."

"I knew you'd do it in the end."

"But how can I say I have stacks of lovers when I haven't a goldarned one?"

Miss Ruth Roye is a female Billy Sunday. Perhaps that's where she got her original hints.

I have asked her. She says that she never copied anyone; I don't really believe she has.

Just then her cue came, and a moment later she did not skip onto the stage, nor dance upon it. She broke loose, she plunged, she hit the spotlight before it could come to her. She crashed right into the middle of it like a small-powered moth, ugly, alive, vibrating (I'm sorry the word has been used before), daring, saucy, sharp-chinned, windmilling her arms, stamping her feet, jerking her head, flinging her curls about, grotesque, living—and all of it only nineteen.

PET SUPERSTITIONS OF SENSIBLE
NEW YORKERS

ONE ALWAYS LOOKS up an authority to avoid quoting him. I looked up Sigmund Freud and so am in a position to go on with this story without further contemporary interruption.

It deals with superstitions, and it also deals partly with the subconscious mind, through which all material things of the body are directed—which sees to it that the heart beats, which is the master behind those indiscretions of discreet moments—that quality, in other words, that does the best work of most lives. To discover just how far the voice of the past has carried and into how many ears it has crept, I questioned the elite few.

I recalled to them that Napoleon always carried with him—or rather, had follow him, on a horse set aside for the purpose—a painting of his young son; how at night he had it placed beside his bed; and how, on the morning of the battle of Waterloo, he arose in the gray of the dawn and stumbled over something. Stooping over, he found the picture of his son lying face down, causing him to say with profound significance, "A very ominous thing has happened on a very ominous day!"

I told them also of Goethe's dread of his own back stairs, down which he was never seen to pass. The secret? In his childhood its carpet dotted with crimson roses had made him dream of blood.

I told them of Oliver Goldsmith, who was encouraged to finish what to him was a very irksome task—*The Vicar of Wakefield*—by the industry of a spider, and how upon completion of the last paragraph he raised his eyes only to behold the spider hanging lifeless in its web.

I ended with Gladstone, who kept a special valet to care for a pet pair of amethyst cuff links.

All of this by way of encouraging them to be brave and come out thus.

Said Chauncey M. Depew, leaning back in his chair and broadening the mouth comforted on either side by the old-fashioned, mutton-chop whiskers, "I am an unsuperstitious man doing superstition grandly. I will sit down to a dinner where I am the thirteenth at the table, though I'd rather not. In three of thirteen cases, the guests have died within the year. In three hundred dinners of fourteen guests that I have attended, sixteen of them have died within the year. Of some four hundred dinners of sixteen guests, something like twenty of the participants have passed out in the following six months.

"So, you see, superstition keeps its hold on the people because statistics are kept of it."

Signor Caruso, who has a voice box in every gesture as well as in his throat, beamed. "Do I believe in superstition? Ah, no! Do I fear the evil eye? No. Am I susceptible to signs? Still no; and yet, to all of my denials I shall have to add, 'Yes.' Superstition is sense without a reason, reason without sense—what you will.

"Shall I illustrate? In Monte Carlo—a place, by the way, where nothing common should happen but where everything common does—I was very fond of motoring. One day my friends and I passed on the road some charming lady priests—those creatures who have sanctified lives. Said my friends: 'Ah! such horrible, such ghastly luck! We must turn back.' But I remonstrated.

" 'Did you not see?' they retorted. 'Those lady priests—it will not do to proceed. We must turn back.'

" 'My dear sirs,' I protested. 'For lady priests one turns back on nothing but one's past. This ride is still a thing of the future. Proceed.' And so they went on, but presently the car stopped of itself. They said, 'You see? The women, the priests.' I said: 'No gasoline.' But in my heart—ah, well."

The Princess Troubetzkoy—she who is haunted ever with the brackets (Amélie Rives)—handed a cup of tea to her tall painter-husband and quoted from a paragraph composed in her youth: "There is a grain of superstition in the stuff all men are mixed of."

She continued: "There is a certain quality in an old fear, which superstition is, that even I can admit; but if one believes in God, how can one believe in peacocks? To the actor there is nothing more portentous than a peacock; yet I have three in my play *The Fear Market*."

The strong face of Mary Austin seemed suddenly to awaken into a fire.

"Superstitions are things practiced after one has none," she observed. "We hold on to everything that we do not believe. Personally, I want no intellectual junk. It is utterly wrong, this separation of thought from action. To pick up a pin is absurd, and yet——"

She studied, her eyes staring before her, the attitude of one who believes and yet does not believe. And still I saw in her no realization that superstition is the very pigment of life, that it strangles the dull monotony of existence and reduces living to one simple system of profound and pangless pains.

Montgomery Flagg, on the other hand, was funny. It seemed utterly impossible for him to think up a thing. He could be neither naturally superstitious nor yet naturally unsuperstitious. He just wasn't anything at all, in spite of the fact that he vowed he'd like to be.

He has very long legs, and he kept walking about above them and shaking his head. He was plainly quite crazy about the subject but could improvise no method by which he could break out into a rash of superstition. In the end, he called in his wife and asked her, comically, what the devil his superstitions were, anyway.

She answered promptly, "Women." He said that wasn't superstition, that was a faculty, and walked about some more.

"I know what," he said finally. "I wish they would get up a correspondence school for superstition. I think life is utterly miserable without a superstition. It's like a prayer rug without knees. Great cats! You've put a new zest into my life. I'm going to cultivate my superstitions. It's absurd for a man with an income to be without them. I don't know what I've been thinking of."

Henrietta Rodman, of the short hair and the brogan gait, came next.

"I refuse to live in a topsy-turvy world," she said flatly. "If it is as silly as superstition would have it, and if superstition is real, then at least I can refuse to see it. After all is said and done, it's only a hangover of yesterday, and I can't be bothered with it."

And so I went away from there. I passed out into the street, still looking, and came upon Dr. Abraham Jacobi, whose thin voice said:

"Superstitions? What are superstitions? I do not feel them; I cannot answer to their message. My body is one vast treble of sciatica."

"Ah!" said I, "my grandmother, too, suffered from that. I am sorry."

"Thank you; you are a good girl. And that about your grandmother establishes a bond between your family and mine, thereby beginning a superstition for ourselves which will hold the world together."

"Not a superstition in me," said Jane Cowl, "unless a hunch is superstition. Once it was about a horse. The owner said he would give me an option on it for a few days. When I returned at the expiration of the period, he had a choice collection of excuses but no horse. Now I always listen to that small, inner voice. Also, I know that if I stay in the country I'll have better health."

Here the unsuperstitious Miss Cowl knocked on wood. Then she laughed, suddenly coloring. "It's only a habit," she said.

Vexed with travail that bore but scant fruit, I came into the golden room of one Frank Harris, a man with the gifted pen but the still more gifted tongue, and put the question to him also.

"The little atavistic superstitions, like skipping certain flagstones and touching parts of the fence, I must confess to. I confess that I am continually counting nine stones and hoping for luck. I find myself looking up, trying to play fair, but all the time acutely conscious just where that ninth one lies.

"I think this is the only superstition I can trace in myself. I rather like whistling, but that is to keep my courage up rather than a super-stition."

And as he believes, so will those who do not and who shall discover that superstitions are put aside for the minutes to betray.

THE LAST PETIT SOUPER
(GREENWICH VILLAGE IN
THE AIR—AHEM!)

I HAVE OFTEN been amused—perhaps because I have not looked upon them with a benign as well as a conscientious glance—to observe what are termed "characters" going through the city and into some favorite cafe for tea.

The proletariat drinks his brew as a matter of pure reason; how differently does our dilettante drink.

He is conscious of the tea growing; he perceives it quivering in the sun. He knows when it died—its death pangs are beating like wings upon his palate. He feels it is its most unconscious moment, when it succumbs to the courtship of scalding waters. He thrills ever so lightly to its last and by far its most glorious pain—when its life blood quickens the liquid with incomparable amber and passes in high pomp down the passage of his throat.

I am not prepared to say that the one gets nothing out of his cup and the other all. I say only what a dreary world this would be were it not for those charming dabblers. How barren and how dull becomes mere specialization. How much do we owe to those of us who can flutter and find decorative joy in fluttering away this small allotted hour, content with color, perfume, and imported accents, and accompanied by a family skeleton made of nothing less amusing than jade.

The public—or in other words that part of ourselves that we are ashamed of—always turns up the lip when a dilettante is mentioned, all in a patriotic attempt to remain faithful to that little home in the Fifties with its wax flowers, its narrow rockers, and its localisms and, above all, to that mother whose advice was always as correct as it was harmful.

There are three characters that I can always picture to myself. Let us call them Vermouth, Absinthe, and Yvette—the last a girlish name ordinarily associated with a drink transmitting purely masculine impulses.

Vermouth I used to see sitting over a cold and lonely cup of French coffee between ten and eleven of the morning, marking him at once above a position and beneath despair. With him he always carried a heavy blond cane and a pair of yellow gloves. He would stare for long minutes together at the colored squares of the window, entirely forgetful of the fact that he could not look out. Undoubtedly he was seeing everything a glass could reveal, and much more.

Sometimes damson jam would appear beside the solitary pot and the French rolls, proving in all probability that someone had admired and carried off some slight "trifle," composed, written, or painted in that simple hour of inspiration.

He was never unhappy in a sad way; indeed, he seemed singularly and supremely happy, though often beset with pains and sustaining himself with his cane as he went out.

If he was sad, one thing alone betrayed it: that quick, sharp movement of the head given only to those special children of nature—the sparrow who cannot rest but must fly, and the mortal who cannot fly and is therefore condemned to rest.

Then there were Yvette and Absinthe. Yvette had his god in his hip pocket. It was unrolled on every occasion, and when it was at last uncovered, it turned out to be merely a "Mon Dieu, my dear!" whereat it was quickly rolled up again, only to come popping out as quickly, like a refrain, to do battle with Vermouth's patient "Lieber Gott!"

Yvette's coat was neatly shaped, frayed but decidedly genteel. It possessed a sort of indefinite reluctance about admitting itself passé. It had what must be called skirts, and Yvette's legs swung imperially beneath them, as the tongue of the Liberty Bell beneath its historical metal.

A soft felt hat was held in a hand sporting several uncut stones, standing in relation to jewelry as free verse to poetry. As he passed, one caught the odor of something intricate such as struggles from between the pattern of an Indian incense burner. And lastly, there came with Yvette the now-famous, silver-wattled cane.

This cane was tall, alert, and partial. It was to him what the stem is to the flower. It enhanced as well as sustained his bloom, while he meant to life what the candle means to the nun.

Absinthe was like this cane: tall, energetic, but acutely pale. He seemed composed of plaster, his lips alone animate and startlingly scarlet. He spoke with that distinct English accent heard only in America.

He had a habit of laying his hands upon his face, presumably for the same reason ferns are laid beside roses. The nails of these hands were long—longer than Japan had ever thrust beneath the cuticle of any native yellow jacket—and they were silvered or gilded with gold.

There are moments in the lives of all of us, or shall I say some of us, that must be lived in French. As these gentlemen had all passed through that stage, dust could, as a consequence, be discovered upon their discourse. They passed each other the snuffboxes of their thoughts as though they were antiques, each statement was as carefully preserved. In other words, they valued that hour.

These men summed up all those little alien things that in their mother country are merely the dialect of the physique, nor were these men ever so pleased with themselves as when they were recollecting.

Yvette had the most unmistakable traces of foreign sojourns of the three; that unconscious product of a conscious program. He was a leopard who had chosen his own particular spots, and this is perhaps that difference between what we call ourselves and those other odd ones who extend their travels beyond ours on into the mental world, on a journey of so-called nonreason.

Yvette was feminine—he could not only look the part, he acted girlish in much that he did. Yet one should have admired him instead of ridiculing him, for it gave him the ease to say: "But my dear fellow, you make a grave mistake. German women are not fat, they are merely plentiful." Or his "Ah me. I miss the reputations of the boulevards far more than their realities."

Vermouth would smile and answer:

"Yes, yes, I know, but just imagine living in a country where one can have miscarriages by telephone and bruises by telegraph."

Thus, one saw how inscrutable Vermouth had grown along with Absinthe. Together they had spent too many hours contemplating a black tasseled curtain, perhaps because of what it contained or because of what it concealed.

He contended that his head was forever in the clouds. To prove it, he ordered chocolate ice cream and tea, and this at twelve at night; for it is a theory of our dilettante that bad dinners make profound diners, and there he was.

And here also am I, at the identical point that I wanted to reach— the twelve o'clock souper and its significance.

In the most profound and religious moments of the philosopher Marcus Aurelius, he came to this conclusion, that each day should be treated as the last.

And there is the secret of the dilettante. He is always about to pass through that incomparable hour, the hour before and the hour after the supper that may prove the last. And so it is that he, dreaming his dreams, making a liquor of his tears to be drunk upon this last and holiest occasion, has discovered that little something that makes the difference between him and the you who have ordered supplies home for a week.

And I, who have been in the presence of this thing, have learned to understand.

GREENWICH VILLAGE AS IT IS

A FRIEND ONCE told me of an artist who had committed suicide because his colors had begun to fade. His canvases were passing like flowers. People looking upon them sighed softly, whispering, "This one is dying," while someone in the background added, "That one is dead." It was the unfulfilled fortune of his future. If he had been less enthusiastic, if he had studied what constitutes permanent color and what does not, he might have left some of those somber pictures that seem to grow daily more rigid and "well preserved." The earliest nudes executed with the most irreproachably permanent colors seem to be clothing themselves slowly with that most perdurable costume—the patina of time. Turner is among those who live by the death of his canvases.

And so people are standing before Greenwich Village murmuring in pitying tones, "It is not permanent, the colors will fade. It is not based on good judgment. It is not of that sturdy and healthy material from which, thank providence, we of the real Manhattan have been fashioned." There are a few who sigh, "It is beautiful in places!" while others add, "That is only an accident."

How charming an answer it was of Nature to make most of her mistakes lovely. Christianity seems to be quite a reprehensible experiment; yet what brings tears so quickly to the eyes as two pieces of wood shaped as a cross?

Why has Washington Square a meaning, a fragrance, so to speak, while Washington Heights has none? The Square has memories of great lives and possibilities therefore; while the Heights are empty, and Fifth Avenue is only a thoroughfare. Here on the north side are stately houses inhabited by great fortunes, the Lydigs and Guinesses and all those whose names rustle like silk petticoats, and on the other side a congeries of houses and hovels passing into rabbit warrens where Italians breed and swarm in the sun as in Naples, where vegetables and fruits are sold in the street as on the Chiaja, and ice cream is made in the bedrooms and spaghetti on the cellar floor. Here is the den where the gunmen conspired recently to shoot down the free-trade butcher and here the row of houses whose inhabitants provide the Women's Night Court with half its sensations. Satin and motorcars on this side, squalor and push carts on that: it is the contrast which gives life, stimulates imagination, incites to love and hatred.

The greater part of New York is as soulless as a department store; but Greenwich Village has recollections like ears filled with muted music and hopes like sightless eyes straining to catch a glimpse of the beatific vision.

On the benches in the Square men and women resting; limbs wide-flung, arms pendent, listless; round the fountains and on the corners children, dark-eyed Italian children shrieking now with Yankee-cockney accent, a moment later whispering to their deep-bosomed mothers in the Tuscan of Dante. Here a bunch of Jewish girls like a nosegay, there a pair of Norwegian emigrants, strong of figure and sparing of speech; a colored girl on the sidewalk jostles a Japanese servant and wonders whether he, too, is colored or if he is thought to be white like "dem dagos."

On every corner you can see a new type; but strange to say, no Americans are to be discovered anywhere. New York is the meeting place of the peoples, the only city where you can hardly find a typical American.

The truth has never been penned about Washington Square and Greenwich Village—names which are now synonymous. To have to tell the truth about a place immediately puts that place on its defense. Localities and atmospheres should be let alone. There are so many restaurants that have been spoiled by a line or two in a paper. We are in that same danger. What can we do? Nothing. The damage has been done, we find, and the wing of the butterfly is already crumbling into dust.

I, personally, have never seen one really good article on Washington Square. The commonest spot is not recognizable. The most daring designs in the shops have all been wrongly colored. As for the long hair of the men and the short hair of the women, that type is to be found on Broadway. Cigarette smoking goes on uptown just as much as it does here; the drinking of wine is just as public; the harmless vanities are displayed in other places quite as blatantly as they are here. The business of making love is conducted under the table beyond Fourteenth Street, but does that establish a precedent forbidding the business of holding hands above the table? Is the touch of kid more harmful than the pressure of boot leather? Of course there are pretenders, hypocrites, charlatans among us. But where are the records that state that all malefactors and hypocrites have been caught within the limits of what we call our Bohemia? And as for crime, have all its victims been found murdered in the beds of Waverley Place and Fourth Street?

Oh! out upon it, this silly repetition about the impossible people living here. Because we let you see us in our curl papers, must you perforce return to your paternal oil stove crying that you never in your life have done your own front hair up in a bang? And must you play forever the part of the simpering puritan who never heard of sex relations? What little story is it that is ringing in your ears, told you one night by your mother about Dad as she sat in the evening yielding up reminiscences, which by day appear to be right or wrong but at night are only clever little anecdotes, timid or sweet adventures of a man now too old for his youth and too wise to try to repeat those things that have made youth the world over the finest and saddest part of life? So forever we rob ourselves of ourselves. We should be born at the age of seventy and totter gracefully down into youth.

Is the beggar of Paris or of Naples any better off than the beggar of Washington Square? And is it not by our beggars that the similarity of a race as well as a group shall be known? These beggars who are the city's finger bowls, wherein the hands of greed have dipped!

What then? We have our artists, but we also have our vendors. We have our poets, but we also have our undertakers. We have our idlers, but have we not also our scrubwomen? We have our rich and our poor. We are wealthier by a mendicant and wiser by a poet.

In reality, Washington Square and Greenwich Village are not one. They have become one above the pavement at the height where men's heads pass; but measured out in plain city blocks the Village does not run past Sixth Avenue. It begins somewhere around Twelfth Street and commits suicide at the Battery.

There are as many artists living off the Square as on it. Some shops are mentioned as these artists are mentioned, because they have caught a certain something that for want of a better word we call atmosphere!

We always speak of Daisy Thompson's shop, of the Treasure Box, of the Village Store and of the Oddity Cellar. Just as many pretty things, however, are to be seen in a small shop on Eighth Street between Fifth and Sixth Avenues. Why is it not also mentioned? Because it is in, and not of, the Village.

There is the pleasant night life of the Café Lafayette. The Brevoort is loved for its basement, where one can catch the lights gleaming between the shrubbery. There, too, is the waiter who has been serving you for ten years past. There is a certain familiarity in everything you eat. You can tell just where you are by closing your eyes. The cold cuts of the Lafayette are superior to those of the Brevoort; the New Orleans "fizzes" are abominable at the latter and delightful at the former. There is a chance that you may meet someone you do not like, as there is a probability that you will meet someone that you do. You decide beforehand what kind of a sneer you are going to throw Billy, just how coldly you are going to look past Bobbie or freeze the spinal column of Louise, who has been your next-door neighbor for months.

The cholera scare populated the place, but the atmosphere entered not much earlier than the advent of one Bobbie Edwards. In nineteen hundred and six he turned what was then the A Club into what later was known as the Crazy Cat Club or the Concolo Gatti Matti—at a restaurant run by Paglieri at 64 West Eleventh Street.

Edwards introduced the habit of pushing the tables back and organizing an after-dinner dance. He sent out cards of invitation to his friends, and they in their turn sent out invitations to their acquaintances. Leroy Scott, Howard Brubaker, and Mary Heaton Vorse were among its earliest members. Thus came the first filterings of what was to be Bohemia.

Yet what does one know of a place if one does not know its people intimately? I know of nothing that I can offer as a substitute that will fit unless it is an anecdote—the skeleton of life.

This is the story of a dancer who came down here on a bus one day last summer, to live here. What she had done in her past we did not ask—what her eyes did not tell we knew was not worth knowing—yet she was vastly frank. One night this girl arose from the table (it was at Polly's) to answer the phone. At her side sat a young Russian, and as she went out she said to him, "Now remember, none of your dirty Slavic tricks, don't you put your fingers in my coffee while I'm gone—mind!" and someone at the other side of the table called out to the boy thus addressed, "Well, you Cossack you, what are you going to do about that?" Instantly the dancer ran back and, flinging her arms about the boy's neck, cried, "A Cossack, how glorious! I have heard of your brutalities."

And so now, having eased my mind by having made at least an attempt to dispel some of the false notions, I can find heart to give this place a body.

On Macdougal Street just above the Dutch Oven is the Liberal Club. It is one more of those things that have come to us from uptown. Margaret Wilson was one of its founders, but needless to say it has changed its tone since its change of locality. Members may bring their friends if they do not bring them too often. Many people have met here, fought, loved, and passed out. The candles of many intellects have been snuffed here to burn brighter for a space until they, too, have given place to newer candles. Here Dreiser has debated and Boardman Robinson sketched, and Henrietta Rodman has left the sound of her sandaled feet. Harry Kemp has posed for his bust only to find on turning round that no one was doing it. Jack Reed and Horace Traubel have been seen here; Kreymborg, Ida Rauh, Max Eastman, Bob Minor, and Maurice Becker; a hundred others.

Whitman dinners are held every thirty-first of May in a private room of the Brevoort. Two seasons ago the heart of the Washington Square Players began to beat here, though the theatre itself was located uptown. A little later Charles Edison—who can really afford to be known for himself, only wearing his father as a decoration—started the Little Thimble Theater with the great Guido Bruno for manager. If they had no successes aside from *Miss Julia,* that was of sufficient importance to have warranted the venture.

Bruno started to make a personal paper, entitled *Greenwich Village.* Allen Norton soon followed with the harmless little *Rogue,* which went out for a while but which is scheduled to return in October or November. Kreymborg put out *Others,* a magazine of verse, blank— the moods of many; a sort of plain-bread-of-poetry—called *vers libres;* and though it was printed in the Bronx it was reeking with the atmosphere of the studios along the south side of the square.

Clara Tice burst into print, and so did Bobbie Locher. The Baron de Meyer began to be seen above a glass of yvette in the cafes, among a score of faces that may have had addresses out of the Village itself but were Bohemians. After all, it is not where one washes one's neck that counts but where one moistens one's throat. And still things are coming, expanding. The very air seems to be improving. There is a rumor that "King" McGrath—or otherwise Jack—backed by some society people, is going to open a tavern on Sheridan Square and, Jack adds to those who will listen, "*With* a license."

George Newton is also planning to erect a Toy Theatre on the same Square. Newton has started a new paper, selling at two cents. The first issue will be out in August. Ah, you see! after all you cannot put out the sun by spitting on its shadow.

And our studio buildings? Our apartment houses? The Judson on the south side of the Square, the hotel Holly, the hotel Earle, the Washington; the promised building where now stands the Village soda fountain and Guido Bruno's garret. The Washington Mews has already been partly demolished to arise again. And of recent past history, what of Louis's at 660 Washington Square South? It is held in the memory, as only a dead woman or a past hostelry can be held: the one for its clasp on the heart, the other for its hold on the mind. Louis's had not only Louis, it also had Christine, a woman who, had she not been born in this century, would have been some great heavy goddess whose presence would have been justice without word of mouth. Louis's was closed because it was running without a license. Perhaps that was one of its charms! Drink there was not mere drink, it was wine *libre*.

And there is the Candlestick Tea Room, and there is Gonfarone's, and there is the Red Lamp, Mori's, Romano's, the Red Star, and Mazzini's.

And so you of the outer world, be not so hard on us, and above all, forbear to pity us—good people. We have all that the rest of the world has in common commodities, and we have that better part: men and women with a new light flickering in their eyes, or on their foreheads the radiance of some unseen splendor.

BECOMING INTIMATE WITH
THE BOHEMIANS

Four o'clock in the afternoon and someone has spilled a glass of wine; it creeps across the tablecloth in a widening pattern of sulky red. It is morning in Bohemia.

In a little back room, with pictures hanging crooked on the wall, lies King McGrath, far from the tumult and shouting, his head in his hand, looking into the face of the Virgin painted on the church just facing his three-plank bed. Yea, for the King has a cold.

Now, while Jack lies there staring at the painted face of the Virgin—while the dusk of a musty hall creeps through an ever-widening keyhole set in a house that was once something, as the ever-widening lips of a drunkard who was once a man—out of her dainty sheets, arising in dimity glory, shaking loose myrrh, long stifled, from crumpled lace, the Queen of Bohemia arises, and I can't tell you her name.

Yes, the day for the Greenwich Villager has begun. The waiters in the Brevoort and the Lafayette begin to preen themselves, for they are the only waiters in the world who feel free to cultivate their innermost longings—in other words, to acquire an individual soul.

Well, isn't Bohemia a place where everyone is as good as everyone else—and must not a waiter be a little less than a waiter to be a good Bohemian? Therefore, say nothing, you of the Bronx, when he openly ridicules you for your taste for parsnips when there are artichokes on the bill of fare. He means nothing, it is only his soul caroling on to higher things. He feels that he has to be negligent before he can be Nietzsche.

Between this hour and six, which is known as Polly's hour or the hour of the Dutch Oven or the Candlestick, the tea tipplers and the cocktail dreamers gather slowly in the basement of the Brevoort. Upstairs is respectability, wife, children, music; a violin plays a sorry tune like melancholy robins on a telegraph wire charged with gossip. In the basement is all that is naughty: spicy girls in gay smocks or those capricious clothes that seem to be making faces at their wearers, such as the gowns of Gaugh. Wild, wild exotics of fabrics—effects of Bakst. Men with arms full of heavy literature, pockets jingling with light coin, resplendent in ties—hold, Allen Norton has described them:

> . . . The arch cravat.
> That maddens like the moon and once looked at
> The moral soldier faints and turns his back.

And again—but no, you have an idea of those winking satin ties, the woven threnodies that make music upon the outside of the throat as the voice box on the inside.

"A liqueur, Tito"—this to her latest lover lounging beautifully, a handsome man of fifty summers, but not these summers; an Italian, perhaps, or a Russian or a Frenchman, for the Bohemians have a preference for foreign make. I personally am with them: the foreigner lies so bewitchingly; he is so cleverly bad. Perhaps it is because he is a better scholar of nature or a better liar—a scholarly man toward unscholarly moments. He has the secret of unalloyed happiness and unalloyed pain. Recognition of both, acceptance of both, love of both, that is all.

Tito orders the liqueur, fingering the coins in his pocket. Has he enough with which to pay? What does it matter? The room is full of just such predicaments as his: no one can pay, and everyone does.

An impressionist sits in the corner with a woman. I know the man very well; he is hawk-faced, thin, and comes into my mind as something worth telling about. He holds his head slightly up, exposing a soft, high collar in which moonstones sulk. On his fingers are red gems and green; these fingers lie over the top of his staff as though they were separate personalities and wanted to be taken notice of. He knows how to smell nicely, gesture tellingly, and above all, he has the art of looking mid-McKinley, with a touch of the frailties of the Louis period. He talks in breathless English, snuffing each little candle of thought one by one, going out in the end in absolute conversational darkness.

The girl I know, too. Her hair is short (a proof that the Bohemians are, after all, so much like others that they are not original even in this); she had a historic past. She is one of the best sports I know—she

has all the maladies in the almanac, and she doesn't care. She was born laughing, and she will die that way—a boy's laugh, a laugh that springs up from the gutter like a flower. She smokes cigarettes, perhaps a hundred a day. I have seen her rummage among the ashes for "makings" while there was yet a faint perfume in the air of others but lately smoked at a dollar a box. I have listened to her and have laughed, but way down deep I knew she was keeping things that she feared lived—children of memory, and those memories' children.

She is quite reckless; she dances through an evening, she gets terribly drunk, for she can no longer stand what she used to do when, some ten summers ago, she was a girl. All that life holds she has borrowed to hold once also in those long, thin hands; only the eyes never change. They are set in her face like a child's peering over a wall where all the refuse of life has been whirled and caught. It is a terrible and a beautiful thing; her name is—let it go at that.

But let us pass on; it is to laugh.

Sometimes a room gathers an atmosphere, and sometimes it gathers a crowd. These rooms, these studios, these cafes in some future day will fall to dust, but the dust will fall singing.

I stood on the corner of Sixth Avenue where it runs past Greenwich Avenue one night, and as I stood there a fur-trimmed woman, heavily laden with jewels, and two lanky daughters hailed me. In her eyes was a restlessness that was strange to me who have been used to looking into the quiet, often lazy, faces of those about me. Her eyes roved; so did the eyes of her daughters. There was a definite air of the loser looking for the lost.

"Where is Greenwich Village?" she asked, and she caught her breath.

"This is it," I answered, and I thought she was going to collapse.

"But," she stammered, "I have heard of old houses and odd women and men who sit on the curb quoting poetry to the policemen or angling for buns as they floated down into the Battery with the rain. I have heard of little inns where women smoke and men make love and there is dancing and laughter and not too much light. I have heard of houses striped as are the zebras with gold and with silver, and of gowns that—— Quick, quick!" she cried, suddenly breaking off in the middle of the sentence and grabbing a hand of either child exactly like the White Queen in *Through the Looking Glass* as she hurried forward. "There's one now!"

And so she left me in pursuit of a mere woman in a gingham gown with a portfolio under her arm.

I heard that she successfully chased her into Polly's and, once there, sat with bated breath—bated with the little giblets of the mind bantered back and forth between tables from the throats of Ada Foster, Adele Holliday, the perpetual and delightful debutante; George Baker, Renée Lacoste, Dave Cummings, Maurice Becker, Marney and Billy, while at another table Harold Stearns talked to Francis Gifford between bites of a fraudulent tapioca pudding.

But still Madam Bronx was not satisfied. She trailed away with her two daughters wobbling after her on uncertain Sheffield Farm-like ankles unto the Dutch Oven, where she listened to Floyd Dell explaining the drama to Max Eastman or caught what she thought might be risque bits in the conversation between Marsden Hartley and Demuth. The girls ordered custard pie and giggled, for it is so that custard pie should be eaten in Bohemia.

Finally, Madam Bronx could stand it no longer. "Are you an artist?" she inquired of a red-haired woman who had somehow forgotten to cut her hair.

The red-haired woman smiled; a twinkle came into her eye. "No," she answered, "I am a pamphleteer."

"What is that?"

"One of the birth controllers," the red-haired lady answered with immovable face.

And from there to the Candlestick, and from the Candlestick to the Mad Hatter, and from the Mad Hatter to the French pastry shop, and from the pastry shop to all the known haunts, ending up in Mazzini's. For this sad little fur-trimmed woman with her certified daughters was ignorant of those lost places that are twice as charming because of their reticence.

No, I shall not give them away, but I'll locate one of them for those of you who care to nose it out as book lovers nose out old editions. It is a basement this side of Sixth Avenue on the odd-number length of Washington Place. I lived there once, but on the night of the disaster to the gunpowder mill in Jersey I was confronted with a house full of wailing women, in the midst of which the rotund landlady, in bare feet, stood crying out upon Manhattan and broken windows in general and moaning for her rosary of beads and her rosary of children.

"They do not shatter glass in Boston like this," she said, and stood shivering until she sank upon the cushions of my couch, calling aloud for a drop of wine to forestall the chills, adding that dynamite was mighty impertinent.

And so I moved. But there in the basement, with pallid Latin faces, are a husband chef and a wife waitress who bring out molding tomes: a cookbook of the early Renaissance, or a favorite recipe of some baron written in his own hand long ago, fading now from the page as a blush from the cheeks of the love-stricken. Or monsieur the chef plays on a bulging mandolin, with twitching blond mustache, while the young composer who lately met with an accident, surviving with a broken leg, sits profiled against the wall, smiling with fine, kind eyes.

This is real—this is the unknown. Even a basement has its basement, and this is one of the basements below Bohemia.

Well, there is Bobby. We cannot forget Bobby, with his row of ukuleles hanging in his studio on Washington Square. Bobby has kept up the old tradition: he has proposed marriage to every girl in the place, hoping devoutly that she would not take him seriously. Bobby, with his hornrimmed spectacles that keep his eyes from stampeding into trouble as a fence keeps cattle from forbidden grounds; Bobby, who steps upon a table at the Black Cat to sing the now justly famous song, "Way Down South in Greenwich Village," and the still more pathetic "Song of the Camel" who desires to forgo the waters of a million pumps to be with his love.

Guido Bruno, in green felt hat, can be seen pondering over his vichy and milk while he writes a last edition on a paper napkin. Or Peggy O'Neill—not the actress, but the other Peggy—comes bouncing in to spill the latest dirt, her hands on her hips as she adds, "Watch me page myself a dinner," later ordering a "flock of lambs," which is nothing more nor less than chops.

A few Radical pests come in with flowing ties and flowing morals, walking from table to table, maintaining that Baudelaire was right when he said, "Be drunk on wine or women, only be drunk on something." Hippolite Havel supports Baudelaire a little better than anyone else, keeping up at the same time what nothing can quite obliterate—education that has been blunted into charlatanism of thought through many, many hard knocks.

There are the evenings in the studios, blue and yellow candles pouring their hot wax over things in ivory and things in jade. Incense curling up from a jar; Japanese prints on the wall. A touch of purple here, a gold screen there, a black carpet, a curtain of silver, a tapestry thrown carelessly down, a copy of *Rogue* on a low table open at Mina Loy's poem. A flower in a vase, with three paint brushes; an edition of Oscar Wilde, soiled by socialistic thumbs. A box of cigarettes, a few painted fans, choice wines (this here the abode of the more prosperous).

And then—a small hall bedroom under the eaves, a dirty carpet lying in rags; a small cot bed with a dirty coverlet. A broken shaving mug with a flower in it, a print of a print on the wall, a towel thrown in a corner, a stale roll and a half-finished cup of tea. A packing box with a typewriter on it, some free verse, a copy of a cheap magazine with a name in the table of contents that corresponds to the name written at the top of the sheet of paper in the machine. A smell of incense, perhaps from the hall downstairs, where the rent is higher, perhaps bought with the last quarter. A pair of torn shoes, a man's body on the bed, with arms thrown out, breathing slowly the heavy breath of the underfed.

Then there are the theatres that have sprung up, the Washington Square Players with a lease at the Comedy, and now the Provincetown Players in a room next to the Liberal Club—which, by the by, in spite of its liberality, threw out a few poker players—and there are to be others.

Of small shops: Daisy Thompson's, the Jolin Shop, the Treasure Box (somebody took some jade rings from here—if they see this, please return). Helena Dayton has clay personalities for sale in some of them; Clara Tice's can be bought in others.

And then in the end, when everything else closes up and the chairs are lifted to the laps of the tables and the lights go out—all together—there is always the Hell Hole on Fourth Street and Sixth Avenue. A slit in the door, a face staring into your face, the dirty back room with its paper cutouts of ladies in abbreviated undergarments, the men at the tables, the close atmosphere, the sordid faces, the unclean jokes; straggling in of colored women and men, a colored sweetheart with a smile set in her face like a keyboard into a night—compliments from him, first embarrassment from her, then preening to end in a mincing exit. The deadening down, down, into a gray, drunken slumber, the still, dead beer; the heavy air, the inert bodies—daylight.

Life's little comedy: comedy's great tragedy—Bohemian night, Washington Square day. Melancholy, the only sign of loyalty to something they once believed. A few friends, a sweetheart playing with two make-believe fires. Real things that are beautiful mixed in dreadfully with that which is sham; a wonderful, terrible hash on the table of life. And the fan keeps on blowing through the world, winnowing the wheat from the chaff. And because the chaff is lighter it blows up and up and turns and shines in the sun, dancing a moment

a mad, wild dance—a dance that turns the gaze from the grain lying
there in a still, fruitful heap. But the chaff dances slower and slower,
down, down, and down; it blows out of sight—it has never been.

Well, in the morning it will be funny again, the morning beginning at four or perhaps as early as eleven. There will be the occasional
balls, the dances at the clubs, the dinners at the inns, the appointments
for a theatre or a moving picture show; the chats in the evening
about art and life, the theories as old as the hills and the newest fads
that are new, the trottings uptown of the interior decorators to match
a shade for a chair or a color scheme for a studio. Anton Hellman
hovering above the legs of chairs arranging their tone as Ziegfeld
arranges the legs of his chorus. The Italian restaurant keepers will
begin to mix the tomato sauce for the evening rounds of spaghetti.
Students will gather in the park. Somewhere out of the rattle of
trolley cars will be heard the sharp, high cry of little bootblacks crying, "Shine, shine, mister; only three cents!" The policemen, swinging their clubs, will stroll past the Mews, talking together. The leaves
crackle under foot, the grass dies, the birds grow scarcer and scarcer.
The endless crowds of "slummers" looking for painted beads and
black tassels will go by. A candle or two will gleam in a studio window to the south. A rattle of music through an open window, the
weeping of a baby in a tenement, the click of a typewriter in a basement, then the Villagers hurrying to their favorite eating place; the
cigarettes once more, once more the round of drinks, once more the
hilarity, a few clever jokes, a jest at free love—night.

FRANK HARRIS FINDS SUCCESS MORE EASILY WON HERE IN AMERICA THAN IN ENGLAND

I WAS DINING at the house of a friend some eighteen months ago when the maid announced Mr. Harris. "Frank, you know," my hostess said as she arose to greet him.

A short man came suddenly into the room, a man with thick, dark hair and a mustache like a mural painting, a decoration to the house of Harris. A man who seemed to be a favorite corridor where life had loved to stroll. When he spoke one became startled: the voice was the deep and rich voice of a large man; let me call it the echo of those who passed.

His eyes were keen at once and kind; not overoften, but once now and again one could see that this man had not flung the harpoon alone.

What more expressive thing can I say to describe him than that life had used him. I like this better than the phrase, he had used life.

This was the only time that I was to meet him and not know him, for he becomes a friend at once or he becomes nothing. He has also the terrible quality that goes with it: he can cease as abruptly and as decisively as he began.

It is a terrible thing that memories of great men die with their contemporaries. For only so short a space can one man say of another, "I knew him well. He used to have a droll little trick—" So soon, too tragically soon, comes the remark instead, "I knew a man once who knew a man—"

This is Harris. With him dies virtually all of the oldest and best in the last century of English letters. An eloquent potpourri of the petals fallen from the flowers of Europe, adding his own fine shower of leaves to the fragrant pile that too soon will pass into the unlimited where all limited things have couch and eternal sleep.

I remember walking up Fifth Avenue one night with him in the fall, and with what awe I watched this man's moods come and go. At one moment running and jumping a brook in the street, and the next denouncing America's insistent crying for "a happy ending." Some editor had got him to change one of his books and he was already beginning to regret it.

A fine strain of piracy runs through the veins of Harris. Like Benvenuto Cellini, he cannot help seeing the beauty of force. Ah, how his eyes shone when mentioning the diamond mines of Kimberley. "There is a living for you," he exclaimed again and again. And even Nellie, his wife, gets a great deal of amusement in watching him, swearing to do her part in holding up the train if he will; both of them amused, but something beyond amusement always in the hot, quick light in Harris's eyes.

I said, "I'll see you swinging yet in Kimberley, see you swinging by the neck in Kimberley."

It had a strange poetic rhythm to it, and Harris looked up and nodded. "That's the way to die," he said. "Go out like a fine, brave fruit, not like a worm."

For me, personally, the social side of Harris is the most charming. He is so human, often brilliant, so caustic, at times so bitter. Undying hate for his enemies and for those who have caused him trouble; such high wrath blazing always for pains brought to the artist's soul by the vulgar bourgeoise; such dynamic contempt for all who cramp and spoil—and yet always so much the gentleman.

This is how I love him, this is where my mind accepts as true the sinister in him.

But there is a business side as well, and to this I had to go also. For when he is being interviewed, he is another man again: not the writer, not the talker, not the host, he is the man who made the *Fortnightly Review* what it was in London and is making *Pearson's* what it is here. And I cannot but feel alienated by the knife that cuts the truth from top to base and lays it a quivering anatomical district before the eye.

Therefore I asked him if he thought he had already reached "safe" with *Pearson's*.

"I believe so," he said. "The circulation manager tells me that the sales have quadrupled in New York in the last four months, and repeat orders are coming in from all parts of the country. Three days after the publication of the February number, we received repeat orders from Philadelphia and Chicago of twenty-five percent—and now another repeat order from Philadelphia for a further twenty percent."

"Success comes running here, where she tiptoes in London?" I queried.

"I can only speak for myself," he replied. "For me, well, I find it more easily won here in America. Let me explain. In England a radical policy is disliked by the classes. Of course, if you get together five or six men of genius such as I had on the *Saturday Review,* an increase of circulation is almost assured. Shaw, Wells, Max Beerbohm, Cunningham-Grahame, and Arthur Symons give a weekly paper distinction and influence, but even in that case the advertiser does not follow the reader. Though I almost doubled the circulation of the *Saturday Review* in the first year, I lost more than half my advertisements. The moneyed classes in England dislike originality and hate all radical theories. The middle-class shopkeeper in England is the most obstinate foe to progress in the world. He is as much the snob as the aristocrat, and has besides an insane love of money and a corresponding hatred of those who hinder him from obtaining it.

"In America, on the other hand, you can reach success through a radical policy. That is, an editor can thus obtain circulation, and advertisements follow circulation. The coming success in American journalism will be a really radical daily paper in New York.

"That is the difference between Europe and America. In Europe you are radical till you get power; then you sell out to the privileged classes and get everything you want for yourself. Like Lloyd George and Briand, who both started as social reformers or Socialists and are now defenders of the privileged classes and money. Mr. Wilson brought in an eight-hour bill while President—a radical reform, a thing unthinkable in Europe.

"America is radical at heart, and if you ever get a Moses, Americans will follow him into the promised land. In Europe Moses' only chance of getting the leadership is to become a lackey of the classes. He frightens everybody by telling them that the Red Sea is a sea of blood.

"My message at present is better than the paper it is printed on," he added, smiling.

Then I asked him if he believed that Lloyd George would be unable to lead the English to success, and if he was not of the opinion that as a popular leader Lloyd George was already lost.

"Completely lost, I'm afraid," he nodded. "He is leaning not on the Liberals, but on the Tories; he is the last hope of the oligarchy.

He thinks that energy, courage, and hard work will make the difference between success and failure in this war. Both the French and the English commanders encourage him in the belief that if sufficient munitions are provided, the Allies can break through on the West and drive the Germans back to their own frontier. He is practically pledged to achieve this by next August. In my opinion, he will fail; but even if he succeeds, he will get no better terms from the Germans than he could get now.

"By rejecting the peace proposal and by making exorbitant demands, he has made himself mainly responsible for at least another year of war; and the next year of war will cost more in blood and treasure than can possibly be gained by any or all of the combatants. He underrates his adversaries, or rather, he does not understand Germany at all or Germany's aims."

"And the result will be?"

"A draw," said Mr. Harris, "with the Germans winners on points."

"Do you think President Wilson could end the war?"

"Yes, a year-and-a-half ago when England was dependent for her munition supply on America. The President could then have forced England to give reasonable terms, by threatening to put an embargo on the exportation of munitions; but now American munitions are not absolutely necessary to Great Britain. Accordingly, President Wilson could hardly enforce peace at the present time. By working for it steadily he may bring it about by next September or October, especially if the Allies fail to drive the Germans out of France or to break their lines. I believe that President Wilson will do all in his power to end it all, but I see no hope of peace until Lloyd George has had his trial and failed."

"Then you think that if the Allies win and drive the Germans back to their own frontier, the war will go on?"

"Probably. The Germans will never accept terms the Allies have put forward till they are completely beaten, and that I regard as impossible."

"What do you think will happen in the United States after peace if made?"

"The United States will either have to socialize her chief industries in order to meet the new competition of socialized Europe, or she will have to erect a high tariff wall and keep out competition, which will have the effect of increasing enormously the social inequality inside these United States. I was very glad to see that Secretary Daniels intends to socialize the manufacture of munitions. That is the best line to take. He seems to be doing much good work.

"I should like to see the telephones and the telegraphs taken over by the state, and the railways; but that will hardly happen the next year, and will never happen if the Frank Trumbulls are listened to."

But I was thinking of Shaw and of Moore and of Wilde and those other brilliant minds that Frank had struck fire against. And so I asked him suddenly, breaking in on a reverie which he had fallen into, his hand set in between the first and second buttons of his coat as one sees them in old photographs.

"Tell me," I said, "something about those men who made up the genius of the *Saturday Review.*"

"You know," he answered, "Shaw and Bertrand Russell are about the only two men in England who have kept their heads in the general smashup. It is astonishing how infectious is the spirit of the herd in England. In America, too, you have persons talking of patriotism as the soul of the nation."

"And Shaw," I asked, "what kind of letters does he write?"

"Shaw's letters are quite as funny as his plays. You had a specimen of that the other day when he replied to the invitation to come to America to speak. He said he was afraid to come, for he liked riding in railway cars with other men's wives—a home thrust for the way we treated Gorki."

"And George Moore?"

"There is a man who writes letters as well as he writes books. Most men who come to the front are sincere—genius especially."

"And what do you think of America in regard to literature and art?"

"There America has everything to do, and has hardly made a start as yet. In the long run, the composite character of America may be a great help. Every state should have a state art gallery, a state theatre and a state conservatory of music, and, of course, state endowment of scientific research.

"Every big city, too, should have its municipal theatre, municipal art gallery, municipal school of music, municipal schools of chemistry and physics. Art, literature, and science must be endowed and fostered, that is the most necessary thing in America today; that is the lesson Germany and France have taught the world. Statesmen should think of themselves as gardeners and not be satisfied till they can show specimens of every flower of genius in the gardens."

"You believe that the endowment of art produces artists, and the endowment of literature, writers of genius?"

"The men of genius are always there," replied Mr. Harris, "but if you do not help them, they will not be able to produce the great works. Shakespeare would never have done his best work, never have written *Hamlet* or *Othello* or *Anthony and Cleopatra,* if Lord Southhampton had not given him the one thousand pounds which made possible his high achievement. The popular taste of his day was worse than ours. His worst play, *Titus Andronicus,* was of the popular type, given hundreds of times in his life, whereas *Hamlet* was only given twelve times, and *Lear* once or twice."

"Only when New York has a municipal theatre and a state theatre shall we be equal to Paris, which has the Odeon and the Comédie Française, and we with a population half as large again. We endow common school education in America; but not the flower of education. We must endow genius in America, and every manifestation of it."

He turned suddenly to the mantelpiece and dropping his lower lip, said, "Ah," as only he knows how to say it. The ejaculation of a man who will not weep when his heart is full, the desolate sound of a man who will not permit himself to be disillusioned; a half-sound between a truce and a challenge.

"It's dreadful, dreadful!" he said, clasping his hands behind him, walking to the window where he could see the park.

I asked him, "What," softly.

"The way they treat a man; the way they treat men of talent and of real worth in America. I don't see how you all stand it."

I knew that he was referring to those of us who have been born with a little reverence for the things that are beautiful, and a little love for the things that are terrible; and I nodded my head.

ALFRED STIEGLITZ ON LIFE AND PICTURES: "ONE MUST BLEED HIS OWN BLOOD"

IT WAS SOME time in the early fall, I think, of 1914, that I strayed into the house of Mabel Dodge toward evening, to show her my pictures. At this time I had half of the "old manner" with me and but a slight hint of the new. The nonchalant classes—the poet, the revolutionist, with their heads always on a sort of ball-bearing system, with bombs and other redeeming munitions of a future social order—were entirely new to me. This class struck me at first as entirely charming, not from the standpoint of wishing to cultivate their immediate acquaintance, but from a gratitude arising from the pleasure of being pointed out the way to the future with an index finger that had previously been dipped in gold ink.

These were my grateful days. I was grateful to Mabel Dodge, who let me eat as many sandwiches as my suburban stomach could hold. I was grateful to Carl Van Vechten for having written the introductory card that had given me access to so much.

I remember how funny I looked in the midst of that artistic atmosphere. I remember that even at that time I asked myself the question, Why is it that all similarity of ideas and tastes has the same manner of dress, of speech and mode of living?

Two or three of the older gentlemen paid some small attention to me, and I wondered at the time if it was because of my lack of *sang froid* or because they liked my drawings. I wondered a little, too, why old men have always had a peculiar liking for me where young men are entirely indifferent—and why at the same time for me there existed no man, young or old, who could draw the slightest, faintest word of interest from me apart from my drawing or some abstract thing connected with themselves. Perhaps it was because love had been much discussed in my family circles, because all the old romances of man and maid had already been read to me. Perhaps it was because, and this surely was it, that art had been something that I felt and not saw, longed for and not possessed, to its outward fullness, hoped for and at last approached.

And yet I was in awe of no one; I attempted not to show the arrogance of my upper lip that would persist in an attempt to curl, probably because I wanted to cry and wouldn't. I felt cold because I wanted so dreadfully to feel warm and hopeful and one with them.

But all of this is entirely out of the way, except to give a small pen picture of myself at the time when Mr. Alfred Stieglitz first came into my life. Mabel Dodge was holding up a painting of mine, extraordinarily bad, too, and she was hesitating between approval and disapproval. "Anyway," she said, "go to 291 Fifth Avenue and ask for Mr. Stieglitz, and show him; perhaps he can help you."

Two ninety-one is at the top of an old-fashioned house overlooking the Avenue. The elevator opened onto a little vestibule and gave a hint of a picture hung well beyond. A man was standing with one elbow on the shelving that runs entirely around this room; his feet were crossed, and he was talking to two or three people, on the same order as those I had met the night before. He did not look up when I entered, nor did he seem to notice me. He was telling some tale beginning, "That makes me remember," interjected with "Well, say."

His hair was longer than usual with men, and turning then iron gray. The eyebrows were bushed, the eyes deep-set and assumed a certain uncertainty. He asserts that he was born in this country, yet I noted then that his mouth had that fine and sudden stoppage of lip seen mostly in the south of Germany. Someone has told me that I have a peculiar habit of noticing mouths. I have, and when I see one that does not merge into the rest of the face, I want the world to know about it, a mouth that is a personality upon a person.

He has a manner of speaking at once quick and hesitating, perhaps a little because he speaks through his nose—I don't know, though I have tried to define and to place it. A very individual speech, an individuality of respiration.

Presently he turned to me and introduced me to those present, at the same time introducing himself to me. They left soon, and he quite naturally took the portfolio with which I was laden out of my arm.

He looked the pictures over and asked me what I thought of them. I had not expected this question, and answered, "I'm quite crazy about them."

He seemed pleased. "You're the first woman," he said slowly, "who has been perfectly frank in that answer. Well, perhaps you're right." He put them back and began to tie them up.

"And what am I to do?" I asked.

"Keep on drawing, if you really care for it, and don't try to sell them or—" There was a pause during which he looked out of the window. "Or keep right on, if you don't want to, and sell them."

That's about the best advice I ever got, and it is typically Stieglitz, though he won't like the word typical. I felt something then which later I analyzed with his help. While he seemed to care for pictures, he did not seem to know pictures; while he gave advice on pictures, he seemed to be giving advice on life.

The type of all his exhibitions has been revolutionary, cubist, impressionist, irrationalist, all of them. There have been Picasso, Matisse, Rodin, Pamela Smith, Brancusi, Toulouse-Lautrec—savage art called "negro," Picabia, Marsden Hartley, Dove, Severini and others, while the newest is a woman, Georgia O'Keefe. Not to forget, of course, the present Marin exhibit and the always oncoming Walkowitz, head down.

Often this man has been called the master faker. I cannot hide behind this statement; I also have thought him the master faker. Many have said, "He must be; he has nothing for sale, yet he has a gallery; he has nothing to gain, apparently, but the futile remarks of those passing." Again I have to confess, but adding, "Well, perhaps he has enough money of his own. In that case, why does he want to amuse himself in such an unamusing way?"

"To meet just such people as you," he said, and laughed.

"Oh," he added, "I'm tired of being America's fool-court fool, jester, buffoon. You have all come here straight-faced, and some of you have gone away smiling, and you did not think I knew. I have been content and patient to know, because that is the only reason for my thirteen years in this garret. You have all thought what you pleased. Why should I enlighten you? Why should I tell you that one must bleed his own blood? It's all right; the other day I thought I had learned all I had come to learn, and the night after, I thought I had learned too much, and I was going to end it. I knew that there was nothing so calculated to expose men as art. They are simple before it or they are the capital liars. What do I know of pictures? Not a thing. What do I know of cubism and all the other things, line and color? Nothing. What do I know of new movements, or old? Nothing. What do I want to know of them? Nothing. But, say, I'll tell you, I've reached the spot where I am about willing to turn down an empty glass. I have had them all here to learn what you Americans are like, and I have learned much. My gallery was only a trap set for humanity, and the trap has worked, season in and out. Who was it who said that he had a gallery, hung on one side with peaceful, pleasing pictures, and the other with horrible and gruesome things, merely to know his friends better? If they stopped before the gentle and the meek representation, he called for his butler to remove the knife he knew would be up their sleeves, but if they stopped at the brutal and the horrible, he had lunch ordered in the green room.

"I have, in other words, had the privilege of laughing at America for thirteen years.

"By their telling me what I am, I have learned what they are. One by one I have lost all my friends to make new ones. They come here and they go away from here, and always I am contented. I do not seek for my life, and that is as it should be. By having open doors the world passes through, and I, I can stand and watch and learn. I have a hunger, a terrible hunger, for that knowledge, and when that knowledge alienates me from the older generation and from the newer generation, I grow afraid, and I ask myself over again. What do they mean when they say no and what when they say yes? Do they have any logical sequence of feeling, is there a before and an after to it? It is the parrot talking in the trees. It is the needle of life reproducing the sounds learned on the mother knee. I do not know."

He went on to talk of women.

"I believe in woman, not in women; I have had enough pain because of them to have made me shut them out of my heart forever, yet I will believe. I can hear 'Nevermore' in the air, and I can out-shout it, 'Evermore.' You say I am a perfect gentleman, nevertheless I say that I have been expelled from the Camera Club. I have never gone away from anything; I have let things go away from me. I have never made the mistake of stepping aside; I have always let things pass up and pass on. That is the only means by which one can find anything out."

"And once you told much about trees."

"That I always went to them and laid my heart upon them and told them my griefs and my pleasure."

"Yes, and once you told about the lake, at Lake George."

"The lake is the most human thing of all, it has neither brains nor heart—as my enthusiasm has neither father nor mother."

"Then nature is the only thing that makes humans possible?"

"Nature is the only thing that explains human nature; we expect too much of the one and nothing of the other.

"Now take women, for instance. They are advanced far ahead of the American man—I have told them often about it. Some of the upper classes used to come here and inquire why their souls would not keep time with their husbands? Why, for instance, they loved Rodin, but that if they bought one and hung it on the wall, their husbands would rebel.

"I answered, 'Because you have kept them working on the nickels and the dimes of the world; you keep them down at business so that you may go gadding about.' 'Did you ever hear of a cat?' I once asked one of them. She hesitated, and laughing asked, 'Do you mean a woman or a real cat?' I assured her that I meant a real cat, 'the kind,' I added, 'who catches a mouse and plays with it, and finally eats it.' She said she had. 'Well,' I answered, 'that's the difference. You women play with the mouse, but you never eat it.'"

"People think you have money?"

"And I have not. I have been in the habit, it is true, of taking four or five of my friends out to lunch. That has stopped; it had to. I would rather keep up 291 than have lunch."

"And now that you have confessed that all these years you have been laughing at us, should we be angry?"

"No—for what? There is no love, there is no art, and I have learned that there are no people. There is only emotional learning, spectacular ABC's and customers."

He laughed.

"And what of thinkers?"

"Brains of insurmountable heights out of which pass incurable thoughts."

"And one should not be in love?"

"One should not be in love, it prevents work; and cool, logical study one should love."

And I thought:

From this place I have been standing eternally, looking out toward the world with my eyes and seeing men pass and look back at me. And I cold and lonesome and increasing steadily in mine own sorrow, which is caught like the plague of other men, until I am full and my mouth will hold no more, and my eyes will see no more, and my ears can stand nothing further. Then do I begin the steady, slow discharge which is called "wisdom," but which is only that too much the eyes cannot see, the ears cannot hear, the mouth cannot hold.

"And so your life from day to day?"

"You see this view from my back window? It is simple and full of a perfect absence of human life. Only a hotel with fire escapes, a lot of blank empty-looking windows, and just lately a few signs painted on it." He began to read, "Hats and gowns, ladies' dresses, A. P. Smith, ladies' cloak maker, neckwear and hosiery." He paused, and I went on, "And petti—"

"Pull down the shade," he demanded. And then we both laughed. Two or three men had dropped in, and I wondered how Mr. Stieglitz has managed to keep from going mad if he has had to listen to all sorts of people, such as I have often seen there. Great droning bores, like buzzards who have come to earth weighed down with a cargo of the heaviest portions of too heavy souls. Or little murky women who hover, in casual life, over rare editions of Emerson, Longfellow and Riley, wearing rubbers and carrying handbags of uncertain leather and speaking with a hissing sound of all s's as though their words were sliding on a well-tiled floor. Or fat ladies burdened with small dogs, who look admiringly at anything providing it isn't a picture, and say that they "adore" all "trends," it is such a great thing for "progress." Still worse, the tourist type, the willowy man with the pliant cane, and the young women who exclaim enthusiastically, "What conception of line and color!" holding some print off at arm's length. All these things puzzled me, as it puzzles me how he can have the patience to talk to them for the length of time that he does.

In looking it over, the question puts itself, what has he done for others, now that we know something of what others have done for him?

One might as well ask what the image of the Virgin in the corner of the darkest church has done for the casual worshipper; might as well ask what the steps have done for the house; might as well ask what the beggar sitting upon the curb has done for the almsgiving pedestrian. Might as well ask to turn things around, what the casual worshipper has done for the Virgin, what the house has done for the steps, what the almsgiving public has done for the beggar.

But often I ask myself when I think no one will hear me thinking, least of all Stieglitz—what has made it necessary for this man to learn life in this way, and what happened in the lives of the others that makes it necessary for them to form a sort of "public society"?

Sometimes I like Stieglitz when he talks too much, and often I find myself liking him when he says too little—very much too little.

THE RIDER OF DREAMS IS HERE

SCENE. THE GARDEN *of Pilate's House at Jerusalem. Time, the day of the new arising of* SIMON, *the cross bearer. At the moment of the opening in the conversation,* ROBERT E. JONES *sits upon a settle at the right of the stage of his own designing; directly in the center stands a Negro of immense build. Upon his head is a cap of silver. He is* SIMON; *but now he is smiling. A little at one side is* JOE *of* The Rider of Dreams, *that infant who has made stealing a divine privilege. His left hand is in his pocket. He looks continually offstage, as though contact with the human eye would make him a little less celestial*

RIDGELY TORRENCE, *author, is speaking to* OPAL COOPER *as I emerge from Pilate's house to left.*

There is nothing lacking but MRS. HAPGOOD, *who will be in later, for out backstage the rest of the Negroes belonging to the Torrence plays at the Garden Theater are laughing and singing among themselves— arranging their throats for the coming of some note of ecstasy which will rest there for a moment and be heard by alien ears only through those throaty walls as something too real to be other than hidden—a song going about its work with the curtains down.*

Here we are, all of us: BOBBY JONES, *the designer and director,* MR. TORRENCE, *the author and the heart, the sense that* MRS. HAPGOOD *saw the possibilities, the actors that at last are coming a little step into their own, and myself—the interrogator.*

One feels the nearness of the circus; one feels the nearness of spring in the air. One balances between tragedy and comedy, and a draught runs between the two—it is called comment.

The story of Simon the cross bearer has come to a close, the cries of the crucifixion have stilled into that silence we term the past, but

89

which is the voice of the future. The cross has been built and has already fallen to dust. The kneebone of the suppliant is one with the hand of the executioner. In the grave of the years they at last come slowly together eon by eon, till the one closes on the other in the clasp of time that brings all things together, articulated by fate.

"Simon the Cyrenian" is now just John Butler plus one superb red cloak by Mr. Jones.

And Granny Maumee is backstage taking the lines of age from her face and the hate from her heart. But the Rider of Dreams is still here, for this is the spirit of the Negro.

R. TORRENCE: And how did you at last feel the part of Madison Sparrow, Opal?

OPAL COOPER: Well—at first I tried to get it in the usual way, Mr. Torrence, by ear—that's no way for a colored man.

MR. TORRENCE: Why not, Opal?

OPAL COOPER: It has to come by way of the feelin's, sir, by the heart. I did it over and over *(he smiles)* this way: *(begins chanting the dream)* I dreamed it las' night, and day befo' yesterday night, and night befo' dat. I heah a voice say, 'Get up and come a-runnin''—and still I couldn't get off the ground, Mr. Torrence. I was still on de stage and I knowed that the thing should be recited with my feet over the tops of the houses, sung as though I was a-lookin' down on the world for a place to spit without hitting things, and I couldn't do it until—

BOBBY JONES: Till?

OPAL COOPER: Till Sam laughed, my friend who came to hear me out. As soon as he laughed, something let go o' my leg and there I was, away up high against the sun.

VOICE OF THE INTERVIEWER: And what did you do then?

OPAL COOPER: Then I say I looks up and sees a fine white saddle hoss, and the hoss say, 'Ride me right and I'll guide you right.'

VOICE OF THE INTERVIEWER: And how did you feel then?

OPAL COOPER: Miss, it was this way: I had the stars for cobblestones and the nighttime for my car, and I done pour all that was in me out in the high places so that you folk way down low in the world, walking around buying and selling and living and dying, could hear the voice of Sparrow singing, 'Off he goes as slick as a rancid transom car.' Come to a high hill, lookin' down on de sun and moon. Hoss says, 'I bring you heah to give you news the world is yours.'

BABY JOE *(still looking offstage):* Wasn't my work good?

VOICE OF INTERVIEWER *(with much approval):* It was positively wonderful, dear. What are you going to do when you are grown up into a big man?

BABY JOE: I shall be a great actor.

VOICE OF INTERVIEWER: Is this your biggest ambition?

BABY JOE: If I get a good part—a good stealing part. But I can't. Big men do not steal.

VOICE OF INTERVIEWER: Then you think the only hope is in remaining five years old, Joe?

BABY JOE *(in a small voice):* Yes.

VOICE OF INTERVIEWER: One can be more natural then, can't one, Joe?

BABY JOE: Yes; that's the only time. *(He moves off slowly.)*

B. JONES: Isn't he the brightest boy you ever saw? He is acting already. He has acquired all the attributes of a matinee idol.

OPAL COOPER: It's in the blood, Mr. Jones. It's in the blood as thick as daisies in a field. Run him along for a space and he will try to run smooth, but there's no preventing him from hitting one of them flowers in the end.

R. TORRENCE *(to* V. OF I.*):* You see how they are. You call them children—when they are children they are grownup. When they are grown-up they are children; we all are—the nicest of us.

OPAL COOPER *(reciting):* Perchance, by praying, a man shall match his god.

> For if sleep have no mercy, and man's dreams
> Bite to the blood and burn into the bone.
> What shall this man do waking?

That were the word of a great poet, Miss. As we pick poets for our ministers, so I want to see poets in our actors—for the stage could be the right-hand man of the church, Miss. When we colored folk get a new preacher, we don't ask that he be educated in the regular sense of the word. He might rattle the Scriptures offhand, easy-like, but it wouldn't be preaching, as we colored folk know it. We says, has he heart or hasn't he heart, do he lose himself in the Lord or do he just stand around on the outskirts a-tickling of Him? Does he ascend, or do he just stay where he's put in the pulpit? Do he teach the gospel or do he stimulate you into believin' what he says? Do he cry,

Miss, in the back of his throat; do he chant and do his soul sing?
Do he be a man standing in a church, or a church standing in
a man?

VOICE OF INTERVIEWER: And you want this in your actors?

SIMON (*speaking for the first time*): We do. If we don't give as much to
the stage as we do to our religion, how can it be worth our time?

R. TORRENCE: There you are. We had hoped to find the dramatic
quality in great abundance in the colored people. Perhaps we were
mistaken; but mistaken or not, it is something to have done.

B. JONES: For me it is a great awakening. I was fast becoming content
with half of myself. To direct a performance as well as to design
it is one of the most astonishing things that has ever happened to
me. Instead of playing around with a color for a bracelet, a shade
for a boot, a certain line for a cloak, suddenly I find myself interested in an arm, the set of a pair of shoulders, a turn of the head,
the position of a mass, the play of a light, a tone in a speech that
is not just right, a sentence that is too high, a remark that is too
low. I have not one string in my hand, but many. I have not one
art, but all art—I have not one ambition, but many ambitions.

R. TORRENCE (*in an aside*): They make a mistake in calling Negroes
children, in thinking that the least praise will carry them away.
It won't, you know—only pleases them, makes them glad to do
their best. They have not been spoiled—they can laugh from the
heart. We have forgotten how, become blasé on many years of
recognition. I want to see this beginning carried out by Negroes
themselves. I want to see a Negro theatre, directed by a Negro,
with plays by Negroes and interpreted by Negroes. How soon
this will come about (*shrugging his shoulders*) I don't know. If it
is left now it will get nowhere. You can't start something as new
as this and drop it suddenly and expect it to stand on its feet. We
have had some plays submitted to us, but, strangely enough, in
the greater number of cases, they were plays dealing with white
people. Sometimes they were low comedy, and often they were
far too exalted to admit of acting except by a company of the
celestially endowed.

B. JONES: Well, you could hardly expect something acted so soon.
Later on—in six months time, perhaps.

OPAL COOPER: Sooner than that, sir. If us colored folks can really
begin to believe that our plays would be given de chance—we are
just a little skeptical yet—we comes forth with fear and much

tremblin', sir. We're like the mole, sir, hidin' low and keeping powerful quiet—but our hide is valuable.

SIMON *(peeling an apple):* We shall yet behold.

R. TORRENCE *(smiling):* That's right, Simon. I hope you will all "yet behold." I have no greater dream.

VOICE OF INTERVIEWER: And through this you hope to be better recognized?

OPAL COOPER: Yes, Miss, but I don't want to see the colored people change theirselves. I don't want to see them trying to be white. You know, Miss, a race is only at its best when it's being racial. You know what I mean—when it's being itself. I am sorry to say that us colored people have a great habit, a great ability, to copy. Some of us have grown up with little knowledge of the dialect and that, Miss, is a sin, same as it's a sin for the Irish to forget their language. It makes a wheat field poor when redtop runs into it, and it makes a race poor when it does not keep its character clean and pure of other people's.

VOICE OF INTERVIEWER: Then you don't want to become Americanized, or like the whites?

OPAL COOPER: No, Miss, we want to develop ourselves and not merge ourselves in another race. We want just enough space to show everyone what is in us—for what it may be worth.

R. TORRENCE *(a mischievous look in his eyes):* Tell her, Opal, why it is that you all wanted a part in *Simon the Cyrenian.*

OPAL COOPER: Because what little chance we have had to show our ability to the theatrical public, Mr. Torrence, has been as comedians! We wants to play something tragic and serious like *Simon the Cyrenian* because that there is the thing we have not been allowed to play.

R. TORRENCE *(with the same twinkle in his eye):* But what is it that you love best?

OPAL COOPER *(with a broad grin):* You knows it, sir—music sure is the colored folks' strong point.

    (In the pause can be heard the voices of the Cleff Club band, singing their songs even when they do not "have to." It rises and swells to a plaintive cry of happiness and dies down again into a humming as of many bees.)

R. TORRENCE *(with a new note in his voice, shaking the long blond hair out of his eyes):* That's right, Opal, and don't you ever lose that talent. Just keep a-hugging it to your heart and nursing it and giving it the encouragement a great art needs. After all, it's better to be happy and to sing than it is to be too cynical and silent.

VOICE OF INTERVIEWER: Shall you write any more colored plays, Mr. Torrence?

R. TORRENCE: I don't know—perhaps. At least I have this off my mind—I have done something for those people who have been so greatly misjudged and ignored. Now I am free to do other things. I want to see of what stuff their dreams are made; if they will stand the hard, critical light of publicity or if 'their dream horses go up in smoke.'

OPAL COOPER (*in chanting lilt*): We are the great black cocks of de world, and we're calling mighty hard upon a sun that is lazy in its bed, but we are a-callin' and a-callin' and a-callin' and when the beak strain, there will come a golden bill all set around that tri-umphant voice. Perhaps it will be a silver bill, and when that breaks and sloughs off from the strain, there will come a golden bill all set around with rubies and all a-waitin' to be sung into, to call up a new day from the darkness. An' when the golden beak is broke and fallen to dust about the black cock's feet, then a little angel will come, and cuppin' its hands about that song will make it reach way up to heaven, and make it arouse the sun where it lies in a drunken stupor from the revelry of the day before. And risin' slowly like a gentleman gettin' out of bed, the sun will say to the moon: 'Moon, go and get my bath ready and get out my sunbeams by the fire, because it's summer, and I am due to shine upon the cold housetops and upon the roofs of little dwellings and upon the wheat fields and the roses, the lakes and the quick leapin' fish and upon the tops of little children's heads. For the fields need me to make the seeds grow, and the houses need me to make the home happy, and the children need me to set their minds a-turnin' on what they shall be when they, too, are men. And den when the black cock has crowed and crowed, and sung and sung his little bit in the ravine, and the little hands of the angel have left him, then he will scratch among the gravel and the grass, and you will think it is for grain, but I know it's for his lost beak of gold—for sometimes he's afraid that he had only the impulse, and some-thing else made his song so powerful and tellin'. (R. TORRENCE *has clasped his hands in front of him, and his kind, keen blue eyes are half-closed. He nods his head, but he does not speak.*)

OPAL COOPER (*continuing*): We mayn't be great and we mayn't be all necessary, we mayn't be powerful and we mayn't be tragic so well as we be glad. But we have de quality if someone will give us a chance to scratch and see if we own the beak or if it's the Lord's.

(B. JONES *gets up slowly with hands behind his back, begins to pace up and down.* R. TORRENCE *remains seated, his hands clasped in front of him.* SIMON *has moved off, leaving nothing behind but the apple peel and a few black apple seeds beside his magnificent cloak of scarlet, but lately fallen from his shoulders. The interviewer has come slowly out of Pilate's house and stands, pencil forgotten in hand.)*

OPAL COOPER: I speaks for my race when I speaks for myself. It's not me only telling you things, it's my mammy and my mammy's mammy before her. What I have forgotten she remembers, and what she has forgotten her mother knows. That's why we linger before we die—to keep alive a little of our heart's blood, a little of our folk song, a little of our dialect and a little of our heritage.

(SIMON *returns with* PILATE'S WIFE.)

PILATE'S WIFE: This way we will find our level.

VOICE OF ACTE AND OF BARABBAS: We shall arise!

VOICE OF PILATE and VOICE OF BATTUS: This way the whites of our eyes shall see across the world!

VOICE OF GRANNY MAUMEE: Thus we shall come a-runnin'!

VOICE OF LUCY SPARROW: For a long time we have been strings curled up in oblivion; now the instrument is stretching us into song.

VOICE OF THE SINGING OVERTURE: At last we are singing up against the cracks of the door. Some day it will swing open.

VOICES OF THE MOCKERS WITH SCARLET ROBE AND CROWN OF THORNS: A crown of thorns for the newborn, a scarlet cloak for a swaddling cloth!

VOICES OF THOSE IN THE GALLERIES: Where's dat nigger heaven now!

VOICES OF THOSE IN THE VESTIBULE: Tickets, that we may see the shell breaking and falling from them!

VOICES OF THOSE IN THE DARK PLACES: We are less by a race!

VOICES OF ROSAMOND JOHNSON AND OF NEGRO SPIRITUALS: Glory, glory, hallelujah!

VOICES OF EXECUTIVE STAFF: To have sewn a bead on, to have mended a broken platform, to have sewn up a torn shoe—this is our share.

VOICES OF THE COLORED PORTION OF THE WORLD *(coming around chair corners and through the cracks of the old theater and down the wings a million on a million):* May our bow arm be strong for the speeding of the arrow tipped with the message!

VOICE OF OPAL COOPER: I dreamed hit last night and day befo' yesterday night, and night befo' dat. I heah a voice say, 'Get up and come a-runnin'.' An' I looks up and sees a fine white saddle hoss, an' the hoss say, 'Ride me right and I'll guide you right.' On I gets, off he goes, slick as a rancid transom car. Come to a high hill, lookin' down on de sun and moon. Hoss say, 'I brung you heah to give you news. The world is yours to pick and choose.'

VOICE OF BOBBY JONES *(calling offstage):* I have a new idea for the lighting of that second play, John. Just switch it on and let's try her now. Ready—that's right.

VOICE OF BABY JOE *(far off stage):* I can't button them up.

VOICE OF INTERVIEWER: I shall try to remember everything.

VOICE OF SIMON: You can't forget, Miss.

VOICE OF RIDGELY TORRENCE: Now we shall see what's in them: if they are great poets, if they are great novelists, if they are great actors, if they are great painters, if they are great producers—or if they are only dreamers singing their dreams over the daily commonplaces that are their lives.

(At this juncture the curtain drops suddenly, blotting out the scene. Then the crooning of many voices singing "Walk Together, Children.")

THE HEM OF MANHATTAN

To TAKE A yacht trip around Manhattan Island is to find yourself in the awkward position of one who must become a stranger in his own house that he may describe it with the necessary color.

How much easier, for instance, to have been sent to Russia to paint a word picture of their afternoon meal and their homes. Or to have gone to France, there to stroll among the ruins of what used to be the descriptive parts of Cousin Milly's letters home; to have walked awhile along the boulevards or to have coveted hats in a window in a street off from that cafe Jules talked of with me the other night. Or to have watched the smoking of French cigarettes, or to have visited Napoleon's tomb or walked where Bernhardt used to walk, or to have tried to find the cafe where Verlaine and Baudelaire wrote their poems, or any one of the million and ten things that one expects to be seen doing when he takes a trip to a foreign country.

There one would notice how the buttons were made because it would be a strange, new person wearing them in a strange, old land. Here one's buttons are never missed until they fall off.

Here one looks upon things because one has eyes. There one has eyes that he may contemplate. This is the inevitable tragedy of being familiar with one's home. Here we live and go through the usual daily program because we must; but it is only when one travels—be it only to Kansas, providing Kansas is a foreign land—that one comes upon the discovery that to appreciate and to understand one should never be on anything but a friendly footing either with architecture or with people.

It's the saying of "How do you do?" that is the educational part of life. The goodbye is only the sad little period to a no-longer-needed paragraph.

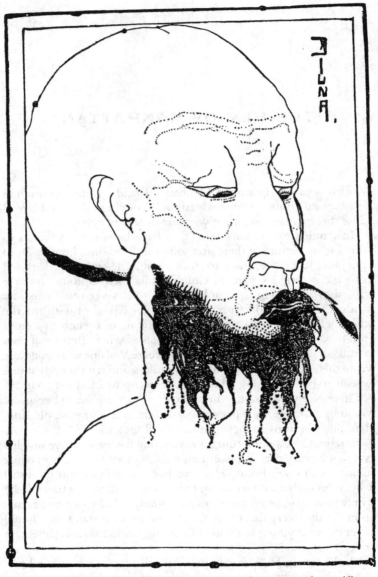

"The gentleman who said, 'You cannot reach into your home.'"

Who was it who said, "My friend, you cannot reach into your home because it is from there you were found reaching out"? And so I am condemned with a thousand million unless I find myself in a lonely place, where I may be profitable in my crying for the echoes I set around me that have never called back since I was born; a place that will be as strange to me as I to it.

It's a pleasant thought, but still I cannot escape my ultimate task: the fact that Manhattan Island has passed before me in review.

I believe this trip is advertised as one of pleasure. Well, perhaps I am melancholy, as I have often been told, but what can one be when to reach the boat one has to cross Death Avenue first? And what is one going to suffer if not despair, when for three hours and a half there pass misery, poverty, death, old age, and insanity?

The two shore lines are separated by a strip of level, uncomplaining water, like two convicts who have between them three links of impassive chain: two terrible positives separated by a negative.

But as the storyteller would say, this is not beginning at the beginning.

I think it was something like two-thirty when I started. The boat was the smallest of its kind I have ever patronized, and as I climbed aboard, the upper deck was already covered with stiff-backed, Middle West school teachers and others, most of whom were bearded gentlemen with gold nuggets mounted and used as tiepins.

They all sat there in uncompromising rows as though they were in a classroom, and off and on they turned their heads just enough to look at the water with determination, because they were there to see, and they would see.

The sun was hot, and you could hear the cordage and the planking creaking. Let me mention that I did not see more than one child on this trip. And after all, this was quite the right thing. Children are taken to Bear Island, or up the Hudson to some camping ground, to some place that resembles at least a definite spot.

Presently, as the yacht pulled out and started moving in a side circle about the Battery, the megaphone man stepped forward and began chanting: "This building to your left is known as the Woolworth Tower, the largest building in the world; it stands so-many-and-so-many feet high," giving the exact number of feet and inches, as though it were growing, and then he turned in the other direction and added casually, "This is a transport steamer to your right, filled, as you see, by our boys in khaki."

Then we heard their voices, hundreds of them, coming to us over the intervening water. A strange cry, a happy cry, an exultant cry, proclaiming doom and death. They all rose up, calling aloud, waving their arms and their handkerchiefs. A few words drifted back to us as we pulled alongside and then moved on. "We'll get the Kaiser," and the often-repeated, "Come on, too." One of them standing a little forward kissed his hand lightly; others thrust their shaggy heads out of the portholes. It made me think of Coney Island and the voice that usually accompanies an outthrust head; "Three shots for a nickel."

I looked around me: everyone was sitting in the same passive manner, stiffly and conventionally and unemotionally.

Looking at the skyline as we rounded the Battery, New York rose out of the water like a great wave that found it impossible to return again and so remained there in horror, peering out of the million windows men had caged it with.

Boats, like pet dogs, were leashed to the docks, and one little tug looking like a spitz growled at our side, sticking its nose out of the green, loose water as though it were trying to bite.

The Brooklyn Bridge, the Manhattan, the Williamsburg, and the Queensboro came into view, stretching away into the distance. The megaphone man came back again, explaining that Steve Brodie was the first man to jump this bridge without loss of life; afterward he kept a cafe and was quite a character.

And then I thought of another trip I had taken once—a cheap excursion trip on a larger and dirtier boat. Somehow I had liked that better; there was something living and careless and human about it. Babies sprawled about the decks in Oriental attitudes crying for the bottle; young people in blouses and open shirts giggled together and sang songs; there was a great disorder about it, dancing, music, fun. Lunches in small uniform boxes, a sandwich, an egg, a piece of cake, and then the mugs of soda water, the bottles of ginger beer, and the occasional splash as one hit the water, thrown from the upper deck by some satiated youth. And I turned in again and looked at this boat's passengers, who sat with folded hands upon gingham and dimity gowns, murmuring to themselves at times that they hoped the educational parts of New York and surrounding country would be visible to the naked eye. Well, they were, but they didn't see it.

The only refuse that cannot be renovated seems to be the human mind. Here at the waterfronts, barges heaped with the city's garbage swayed in the greasy, dark water, great mounds of a city's refuse suspiring in the sun like a glutton lolling after an orgy. One felt that, had one listened sharply enough, one would have caught its thick, throaty breathing; the mounds seemed to move, rising slowly, falling slowly, a great stomach on a couch. Ah, our modern lily maids of Astolat are the unnamed dead from the morgue who are rowed up to potter's field past the hospitals and this great, unending, daily birth of the city's dead food. I never realized before that there are places more terrible than the cemetery. They are the dumping grounds, and like carrion birds that sweep over a battlefield, men move in among this filth and decay, picking out wood for kindling, paper for the mills, and rags for the paper factories, and God knows what else for what, and someone making a million upon this terrible resurrection.

It was from the water's edge that we crawled in the days of our oblivion and first started that slow ascent into the life of man, and it is to the water's edge that we are brought back again in the end, the great, wet tomb that dries all tears, that gives the raw material and takes back the finished tool and knows neither pleasure nor pain; for "This is the end of all the songs men sing."

And as I said, "Man is the only thing that has no further use after something goes amiss." Look for yourselves and see. Exactly opposite this line of refuse, these heavy-laden barges, is a home for the insane. There is no hand moving in these poor, disordered brains in search of some one thought that could be used again. No man pays the city for the privilege of saving some lost and beautiful thing among this sad refuse; no hired hands thrust their fingers in to save some little kindling from this wrecked house, nor is anything profitable to be found for the decay of the garden.

And side by side, the Old Men's Home. Gray figures bent like hooks move about the splendid lawns and pause beneath the great trees spilling their green bloom to the ground; Old men like futile pollen in a breeze whose scattering will bring no profit to the world.

And you will say, "Enough, enough; this was a pleasure trip! Pass on, and describe its beauties." How can I, when there was nothing beautiful nor pleasant to see, save the ever-lovely sky, the green of the grass and the trees, and an occasional handsome spire?

We progressed, the megaphone man cutting the trip up in two jokes, one to the effect that dogs wagged their tails up and down instead of sideways in the Flatiron Building, and another that no deaf man had been ever condemned—this as we passed a prison—for the simple reason that he must be given "a hearing."

And when I looked at this island with its old men and its prisons, hospitals, and home for incurables, I thought again of that day I had spent on a strip of land just on the other side of Hell Gate with a young boy who had found society too difficult to understand. It was a lonely, flat stretch of marsh, thick with wild, high grass set in water. Planking ran from the broken-down house to the edge of the bank where a boat was anchored. This island, with its broken bits of wreckage and its ooze and salty smell at low tide, made me think of these human beings. Sometimes nature has an ailment: this island was one of them. Across the water, late in the afternoon, came the cries of the mad—a wild, sad scream that was taken up by the others gradually, as though they were playing a game at madness—and a shiver ran through me, and I wanted to cry also, and I asked him how he could bear it. He was smiling. "Sometimes," he said, "I think we are the loony ones. You have songs on which to go to battle; why shouldn't they have their songs on which to go to death?" Afterward he said that often they swam across and played together quite amicably.

Well, that has passed—the island lies under the sun and rain now, and the boy has gone—where, no one knows—a tramp perhaps—an inmate of one of the houses on the other side of the island. But I know one thing, that wherever he has gone he has taken with him a little of the freedom of a wild life that no standard insanity can harm.

Presently we passed the last bridge in the Harlem series, where a soldier stood, gun over shoulder—and came out into the half-moon of Spuyten Duyvil Creek. Little naked children ran hither and thither in the wooded banks and dropped, sighing, down upon the leaves like acorns. Others looked at us with small, water-wet, squinting eyes and waved, diving off hastily that we might accord them due praise for their excellent agility.

We took the turn in Spuyten Duyvil Creek well, watching these children until we could see them no more. It was here that I drew my first contented breath. Up on the heights several handsome houses peeped between the trees, and in the coming evening the Palisades stood out no heavier than a puff of smoke.

There was a hint of rain in the air, too. A small motor-boat shot past us, a brown-armed boy shouting hello as he steered. A three-oared canoe with a girl up front turned in from the creek behind us, the oars in steady, rhythmic motion dripping fine, silver beads of water.

A boy crying "Ice-cold soda here" came out of the hot cabin. A chocolate vendor stepped on my hat—I smiled.

The pilot, brown and lined of face, turned the wheel slowly, looking away into the distance. The megaphone man told us to pay strict attention to a white house on the drive: "Made possible by cigarettes," he said. We all leaned forward. Then he called attention to the college. All the Middle Western schoolmarms got to their feet.

"I wonder," one of them said, "if they discuss higher mathematics there." And another answered laconically, "Spinoza." They sat down again.

Somewhere, everywhere over there in that world that we had been around, and against which only one voice was raised—that of the megaphone man—actresses were getting their beauty sleep or were at school learning arduously a new dance. Somewhere a man was killing a gnat and somewhere else a man building a bomb. Someone was kissing, and someone was killing, someone was being born, and someone was dying. Some were eating and drinking and laughing, and others were starving. Some were thinking, and others were not. Waiters moved about in the great hotels, dragging their servility with them like trains. Pompous gentlemen in fat rings discussed politics amid spittoons, and handsome women read yellow-backed novels and gave their hands to be kissed by gallants. And there some were walking about, looking over at us as we looked back at them.

The tall buildings threw their shadows down on little buildings, great men on small men, joy on sorrow.

Someone was yawning at my side and buying postal cards, thirty-five views for a quarter, and I had a thousand for nothing!

And yet the city gave out only a faint sound of fabric being rent: one-half of the mass pulling one way and the other half in an opposing direction. Another self-sufficient tugboat hooted at us from the docks, and factory whistles shrieked back at them like masters calling them home. An electric sign stood up against the sky advertising some brand of chewing gum and beside it the steeple of a church. Great warehouses and grain elevators supported flaring advertisements; it looked as though the whole of Manhattan were for sale.

A dark line of boats to the left of us—Holland, German, Italian.

And somewhere in all this tangle of lives and tangle of buildings, inland out of sight of the sea and fog, there was my own particular little studio called home.

And "There's no place like home," chiefly because here we can best forget.

YVETTE GUILBERT

THE ROOM IS not large. An odor of a city autumn is in the air. Not that autumn which brings death and decay and trampling out of flowers, but that Manhattan autumn into which alien blossoms suddenly thrust their pink and purple opulence: the spring of the year for hothouse blooms.

The pink chair of gray enameled wood rests on a carpet still a little heavier with shades of rose. The high screen, with its false plumed birds and its great rusty dahlias, stands aside just enough to expose the portrait of a small Parisienne in white gown and cupid-shaped straw hat, who, lifting her skirt ever so little with that conscious coquetry that always goes before an ankle, smiles at the gentleman leaning out of the latticed window.

Suddenly the pink and gray chair is obliterated, the screen and the grisette forgotten, for Madame Yvette Guilbert has swept into the room and is leaning forward, her two white-clad arms upon the glass top of the table.

She is a large woman with low-curling blonde hair. Her years sit on her kindly indeed, more like a decoration than a calamity, more like a friendship between her and life.

Her smile is quick and broad. I remember once hearing her sing something with "hips and haws" as a refrain; and now, looking on her some ten or twelve years later, I saw the same intelligent eyes, the same mobile but thin lips and the large, slightly tilted, clever, cynical nose; and I knew that one is bound to be at home wherever this singer is.

It is impossible to catch and render on paper her manner of pronouncing English; it is not a matter of letters, it is entirely a matter of the back of the throat. Therefore, I shall not attempt it at all.

"Sometimes I think," she said, leaning forward, "that the world does not understand anyone. The artist, no matter in what country, has so many terrible and pitiful hours to pass through, and if finally someone does pay attention to him and does give him a chance, it is only to have him grossly misunderstood.

"You ask me about my songs; you say, Madame Guilbert, are you not sorry that you can no longer sing the little saucy songs you used to sing—ah." She throws up her expressive hands, draws her lips together, bows her head. "Ah, ah that such a thing should be said, that anyone should misunderstand me like that. They were not naughty songs, mademoiselle, they were life. They were flowers tossed from the gutter into heaven; they were strands of martyrs' hair blowing across the centuries; they were drops of blood from the heart; they were human passions and all-too-human forgetfulness. For alas, alas, the world forgets so soon and so easily.

"No, mademoiselle. They were irreverent and they were sarcastic and they were cutting—they were never risque. They were the little penknife blade with which one cuts the wrist of malice and deceit—this and nothing more.

"I am not a tragedienne, nor am I a heavy and emotional actress who tears her hair out in teaching a truth. These things I cannot do, but this other I can. I want to be like Pierrot, to play the fool, the gay one; and as I smile, appear to weep, and as I live, appear to die. If I pull out one single strand of hair, it shall seem as terrible as if I tore out the whole; if I make one shake of the head, it shall be as if some hand took all humanity by the ankles and shook it loose eternally from life.

"When I appear this winter at the new French theatre, the Théâtre du Vieux Colombier, I am going to present a Pierrot that I have based on the poems of two brilliant men, and then I shall prove to you all that Pierrot is a gay blossom, but that his roots go deep and are wound about the eternal corpse of the world, as a ribbon is wound around a lovely gift."

She laughed, tossing her great head back, and suddenly I knew that she was beautiful: the crooked smile, the bright eyes, the sensitive under-curve of the nose. With these things Madame Guilbert is as clever as with her songs.

"I am always trying to teach someone some few things. Is it silly, impossible? I do not know. You see, I was ten years before my time. I set out to destroy deceitfulness by truth, and the future shall see such things attacked; not in their reality alone, but in their spirit.

"You see," she went on, bringing her hands back from a last gesture, "we need to know each other better, America and France. We have always made mistakes in judgment about each other. You think we are naughty and off-color and trivial, and we think you are giddy and cruel and ignorant. We think of you as society women, who have a flower trained to your corsage as we train flowers to our verandas, who carry about little dogs and spend your hours in idleness. Now it is time that we know what is in the heart of the other. We are allies fighting for the one cause, and we should not be strangers to each other in life if we can be such comrades in death.

"The Théâtre du Vieux Colombier is such an attempt—a medium through which we can learn to know ourselves and to know you better than through any one other thing perhaps. But ah—" Again she tossed her hands into the air. "What is one going to do if you insist that our writers are 'naughty' and our entire life a little what it should not be? But I tell you—," and here she brought her fist down upon the table top, "—there is not one indecent song in France, nor one immoral poet."

"Tell me about France," I said.

"Ah, France—can one speak of it?" She lowered her lids slowly, looking at her hands. "You know, I have had some letters, many letters from the *poilu*—I am godmother to many of them. Ah, mademoiselle, and such letters, such letters! One wrote me, 'I had hoped to keep a thumb or two to press buttons with when I came back from the war, but, madame, will you believe it, they are dead; they will push nothing further. I am sorry; there are so many things I will no longer be able to do.' And another—a man unable to move his legs, with one eye only a blind groove where sight had been—he said, 'It is well, I shall go back to the trenches when they will let me.'"

There were two spots of wet upon the table, and Madame Guilbert put her crossed hands over them quietly. "And there are others, mademoiselle, many others. No, they do not say, 'Ah, the Germans, how we hate them.' Instead they say nothing. One cannot say anything; one can only die. Europe is an immense field of fragments, and these fragments are moving. Some of them still have eyes, some of them still have mouths, some hands, others feet; but they are terribly scattered. They lie in the four corners of the earth, piling up slowly, and always as dust gathers in a forgotten corner."

She looked out of the window, turning her head. "One of them said to me, 'There was a parade, a charity parade or something—you were not there—that is right. We knew we could trust you, we knew you would not disguise yourself in the carnival patriotic.' "

She repeated it and laughed a hard, quick laugh. "Ah yes, mademoiselle, so are our men; they cannot stand any hypocrisy longer—any more lies, anything false. God! If anyone can know where things begin and end, it is they.

"When will it end?"

She turned to me. "Have you read *Le Feu*? That man told the truth—he knows. We who do not know should keep our peace, should be still. It is only an insult to our dead."

"And what will be the end of it all? Will there be a revolution, or will there be nothing changed?"

"There will be a great rebirth of religion, mademoiselle. One needs God."

"Do you mean by that universal brotherhood, without revolt?"

"I do not know; all I know is that after this, one will no longer dare to hate."

"And do you see anything happening that portends upheaval?"

"Again, I do not know. Somehow I don't see how there can be any more energy for revolt. One must be angry for that, and the people are terribly tired."

"But love by fatigue is not lasting love."

"It will be more than that—infinitely more than that; but you who have not been there cannot know."

"Yes, I think a few of us know—those with intelligence."

"Ah," her eyes snapped, "there you have it. With intelligence even stupidity is understood; with intelligence Europe could have had this war without a single dead man."

She continued, "No, no, no, after this no one alive will be the same person he was before. You go through the 'face hospital,' you see that 'thing' lying there, a red slanting plane for a face—out of which, in the place where the mouth should be, oozes a little saliva and blood—a cross section of flesh. There are no ears to hear with, yet they have heard all; there are no eyes, yet this body that we call a 'thing' by its very sacrifice, sees all; and shorn of lips, it speaks in such a thundering voice that it must be heard to the uttermost ends of the earth.

"One's parents and children, husband and lover are in it. In peace one may be an individual, but in times like these one is only that flesh which is a little to one side of the wound.

Yvette Guilbert

"You know," she said, "I am quite angry at your society, at the society woman. They are very ignorant of the proper manners. They assume that money makes up for everything, instead of having discovered that money pays for everything, even an education." She laughed in a good-humored way, very generously and forgivingly. "I have had some funny—what do you call them—run-ins with society when it wants to give a benefit and does not seem to know enough to take the same amount as they would make out of their own pockets, instead of making all that fuss and show for a few dollars. But then," she shrugged her shoulders, "I suppose one must have misfortunes, or where would they get their 'benefits' from."

She stooped and, lifting a handful of manuscripts up, began to turn the leaves over.

"I have composed a few songs in my life, mademoiselle, and I made out very well and seemed to please. But lately I have found two artists that I love to sing: Rictus and Laforge. One poem—ah, so splendid, so magnificent—to Christ. He says to him, 'Do not weep, old chap, yet there is nothing else for you to do.' Ah, ah, ah, such men as these in all countries alike are left to starve and to break their hearts—and then to die understanding, but misunderstood."

"What of the artist in America?"

"If you Americans would only be patient in the presence of life it would be well, but you won't. Everything real shocks you. Not all of you, of course. I mean the crowd, the poor tragic crowd; when will they know—will they ever know?"

She stood up. "And now, mademoiselle, let me see what you have been drawing." She came up behind me, placed her arm about my shoulder and said:

"It is like an antique, a carving in wood. Perhaps it is like me, and perhaps it is not."

"No," I shook my head. "Something is wrong."

"It is the nose," she said, and tilted it a little, laughing. She walked away from me again, her hands behind her back.

"And do you, as an artist, find anyone in your life who understands you?" she inquired, looking at me searchingly.

"Yes, yes, I see," she said, quickly smiling again and, putting a hand on my shoulder once more, she said:

"It is nice, is it not, even if there is only one who really understands."

WOMAN POLICE DEPUTY IS WRITER OF POETRY

IMAGINE A DAY on Centre Street, overcast and threatening rain; a day through which shuffle flickering tramps like wicks that are dying. Centre Street with its hurrying businessmen, its thin clerks carrying brief bags, the Criminal Courts Building, that edifice of anticlimaxes on whose steps people are obscured into a sameness of sorrow—men with hurt mouths, women in black talking in Italian and children playing noiselessly, as if they were the innocent ashes of some despair. Imagine the cries of someone in a vacant lot raised high above the multitude on a soapbox with wide, imploring, heedless arms crying for volunteers. Then imagine the long, cold corridors of Police Headquarters, the uniformed men with their badges winking sleepily above their hearts, the rows of prize beakers in a glass case, and then the room on whose door is the sign FIFTH DEPUTY COMMISSIONER. In here, by an imposing and legal desk, in a blue serge dress trimmed with lace, sits a well-built woman, her face at once stern and humorous. Imagine all this, and you have the environs and the person of Mrs. Ellen O'Grady, Fifth Deputy Police Commissioner.

Her eyes are set close together and slanting, the nose is of gentle modeling, and the mouth one of which one would say, "That moves for the state." My first impression was of a woman who was afraid of being too homelike in an office of business.

She is a woman to whom you put impersonal questions last. Therefore I asked her about her immediate work.

"I am interested in the saving of girls before they have taken the last step," she said. "I do not mean that I am not also interested in and careful of the girl who has already fallen—that goes without saying; but I do think that more things should be done to prevent and less to attempt cures. It is better far to save a girl before she is in

110

dire need of saving than to try to save her after it is too late. Not but that girls can be reclaimed, but is it not better never to have made a mistake than to have made one?"

She went on, turning over a ruler. "True, I believe in the benefits of suffering; the worst of us are always better for having done something for which we can truly suffer. But there are some who can be saved and yet gain their knowledge and be as purified as if they had gone through the last fires and out on the other side of Fiddler's Green." For the first time she smiled a little.

"I believe in women; I love them; there is a kindliness and an understanding and a sympathy in women that no one, not even an animal, possesses. Oh, you needn't smile at the animal; they are unequalled for blind devotion—which, of course, has its limits.

"Because of this love of beauty, because of this reaching out for something better and brighter and of more worth, our girls fall into trouble. It is for this very reason that those cast into the shadow by poverty and ignorance, by pain and suffering, by neglect and misfortune, grope toward the only thing that they know as beautiful: love. It is for this reason that since the war began there have been more cases of small girls going astray. Let me explain."

She turned around in her chair, facing the window.

"Somehow a uniform has always appealed to a woman—it appeals to men also, but they can wear it, you see. She connects it with something holy and something to be investigated, something at once to be venerated and to be familiar with. For a girl of fourteen—and the girls who go astray are younger than ever—nothing has ever come so close to her dreams as these uniforms. Anything she might do is jumbled up with a sort of patriotic fanaticism; thus, she pretends to herself that her feelings are somehow made divine and noble."

"How then are you going to prevent it?"

"I look into those conditions which are likely to lead up to such a climax. Now take, for instance, the girls doing messenger service. They have to go through the back entries of houses, or so I have been advised. When such a case is brought to my attention, I write to the company employing them and ask that they be allowed to enter through the front.

"And then, too," she continued with some firmness, "there is the problem of the 'masher,' a man who is not only a nuisance to himself but a menace to humanity. I mean to see to it that young girls are shielded from the attention of these men.

"The first thing to do is to watch furtive sweetmeat shops, with their rows of bottles filled with brilliantly colored soda water fruit syrups and the little back rooms; the pseudo motion-picture schools, which help to recruit the great army that Lecky spoke of as the 'sacrifice on the altar of the nation's purity'; the spurious 'theatrical agency'; and all the many other forms used to lure young girls to their ruin.

"You will realize that there could hardly be a more important thing to tackle—unless, of course, you mention the matter of national defense."

"Do you think that general public service is unfit for women?"

"I most certainly do. Such work as that of the streetcar conductor and running an elevator is very bad for women; they are subject to the passing insults of the crowd. You will say that women are subject to this anyway; that is quite true, but in ordinary life they are in a better position to protest."

"And," said I, "what do you think of crime in general? To me personally it has a strong appeal—I like crime, provided it is well committed."

She smiled, shaking her head. "That sounds nice, but of course that is the artist's point of view. Crime, murder, love, hate, all appeal to the artist; but you see," she added, "there are only a very few artists in the world, and the unavoidable crimes will always be enough for them.

"The criminal who is one through a moment's great feeling, through a sudden climax of passions, I forgive always in my heart. There is so little feeling in the world that even when it takes the wrong method of expressing itself it is something that the world cannot do without. There is too little love and therefore no really great and profound hate; too few people move with a 'certain somber fury.'"

"Will crime ever be uprooted? That is, will the court and the judgment seat and the prisons ever be done away with?"

"Never, not so long as humanity is inhuman. The gallows tree has not shut the mouth of all the angers, nor has the rope strangled the universal cry of despair."

"But the cause of most crime, is it not poverty?"

"Oh, yes; poverty is the greatest of all evils, because people do not understand how to be poor. Poverty drives the children into the street, we all know that, and from there to the saloons; but why? Because their own homes are not only poor but dirty."

"But soap costs money, Mrs. O'Grady."

"I know, I know, but some there are who have proved their divine ability, some who reach heaven little but skin and bones; but this kind He loves best."

> The sum of thy past agony shall shake
> The very marrow of thy bones, and move
> The oblivious skin upon thy nerveless veins

—I quoted.

Mrs. O'Grady looked up sharply.

"What is that?" she inquired. "I, too, love poetry, but there!" she added sighing, "I must learn not to speak of poetry in business hours."

"But you yourself write it, I have heard."

"Oh, yes; I write it, but I do not speak of it excepting to those nearest me—my daughters, a friend or two, and that is all."

"Yet," said I, "what of:

> O marvelous man, must thy heart beat high
> As with frozen limbs 'neath the northern sky
> You planted the flag Old Glory there,
> Your thanksgiving hymn, your voiceless prayer,
> Was freedom's flag at the Pole unfurled;
> The Stars and Stripes at the top of the world.

"Yes, yes," she said, coloring a little. "Those naughty boys on the papers got that. They played a trick on me, but I don't mind. The papers have always treated me kindly and justly; though I would like you to say for me that the newspapers no longer mold the public opinion, as was proved by the last election."

"But, for goodness sake, do not let us get away from our subject—crime and death. Now, death is something I am really keen about," I interrupted.

This time she laughed heartily.

"You're a funny girl," she said. "You love crime and now you adore death—I see you have the artist's soul.

"The saddest part of it all is that it really takes a lifetime to understand a person, and no one can spend a lifetime judging a criminal. Crime takes but a moment but justice an eternity. Therefore the best that we can do, the best that the judge can do, is to be as good a character reader as possible, a person who has almost occult powers, one who can discern at a glance all the little complexities that have gone into the making of the mistake."

"What of psychoanalysis—Freudism, you know?"

"I don't believe in it very much. It goes too far—digs down too deep; but I do believe in the psychological moment. Take a person at the edge, just before he goes over—a person with the knife lifted, one with the poison to his lips, he who is about to shoot—and you have a chance for redemption such as you will never have again and which you could not have had before. One always saves and loses the most at the edge of things."

"Do you think that Osborne's prison reform would have worked out well for the criminal?"

"I don't like to say yes or no to that. I do think that his ideas were good ones. I do think that prison reforms are good things. But the prisons as they were before were not as bad as they were painted."

"What about a colony for criminals: a whole town, if you like, walled in as China is walled in, through which the criminal could express himself; a place with libraries, public squares, town hall, opera house, movies, and garden—a place where crime could be developed into something beyond crime, beyond good and evil?"

"Ah, what a dreamer's idea that is!" she said.

"Yet, cannot criminals and fallen women teach things that none of us know, such things that we might be the better for?"

And now she rather surprised me.

"Yes, very many things," she replied. "I know of no honor that is at times more beautiful than that among thieves. I know of nothing more terrible and more tragic and more splendid than the feeling of fallen women for another who might fall. The honor among thieves reaches very often a sublime point; the effort of a fallen woman to save a sister has often brought tears to my eyes—but yet such honor and such unselfish feeling cannot enter our world, cannot mean anything for the great masses, cannot save or make better or count in the great world which, at large, is honorable and upright and fine."

"Yet, at any moment any one of us might commit a murder."

"It has been said quite truly that we are all potential criminals. It is true that environment makes most of us what we are; then we must change the environment."

"How? Through Socialism?"

"Certainly not." She looked displeased. "Socialism has nothing to do with it. Socialism is another dream of a class of people who see wrongs but no rights. No, I think it can only be attained by education: education of the senses and of the mind, education in what is desirable because it is best, education of the heart, teaching it to reach that point where it will not be an effort but a pleasure to respond to those things which are fine in themselves and which neither outrage the heart nor the theory."

"But is such a thing possible?"

"It becomes impossible only so soon as you give up all hope of the human race—and that I have not done."

"And what of death?"

"But that is a subject of which I know so little."

"That is why I want you to talk about it—it is the one medium by which one has to come to a conclusion through feeling and not theory."

"Well, death has always touched me very deeply. Why? Because it is so inevitable, so lasting, so unexpected, so imminent. Why do you regard it as you do?"

"Because it is so terrible to see all the gestures gone."

She half closed her eyes, turning a golden whistle over and over in her palm. Leaning forward, I saw that it was a police whistle and that on the table lay a badge.

"My jewelry," she said. "The only jewelry one should wear—the symbol of one's labor for humanity. Jewelry, by the way, is the first mistake made by mothers. They should forbid their children the wearing of rings and necklaces—thus many a girl has been led to her ruin. Jewelry is vanity, and vanity is destruction."

"And now, tell me about yourself."

"I am Irish; you can tell that, can't you? Yes, Irish all the way from Ireland. I married in 1888 after having studied to become a teacher. My husband, who was an expert accountant with a firm of importers, died in 1898, leaving me with five daughters. I took up dressmaking. Two of my daughters died. It was a hard struggle, but I have never been afraid to work.

"About this time I grasped the civil service idea, passed my examinations, and was appointed probation officer and served so for eleven years in the New Jersey Avenue court, Brooklyn."

"But most women left without support and with a family could not have done as well. Too many women are ignorant of life, and too many are without a practical means of support."

"Very true; that is the tragedy of it. Women, you know, I have great faith in, especially women who have borne children; for through the bearing and rearing of children comes wisdom. My advice to all women is first to learn a trade, have something at their fingertips and then to marry and have a family. A woman who has not had children knows no more of life than one blind. This does not mean that I am advocating the rearing of six or seven children. It really does not matter so long as you can say, 'I have borne.'

"I think that women are fitted for a great many things. There are plenty of places in public life where they can serve. They are excellent secretaries; they make good waitresses; they are librarians of the most careful type. There are hundreds of things that they can do besides vote.

"I do not like to see them doing work, however, that is entirely unsuited to them, as I said before. Housework is, after all, their master art. Did you ever see a man who could keep a house in perfect shape? No, and the state, the world, the entire administration and public life—what is it if not housekeeping on an immense scale? This does not imply that they must necessarily run cars any more than one would expect them to bring in the coal or kill the hogs.

"In my work there are many things that only a woman could understand. It takes a woman to know the temptations of women. That is why I have women detectives; that is why I would like to have women at every dance hall and every moving picture and along the beaches in summer. That is why I should deeply regret the removal of women from the outside world."

"And your daughters, Mrs. O'Grady—what do they think of their mother?"

"They think it most scandalous," she said with bright eyes, "that a woman of my age should be sitting in Police Headquarters at the beck and call of every unfortunate. Yet I love the work, and I don't think I have an enemy in the world."

"And now," said I, reaching for the door, "tell me what you think of the Russians?"

"Ah," she sighed, turning to her papers so that I saw only the parting in the pretty white hair, "I enjoy Tolstoy a little more than anything else in the world."

JAMES JOYCE

THERE ARE MEN in Dublin who will tell you that out of Ireland a great voice has gone; and there are a few women, lost to youth, who will add: "One night he was singing and the next he wasn't, and there's been no silence the like of it!" For the singing voice of James Joyce, author of *A Portrait of the Artist as a Young Man* and of *Ulysses,* is said to have been second to none.

The thought that Joyce was once a singer may not come as a revelation to the casual reader of his books. One must perhaps have spent one of those strangely aloof evenings with him, or have read passages of his *Ulysses* as it appeared in *The Little Review,* to have realized the singing quality of his words. For tradition has it that a singer must have a touch of bravado, a joyous putting-forth of first the right leg and then the left, and a sigh or two this side of the cloister; and Joyce has none of these.

I had read *Dubliners* over my coffee during the war. I had been on one or two theatrical committees just long enough to suggest the production of *Exiles,* his one play. The *Portrait* had been consumed, turning from one elbow to the other, but it was not until I came upon his last work that I sensed the singer. Lines like: "So stood they both awhile in wan hope sorrowing one with the other"; or, "Thither the extremely large wains bring foison of the fields, spherical potatoes and iridescent kale and onions, pearls of the earth, and red, green, yellow, brown, russet, sweet, big bitter ripe pomilated apples and strawberries fit for princes and raspberries from their canes"; or still better, the singing humor in that delicious execution scene in which the "learned prelate knelt in a most Christian spirit in a pool of rainwater."

117

Yes, then I realized Joyce must indeed have begun life as a singer, and a very tender singer. And, because no voice can hold out over the brutalities of life without breaking, he turned to quill and paper, for so he could arrange, in the necessary silence, the abundant inadequacies of life, as a laying-out of jewels—jewels with a will to decay.

Yet of Joyce, the man, one has heard very little. I had seen a photograph of him, the collar up about the narrow throat, the beard, heavier in those days, descending into the abyss of the hidden bosom. I had been told that he was going blind, and we in America learned from Ezra Pound that "Joyce is the only man on the continent who continues to produce, in spite of poverty and sickness, working from eight to sixteen hours a day." I had heard that for a number of years Joyce taught English in a school in Trieste—and this is almost all. Of his habits, of his likes and his dislikes, nothing, unless one dared come to some conclusion about them from the number of facts hidden under an equal number of improbabilities in his teeming *Ulysses*.

And then, one day, I came to Paris. Sitting in the cafe of the Deux Magots, which faces the little church of St. Germain des Près, I saw approaching out of the fog and damp, a tall man, with head slightly lifted and slightly turned, giving to the wind an orderly distemper of red and black hair, which descended sharply into a scant wedge on an out-thrust chin.

He wore a blue-gray coat—too young it seemed, partly because he had thrust its gathers behind him, partly because the belt which circled it lay two full inches above the hips.

At the moment of seeing him, a remark made to me by a mystic flashed through my mind—"A man who has been more crucified on his sensibilities than any writer of our age"—and I said to myself, This is a strange way to recognize a man I never laid my eyes on.

Because he had heard of the suppression of *The Little Review* on account of *Ulysses* and of the subsequent trial, he sat down opposite me, who was familiar with the whole story, ordering a white wine. He began to talk at once. "The pity is," he said, seeming to choose his words for their age rather than their aptness, "the public will demand and find a moral in my book—or worse, they may take it in some more serious way, and on the honor of a gentleman, there is not one single serious line in it."

For a moment there was silence. His hands, peculiarly limp in the introductory shake, and peculiarly pulpy-running into a thickness that the base gave no hint of—lay, one on the stem of the glass, the other, forgotten, palm out, on the most delightful waistcoat it has ever been my happiness to see. Purple with alternate doe and dog heads. The does, tiny scarlet tongues hanging out over blond lower lips, downed in a light wool, and the dogs no more ferocious or on the scent than any good animal who adheres to his master through the seven cycles of change.

He saw my admiration and he smiled. "Made by the hand of my grandmother for the first hunt of the season." There was another silence in which he arranged and lit a cigar.

"All great talkers," he said softly, "have spoken in the language of Sterne, Swift, or the Restoration. Even Oscar Wilde. He studied the Restoration through a microscope in the morning and repeated it through a telescope in the evening."

"And in *Ulysses?*" I asked.

"They are all there, the great talkers," he answered, "them and the things they forgot. In *Ulysses* I have recorded, simultaneously, what a man says, see, thinks, and what such seeing, thinking, saying does to what you Freudians call the subconscious—but as for psychoanalysis," he broke off, "it's neither more nor less than blackmail."

He raised his eyes. There is something unfocused in them—the same paleness seen in plants long hidden from the sun—and sometimes a little jeer that goes with a lift and rounding of the upper lip.

People say of him that he looks both sad and tired. He does look sad and he does look tired, but it is the sadness of a man who has procured some medieval permission to sorrow out of time and in no place; it is the weariness of one self-subjected to the creation of an overabundance in the limited.

If I were asked what seemed to be the most characteristic pose of James Joyce, I should say that of the head, turned farther away than disgust and not so far as death. The turn of displeasure is not so complete; yet the only thing at all like it is the look in the throat of a stricken animal. After this I should add, think of him as a heavy man yet thin, drinking a thin cool wine with lips almost hidden in his high narrow head, or smoking the eternal cigar, held slightly above shoulder-level, and never moved until consumed, the mouth brought to and taken away from it to eject the sharp jets of yellow smoke.

Because one may not ask him questions, one must know him. It has been my pleasure to talk to him many times during my four months in Paris. We have talked of rivers and of religion, of the instinctive genius of the church which chose, for the singing of its hymns, the voice without "overtones"—the voice of the eunuch.

We have talked of women; about women he seems a bit disinterested. Were I vain, I should say he is afraid of them, but I am certain he is only a little skeptical of their existence. We have talked of Ibsen, of Strindberg, Shakespeare: "*Hamlet* is a great play, written from the standpoint of the ghost"; and of Strindberg, "No drama behind the hysterical raving."

We have talked of death, of rats, of horses, the sea; languages, climates and offerings. Of artists and of Ireland. "The Irish are people who will never have leaders, for at the great moment they always desert them. They have produced one skeleton—Parnell—never a man."

Sometimes his wife, Nora, and his two children have been with him. Large children, almost as tall as he is himself, and Nora walks under fine red hair, speaking with a brogue that carries the dread of Ireland in it; Ireland as a place where poverty has become the art of scarcity. A brogue a little more defiant than Joyce's, which is tamed by preoccupation.

Joyce has few friends, yet he is always willing to leave his writing table and his white coat of an evening, to go to some quiet nearby cafe, there to discuss anything that is not "artistic" or "flashy" or "new." Callers have often found him writing into the night, or drinking tea with Nora. I myself once came upon him as he lay full length on his stomach poring over a valise full of notes taken in his youth for *Ulysses*—for as Nora says, "It's the great fanaticism is on him, and it is coming to no end." Once he was reading out of the book of saints (he is never without it) and muttering to himself that this particular day's saint was "a devil of a fellow for bringing on the rain, and we wanting to go for a stroll."

However it is with him, he will come away for the evening, for he is simple, a scholar, and sees nothing objectionable in human beings if they will only remain in place.

Yet he has been called eccentric, mad, incoherent, unintelligible, yes and futuristic. One wonders why, thinking what a fine lyric beginning that great Rabelaisian flower *Ulysses* had, with impartial addenda for foliage, the thin sweet lyricism of *Chamber Music,* the casual inevitability of *Dubliners,* the passion and prayer of Stephen Dedalus, who said that he would go alone through the world. "Alone, not only separate from all others, but to have not even one friend."

He has, if we admit Joyce to be Stephen, done as he said he would do. "I will not serve that which I no longer believe, whether it call itself my home, my fatherland, or my church; and I will try to express myself in my art as freely as I can and as wholly as I can, using for my defense the only arms I allow myself to use: silence, exile and cunning."

This is somehow Joyce, and one wonders if, at last, Ireland has created her man.

Fiction

PAPRIKA JOHNSON

EVERY SATURDAY, JUST as soon as she had slipped her manilla pay envelope down her neck, had done up her handkerchiefs and watered the geraniums, Paprika Johnson climbed onto the fire-escape and reached across the strings of her pawnshop banjo.

Paprika Johnson played softly, and she sang softly too, from a pepsin disinfected throat, and more than reverently she scattered the upper register into the flapping white wash of the O'Briens.

Sitting there in the dusk, upon her little square of safety, in a city of a million squares, she listened to the music of the spheres and the frying of the onions in Daisy Mack's back kitchen, and she sang a song to flawless summer, while she watched Madge Darsey loosen her stays in the tenement house opposite.

Below Paprika, straight as a plumb-bob would direct, sat the patrons of Swingerhoger's Beer Garden, at small brown tables that had once been green, perhaps, or blue. Paprika, unconscious of the laws of state, the rules of Sanskrit, and of the third dimensions, was also unaware of the trade that waged below her; was unaware of the hoisting of hops and of dilettanteism.

Also, in the beginning, she was unaware of the existence of the boy from Stroud's. This is beginning at the beginning.

Paprika had a bosom friend, in the days when roses found no hedge from her neck to her hair, when she allotted to them no design, save the generous and gentle smiling bow that was her mouth. And her bosom friend, like all bosom things, was necessary and uncomfortable.

She borrowed incessantly, did Leah, she borrowed Paprika's slippers out of bed, and her shifts into bed, and she borrowed her face powder, and her hair ribbons and her stockings. And she borrowed, most of all, Paprika's charm.

Leah was thin and pock-marked and colorless, and still, without the stiffness of a wall flower was one, and chose Gus to lean on.

It goes without saying that Gustav was blind, as blind as a man in a rage and as a man in love.

He listened to Paprika's soft voice, and not being able to estimate the distance that sound carries, put his arm about Leah's waist while Paprika sat upon the other side of the table.

Leah would have been just as well pleased to have had Gus in her own room, but that was impossible, as it was chaperonless.

Paprika was safe, because Paprika had a moribund mother under the counterpane, a chaperone who never spoke or moved, since she was paralyzed, but who was a pretty good one at that, being a white exclamation point this side of error. Therefore, Leah was hugged in Paprika's presence.

Gus thought he knew what he was doing, because on his trip to the back sink in the hall, he heard things about Paprika that were kind and good to listen to, and he thought they were said of the one he hugged. Therefore, he shaved and was happy.

Now, listen; I'll tell you something.

Gustav kept behind his ninety-eight-cent alarm clock, where he could not lose it, the address of an oculist who would cure him for a remuneration. No one is sending perfect cattle to heaven without pocket padding, so Gus waited until he could pay to see again, and in the meantime, toiled up to the eighth floor of evenings and sat with the girls. And Paprika being a bosom friend worth having, lent Leah her violet extract.

At night when she dug into bed, Paprika exchanged notes with Leah about their mutual work. Paprika typewrote and Leah pushed Sloe Gin Fizz toward erring youths, who drank with averted faces.

Which proves without my saying it, that Leah was all right on the inside—perhaps—but that her intentions were a lot better than her claims on beauty.

Yet, Leah realized and gave worship for the part that Paprika had played for her, she comprehended, and was almost humble by the devotion of her friend, in keeping Gus's arms about her waist. She whispered her loyalty into Paprika's ear in the silence of the night, while Paprika pushed her gum into the leg of the bed.

Among other things, Leah said that she would do as much for her sometime, in another way—if she could, and lay back, knowing that the dark was doing as much for her as it was for the hole in the carpet.

Paprika was touched and bought a banjo.

So on evenings when she had talked Gustav's arm half way round Leah's waist, she took her banjo out upon the fire escape, and practiced a complicated movement from Chopin.

Across the cliff she looked and watched the moon grope its way up the sky and over condensed milk signs and climb to the top of the Woolworth Building. And Paprika wondered if her time was soon coming and smiled, for she knew that she was as good to look upon as a yard of slick taffy, and twice as alluring.

Unconsciously, Paprika was the cabaret performer of the beer garden. The men about the tables put their hands into their shirt bosoms, and felt the ticking of the tolerably good clock their mother had given them. Or others felt into the breast pockets and felt the syncopated beat of the watch their father had given them (from frequenting just such a garden). And others, without any inherited momentum, looked wanly upon the open faces of dollar Ingersols, and sipped with slow, bated breath.

The combination of Paprika, beer and the moon got into the street and nudged the boy off his stool at the head of Stroud's donkeys stabled in lower Bleecker Street; edged him off, and after a while it was said that the boy from Stroud's was becoming a man in Swingerhoger's beer garden.

The boy from Stroud's was a tall blond wimpet who had put his hands into his mother's hair and shaken it free of gold; a lad who had painted his cheeks from the palette of the tenderloin, the pink that descends from one member of a family to the other, quicksilver running down life's page. And the fact that at twenty the boy from Stroud's still had it, proved that he was his mother's only child. He also had great gray eyes, and an impassible mouth, a hand that was made for soft-brimmed hats and love notes, and a breaking voice like a ferryboat coming in from Staten Island.

He sat in the beer garden three nights before he dared follow up the music from above. When he looked, he decided that the perspective on Paprika made her very alluring. And so the boy from Stroud's, who had turned the donkeys around for supper, crowded down, into the portfolio of his soul, the pattern of P. Johnson.

And she, all oblivious and smelling of white roses and talcum, might have gone on indefinitely, but one night, stumbling up the stairs in the dark, came against a little packet. She picked it up and, woman-like, tried to read it in the hall. Failing, and being over-anxious to discover its contents, she tried again at the crack of light running along Daisy Mack's door, and on to the fifth floor, running up a little higher and balancing herself vertically over a vertical package at Eliza Farthingale's. But Eliza burned only one candle, and Paprika could make less of it than ever, and finally, having got to her room by a long stage of short runs, read it in the light from her open door, saw that the hand was a masculine one. And being Paprika and a woman, and thinking that she had nothing on her bosom friend, she sidled in backward and dropped it in among the bananas on the sideboard.

After supper she took it and the banjo out upon the fire-escape, and read it by the light of the moon.

The involuntary suicides in the beer garden sipped slowly and finally ceased altogether, and Swingerhoger, who had hopes of rolling up silk sleeves out of them, became uneasy at the sight of bricklayers whining over their brew. He did not know that all the trouble came of a silent banjo. Paprika wasn't playing, she was reading the note from the boy. Inside the note was a photograph taken side face with a soft look and collar; his fine Roman nose was enchanced by a dark background. What did it matter to her if he was turning the donkey around?

About this time, when Leah, who had lost part control of her hands, never being sure when she could use them—lost control of her one finger on the left hand altogether, it being weighed down by the weight of a diamond, purchased by Gus.

Paprika kissed her, and Leah went down upon her knees and thanked God for a willing sacrifice, and, by way of surety, prayed that Gus might remain forever in the dark. Then arising, she dusted her knees and inquired of Paprika if she looked well in curlpapers, and got into bed.

"My dear," said Paprika, wiggling her toes in the last effort to get comfortable, "Don't let him know anything about it—ever—me, I mean. And if, after you are married I can do anything, just whoop and I'll be there. By the way, are you going to start in, in Yonkers, where they have Gaby Deslys and cats, or in the Bronx, where you get commuter's grouch and new laid eggs?"

Leah answered from the depths of the bed and Paprika's warm arm. "Neither. You see, dear, Gus is a sort of cousin to Mr. Swingerhoger, and Swingerhoger is going to let Gus run a part of the business, and pay him a salary, and so we are not going to leave you, only to move in downstairs, into the second floor front. And I'm so glad."

"Why?" demanded Paprika, losing forever the vision and the hope of the second floor front.

"Because I'll be near you, dear—don't you understand?"

And Paprika, being a good bosom friend, understood.

Now, the boy from Stroud's, having gotten tired of picking straw out of the donkey's ears, decided to take a risk and pick a wife out of the sky.

He had seen Paprika from the beer garden, but Paprika was eight floors distant, and though his soul's eyes were extra keen, they were not keen enough to discover, with any directly satisfying accuracy, whether Paprika's petticoats were three or two, as he got her, a silhouette aginst Manhattan, enchanted keen, they were not keen enough to discover, with any directly satisfying accuracy, whether Paprika's petticoats were three or two, as he got her, a silhouette against Manhattan, enhanced as she was by the whole of the left side of the Hudson, he came to the conclusion that she was fit for a flat off Bleecker Street with eggs for breakfast.

And so it was that Paprika presently bought a yard of baby blue ribbon and tied up a bunch of letters and put them beneath her chemises in the lower drawer.

She did not think that she was taking a risk. She had seen the picture of the boy, and he was a good cameo, so she allowed her heart to keep pace with him, as Dan Patch with his shadow. In her mind's eye she was already carrying the shaving soap into the dressing room.

In a flurry of hot ginger tea and white voile, Leah was married. For the last time, a single girl, without as yet the knowledge of the one-sided effect of a dresser with military brushes on one corner, and an automatic stop on the other. She hugged and kissed Paprika and cried a lot down her neck and felt that she was being parted by the whole of a geography and an isthmus. And after they carried her Swedish trunk and her bouquet down to the second floor front and she and Gus turned at the landing and threw kisses back to Paprika, who leaned over the banister.

Paprika hitched up her one-fifty "American Madame," patted her back hair and went and sat down upon the china chest.

She was grateful to circumstances that had made it possible to swap the boy for Leah. Also she sang as she played her banjo, and didn't care that the night got in front of the Municipal tower and shut out the million lights.

But the man in the beer garden, who was nobody in particular, spoke to Swingerhoger.

"Why haven't you discovered for yourself that the drawing card here is that little girl who comes in about three beer time, and after pinning her handkerchiefs to the sash, yanks the strings of the banjo into the harmony of the human breast?"

Swingerhoger made a warp of his fingers to catch the woof of his gold seals, and looked worried.

"Are you perfectly sure that they come here to hear her play as much as for anything?"

"As much as for anything," answered the man, who was nobody in particular. "They think they have found the spring and the song, which has left the city altogether, and the cry of the birds and the plaint of a woman, the rarest things I know in little old New York."

"Perhaps you're right," said Swingerhoger. "Perhaps if I put it to her delicately, she will take it in the right way, which is, that it is a compliment and an honor to play to Swingerhoger guests, and she may put in more of her time at it."

The man who was nobody in particular looked a long while into the inherited vapid face of the garden owner, and he did not think of the arrangement of that gentleman's mind.

"You must pay her," he said.

"Pay her? What for?"

"To play and sing, my friend. She has a job somewhere in this lonesome city, and she must fill the hours. If you pay her she can play for you from, say, four to twelve p.m., and then you are already a wealthy man."

"But," said Swingerhoger, dropping his seals, "no other beer garden is doing this."

"And that," said the man who was nobody in particular, "is where you get in your start. When the thing gets winded all the gardens will take it up, and then you're done. But until then the chance is yours."

To Paprika, therefore, Swingerhoger took the proposition.

The man from nowhere, who was nobody in particular, got a free beer.

"Play for you?" queried Paprika, keeping him out by the chain on the door. "How can I? I have a stenographer's job to fill, in a silk office. I'm getting ten per, and it just keeps tapioca in mother's mouth and the pepsin in mine, and it hangs out a few starched things and a ride now and then on the cars."

"You don't understand. I pay you ten dollars just the same and all you got to do is lie in bed all day until four and then you play for me until midnight and hit the mattress again, see?"

"Gee!" gasped Paprika, "in bed all day. I'm dreamin', but say, I can't do it anyway, because," she blushed this time, "I'm leaving soon." She smiled, the last letter from the boy lay next her fifth rib.

"But," he protested, walking down backward, as she followed, "you don't understand. Nothing to do all day and then only play an easy tune now and again, between bites of the pralines and sips at the sherry lemonade. I'm getting rich on you, Miss Johnson. Think it over. Why, only today I gave my cousin Gus a bank account on you."

Paprika smiled again and shook her head. "I'm changing my tune anyway," she said, and added softly, "to a lullaby."

And so at last, though she had never seen the boy from Stroud's face to face, she put the chair over the rent in the carpet, the vase over the moth hole in the piano scarf, and the stain just back of the hat rack she covered with a picture of three pink gowned girls walking over a brittle paper stream.

Her heart beat terribly fast. She got that same sensation that Leah had gotten. She felt that nothing was going to be as it had been. She took a dose of soda water, but it was not the treatment for the trouble. Therefore, resigning herself to her best dress and a peach of a haircomb, she waited for the boy from Stroud's who was coming to see her.

The little hands on the clock came coquettishly in front of its gold face and parted suddenly as if saying, "Oh, all's well, I need not hide," with the pettish nonchalance of ninety-eight cent clocks.

Paprika fussed a bit with the position of her feet and decided, after all, that she looked better standing up, and had gotten a pose to suit every one, herself included, half drooping over moth-eaten geraniums, when Leah hurled herself into the room.

"Oh, my God!" she said, stumbling over to the mantle-piece, and stood there shaking.

"He got it from behind the clock," she wailed, "and now the oculists have taken their last diagnosis, and they say that he can have the bandage removed, and I didn't understand and I'm done, I'm done." She took to shaking the mantle and its blue array of willow-ware and the peacock feathers sticking in the mucilage. Also she shook Paprika.

"What can I do?" asked Paprika, and Leah fell upon her.

"This once—this once—he would never get over the shock—and I can't, I can't!"

"You can't what?" demanded Paprika.

"It's Gus, you don't understand. The oculists have just left him and he can *see!*"

"*Well?*"

Leah took a step toward the girl who had been her bosom friend, and she heaved her forty-nine-cent belt up. "He mustn't see me— yet."

And so she stood. Leah, the friend who had got a husband in the dark, and now must stand before him in the light that had come to him with his prosperity, gotten by the playing of Paprika. And Paprika, realizing this, did not know what to do.

Leah came to her and took her arms in both her hands, nursing them between her palms with long frightened fingers, and looked at Paprika and could not speak.

Paprika had forgotten the boy from Stroud's. She had forgotten her best dress and the sense of back thrust feet, and she put her chin out.

"You want him to pin his eyes on *me?*"

And Leah nodded her thin head back and forth, and took her lip in between her teeth. "He won't be so sorry, after—when he gets used to it and me, when I come in later and you straighten things out. He will be too much a man to be a quitter."

And Paprika understood what it meant to a woman to be willing to keep her own at such a cost. Also Paprika thought she was over-estimating Gus's sense of beauty.

So she said "all right," looked at the clock and thought, at a rough estimate, that she had time, and descended to the second floor front.

She stirred as she sat by Gus's bed at the step on the stair that halted a bit, and then went on up. She remembered that she had told nothing to Leah about his coming, and Leah was up there in the dusk— but Gus was taking the bandages off.

In the dim light, the boy from Stroud's took off his hat. He was breathing hard from the eight flights and a heart full of a sensation that was like being run over with molasses and crowned with chocolate meringue. In the corner he saw the dim shape of a woman. He never looked toward the bed where slept the perfect chaperon. He shut the door reverently and came a step in. The figure in the corner moved and moaned like a seal at twelve p.m., moved and moaned and put her hand to her unlovely hair and blinked at him from, startled blue eyes with her mouth open.

The banjo leaning in the corner caught his eye as he leaned forward, and he laughed suddenly, shortly, with a hard disillusioned break, and suddenly, without a word, caught up his hat and ran pantingly down the stairs. Heedless, he ran past the second story front on to the first, and fell into the murky light of Swingerhoger's beer garden, threw up his hands and cried something about "perspective and a picture plane" and darted out of the garden and disappeared in the direction of Bleecker Street.

Well, that's about all, excepting as we said, Paprika Johnson still holds the job as the first cabaret artist, at thirty years old. Still of evenings she sits upon the fire-escape and plays her banjo as her handkerchiefs dry, just as she did on that afternoon three minutes after Gus had taken the bandages off and she had come into the garden to get a pitcher of lemonade to celebrate, and leaning across the counter, she had said, "All right, I'll take that job."

Also she never told Leah that her chance "to do as much for her sometime, in a different way," had come and gone.

A NIGHT AMONG THE HORSES

TOWARD DUSK, IN the summer of the year, a man dressed in a frock coat and top hat, and carrying a cane, crept through the underbrush bordering the corral of the Buckler farm.

As he moved small twigs snapped, fell and were silent. His knees were green from wounded shrubbery and grass, and his outspread hands tore unheeded plants. His wrists hurt him and he rested from time to time, always caring for his hat and knotted yellow cane, blowing through his moustache.

Dew had been falling covering the twilight leaves like myriad faces, damp with the perspiration of the struggle for existence, and half a mile away, standing out against the darkness of the night, a grove of white birches shimmered, like teeth in a skull.

He heard the creaking of a gate, and the splashing of late rain into the depths of a dark cistern. His heart ached with the nearness of the earth, the faint murmur of it moving upon itself, like a sleeper who turns to throw an arm about a beloved.

A frog began moaning among the skunk cabbages, and John thrust his hand deep into his bosom.

Something somnolent seemed to be here, and he wondered. It was like a deep, heavy, yet soft prison where, without sin, one may suffer intolerable punishment.

Presently he went on, feeling his way. He reached a high plank fence and sensing it with his fingers, he lay down, resting his head against the ground.

He was tired, he wanted to sleep, but he searched for his hat and cane and straightened out his coat beneath him before he turned his eyes to the stars.

And now he could not sleep, and wondered why he had thought of it; something quick was moving the earth, it seemed to live, to shake with sudden immensity.

He heard a dog barking, and the dim light from a farm window kept winking as the trees swung against its square of light. The odor of daisies came to him, and the assuring, powerful smell of the stables; he opened his mouth and drew in his moustache.

A faint tumult had begun. A tremor ran under the length of his body and trembled off into the earth like a shudder of joy,—died down and repeated itself. And presently he began to tremble, answering, throwing out his hands, curling them up weakly, as if the earth were withholding something precious, necessary.

His hat fell off, striking a log with a dull hollow sound, and he pressed his red moustache against the grass weeping.

Again he heard it, felt it; a hundred hoofs beat upon the earth and he knew the horses had gone wild in the corral on the other side of the fence, for animals greet the summer, striking the earth, as friends strike the back of friends. He knew, he understood; a hail to summer, to life, to death.

He drew himself against the bars, pressing his eyes under them, peering, waiting.

He heard them coming up across the heavy turf, rounding the curve in the Willow Road. He opened his eyes and closed them again. The soft menacing sound deepened, as heat deepens, strike through the skin into the very flesh. Head on, with long legs rising, falling, rising again, striking the ground insanely, like needles taking terrible, impossible and purposeless stitches.

He saw their bellies, fawn colored, pitching from side to side. flashing by, straining the fence, and he rose up on his feet and silently, swiftly, fled on beside them.

Something delirious, hysterical, came over him and he fell. Blood trickled into his eyes down from his forehead. It had a fine feeling for a moment, like a mane, like that roan mare's mane that had passed him—red and long and splendid.

He lifted his hand, and closed his eyes once more, but the soft pounding did not cease, though now, in his sitting position, it only jogged him imperceptibly, as a child on a knee.

It seemed to him that he was smothering, and be felt along the side of his face as he had done in youth when they had put a cap on him that was too large. Twining green things, moist with earth-blood, crept over his fingers, the hot, impatient leaves pressed in, and the green of the matted-grass was deathly thick. He had heard about the freeness of nature, thought it was so, and it was not so.

A trailing ground pine had torn up small blades in its journey across the hill, and a vine, wrist-thick, twisted about a pale oak, hideously, gloriously, killing it, dragging it into dust.

A wax Patrick Pipe leaned against his neck, staring with black eyes, and John opened his mouth, running his tongue across his lips snapping it off, sighing.

Move as he would, the grass was always under him, and the crackling of last autumn's leaves and last summer's twigs—minute dead of the infinite greatness—troubled him. Something portentuous seemed connected with the patient noises about him. An acorn dropped, striking a thin fine powder out of a frail oak pod. He took it up, tossing it. He had never liked to see things fall.

He sat up, with the dim thunder of the horses far off, but quickening his heart.

He went over the scene he had with Freda Buckler, back there in the house, the long quivering spears of pot-grass standing by the window as she walked up and down, pulling at than, talking to him.

Small, with cunning fiery eyes and a pink and pointed chin. A daughter of a mother who had known too many admirers in her youth; a woman with an ample lap on which she held a Persian kitten or a trifle of fruit. Bounty, avarice, desire, intelligence—both of them had always what they wanted.

He blew down his moustache again thinking of Freda in her floating yellow veil that he had called ridiculous. She had not been angry, he was nothing but a stable boy then. It was the way with those small intriguing women whose nostrils were made delicate through the pain of many generation that they might quiver whenever they caught a whiff of the stables.

"As near as they can get to the earth," he had said and was Freda angry? She stroked his arm always softly, looking away, an inner bitterness drawing down her mouth.

She said, walking up and down quickly, looking ridiculously small:

"I am always gentle John—" frowning, trailing her veil, thrusting out her chin.

He answered: "I liked it better where I was,"

"Horses," she said showing sharp teeth, "are nothing for a man with your bile—poy-boy—curry comber, smelling of saddle soap—

lovely!" She shrivelled up her nose, touching his arm: "Yes, but better things. I will show you—you shall be a gentleman—fine clothes, you will like them, they feel nice." And laughing she turned on one high heel, sitting down. "I like horses, they make people better; you are amusing, intelligent, you will see—"

"A lackey!" he returned passionately throwing up his arm "what is there in this for you, what are you trying to do to me? The family—askance—perhaps—I don't know."

He sat down pondering. He was getting used to it, or thought he was, all but his wordy remonstrances. He knew better when thinking of his horses, realizing that when he should have married this small, unpleasant and clever woman, he would know them no more.

It was a game between them, which was the shrewder, which would win out? He? A boy of ill breeding, grown from the gutter, fancied by this woman because he had called her ridiculous, or for some other reason that he would never know. This kind of person never tells the truth, and this, more than most things, troubled him. Was he a thing to be played with, debased into something better than he was, than he knew.

Partly because he was proud of himself in the costume of a groom, partly because he was timid, he desired to get away, to go back to the stables. He walked up to the mirrors as if about to challenge them, peering in. He knew he would look absurd, and then knew, with shame, that he looked splendidly better than most of the gentlemen that Freda Buckler knew. He hated himself. A man who had grown out of the city's streets, a fine common thing!

She saw him looking into the mirrors, one after the other, and drew her mouth down. She got up, walking beside him in the end, between him and them, taking his arm.

"You shall enter the army—you shall rise to General, or Lieutenant at least—and there are horses there, and the sound of stirrups—with that physique you will be happy—authority you know," she said shaking her chin, smiling.

"Very well, but a common soldier—"

"As you like—afterward."

"Afterward?"

"Very well, a common soldier."

He sensed something strange in her voice, a sort of irony and it took the patience out of him:

"I have always been common, I could commit crimes, easily, gladly—I'd like to!"

She looked away. "That's natural", she said faintly, "it's an instinct all strong men have—"

She knew what was troubling him, thwarted instincts, common beautiful instincts that he was being robbed of. He wanted to do something final to prove his lower order; caught himself making faces, idiot faces, and she laughed.

"If only your ears stuck out, chin receded," she said. "you might look degenerate, common, but as it is—"

And he would creep away in hat, coat and cane to peer at his horses never daring to go in near them. Sometimes when he wanted to weep he would smear one glove with harness grease, but the other one he held behind his back, pretending one was enough to prove his revolt.

She would torment him with vases, books, pictures, making a fool of him gently, persistently, making him doubt by cruel means, the means of objects he was not used to, eternally taking him out of his sphere.

"We have the best collection of miniatures," she would say with one knee on a low ottoman, bringing them out in her small palm. "Here, look."

He would put his hands behind him.

"She was a great woman—Lucrezia Borgia—do you know history—" She put it back again because he did not answer, letting his mind, a curious one, torment itself.

"You love things very much, don't you?" she would question because she knew that he had a passion for one thing only. She kept placing new ladders beneath his feet, only to saw them off at the next rung, making him nothing more than a nervous irritable experiment. He was uneasy, like one given food to smell and not to taste, and for a while he had not wanted to taste, and then curiosity began, and he wanted to, and he also wanted to escape, and he could do neither.

Well, after he had married her, what then? Satisfy her whim and where would he be? He would be nothing, neither what he had been nor what other people were. This seemed *to* him, at times, her wish—a sort of place between lying down and standing up, a cramped position, a slow death. A curious woman.

This same evening he had looked at her attentively for the first time. Her hair was rather pretty, though too mousy, yet just in the nape of the neck, where it met the lawn of the collar it was very attractive. She walked well for a little woman too.

Sometimes she would pretend to be lively, would run a little catch herself at it, as if she had not intended to do it, and calm down once more, or creeping up to him, stroking his arm, talking to him, she would walk beside him softly, slowly that he might not step out, that he would have to crawl across the carpet.

Once he had thought of trying her with honesty, with the truth of the situation. Perhaps she would give him an honest answer, and he had tried.

"Now Miss Freda—just a word—what are you trying to do? What is it you want? What is there in me that can interest you? I want you to tell me—I want to know—I have got to ask someone, and I haven't anyone to ask but you."

And for a moment she almost relented, only to discover that she could not if she had wished. She did not know always what she meant herself.

"I'll tell you," she said, hoping that this, somehow, might lead her into the truth, for herself, if not for him, but it did not. "You are a little nervous, you will get used to it—you will even grow to like it. Be patient. You will learn soon enough that there is nothing in the world so agreeable as climbing, changing."

"Well," he said trying to read her, "And then?"

"That's all. you will regret the stables in the end—that's all" Her nostrils quivered. A light came into her eyes, a desire to defy, to be defied.

And then on this last night he had done something terrible, he had made a blunder. There had been a party. The guests, a lot of them, were mostly drunk, or touched with drink. And he too had too much. He remembered having thrown his arms about a tall woman, gowned in black with loose shoulder straps, dragging her through a dance. He had even sung a bit of a song, madly, wildly, horribly. And suddenly he had been brought up sharp by the fact that no one thought his behavior strange, that no one thought him presumptuous. Freda's mother had not even moved or dropped the kitten from her lap where it sat, its loud resolute purr shaking the satin of her gown.

And he felt that Freda had got him where she wanted him, between two rungs. Going directly up to her he said:

"You are ridiculous!" and twirled his moustache, spitting into the garden.

And he knew nothing about what happened until he found himself in the shrubbery crawling toward the corral, through the dusk and the dampness of the leaves, carrying his cane, making sure of his hat, looking up at the stars.

And now he knew why he had come. He was with his horses again. His eyes, pressed against the bars, stared in. The black stallion in the lead had been his special pet, a rough animal, but kindly, knowing. And here they were once more, tearing up the grass, galloping about in the night like a ball-room full of real people, people who wanted to do things, who did what they wanted to do.

He began to crawl through the bars, slowly, deftly, and when half way through he paused, thinking.

Presently he went on again, and drawing himself into the corral, his hat and cane thrown in before him, he lay there mouth to the grass.

They were still running, but less madly, one of them had gone up the Willow Road leading into a farther pasture, in a flare of dust, through which it looked immense and faint.

On the top of the hill three or four of the horses were standing, testing the weather. He would mount one, he would ride away, he would escape. And his horses, the things he knew, would be his escape.

Bareback, he thought, would be like the days when he had taken what he could from the rush of the streets, joy, exhilaration, life, and he was not afraid. He wanted to stand up, to cry aloud.

And he saw ten or twelve of them rounding the curve, and he did stand up.

They did not seem to know him, did not seem to know what to make of him, and he stared at them wondering. He did not think of his white shirt front, his sudden arising, the darkness, their excitement. Surely they would know, in a moment more.

Wheeling, flaring their wet nostrils, throwing up their manes, striking the earth in a quandary, they came on, whinnied faintly, and he knew what it was to be afraid.

He had never been afraid and he went down on his knees. With a new horror in his heart he damned them. He turned his eyes up, but he could not open them. He thought rapidly, calling on Freda in his heart, speaking tenderly, promising.

A flare of heat passed his throat and descended into his bosom.

"I want to live. I can do it—damn it—I can do it. I can forge ahead, make my mark."

He forgot where he was for a moment and found new pleasure to this spoken admission, this new rebellion. He moved with the faint shaking of the earth like a child on a woman's lap.

The upraised hoofs of the first horse missed him, but the second did not.

And presently the horses drew apart, nibbling here and there, switching their tails, avoiding a patch of tall grass.

THE TERRIBLE PEACOCK

It was during the dull season, when a subway accident looms as big as a Thaw getaway, that an unusual item was found loose in the coffee.

Nobody seemed to know whence it had come. It dealt with a woman, one greater, more dangerous than Cleopatra, thirty-nine times as alluring as sunlight on a gold eagle, and about as elusive.

She was a Peacock, said the item, which was not ill-written—a slinky female with electrifying green eyes and red hair, dressed in clinging green-and-blue-silk, and she was very much observed as she moved languorously through the streets of Brooklyn. A Somebody—but who?

The city editor scratched his head and gave the item to Karl.

"Find out about her," he suggested.

"Better put a new guy on," said Karl. "Get the fresh angle. I got that Kinney case to look after today. What about Garvey?"

"All right," said the city editor, and selected a fresh piece of gum.

Garvey was duly impressed when Karl hove to alongside his desk and flung his leg after the item onto it, for Karl was the Star.

Rather a mysterious person in a way, was Karl. His residence was an inviolable secret. He was known to have accumulated money, despite the fact that he was a newspaperman. It was also known that he had married.

Otherwise, he was an emergency man—a first-rate reporter. When someone thought best to commit suicide and leave a little malicious note to a wife who raved three steps into the bathroom and three into the kitchen, hiccuping "Oh, my God!" with each step, it got into Karl's typewriter—and there was the birth of a front-page story.

"So you're to look her up," said Karl. "She's dashed beautiful, has cat eyes and Leslie Carter hair—a loose-jointed, ball-brearing Clytie, rigged out with a complexion like creamed coffee stood overnight. They say she claws more men into her hair than any siren living or dead."

"You've seen her?" breathed Garvey, staring.

Karl nodded briefly.

"Why don't *you* get her, then?"

"There are two things," said Karl judicially, "at which I am no good. One is subtraction, and the other is attraction. Go to it, son. The assignment is yours."

He strolled away, but not too late to see Garvey swelling visibly at the implied compliment and caressing his beautiful, lyric tie.

Garvey didn't altogether like the assignment, nonetheless. There was Lilac Jane, you see. He had a date with her for that very night, and Lilac Jane was exceedingly desirable.

He was at that age when devotion to one female of the species makes dalliance with any others nothing short of treason.

But—he had been allotted this work because of his fascinations for slinky green sirens! Garvey fingered the tie again and withdrew his lavender scented handkerchief airily, as an alterboy swings a censer.

At the door he turned under the light and pushed back his cuff, and his fellow workers groaned. It was seven by his wristwatch

Outside he paused on the corner near the chophouse. He looked up and down the gloomy street with its wilted florist-window displays and its spattering of gray house fronts, wishing there were someone with him who could be told of his feeling of competence in a world of competent men.

His eyes on the pavement, lost in perfervid dreams of Lilac Jane, he wandered on. The roaring of the bridge traffic disturbed him not, nor the shouts of bargemen through the dusk on the waterfront.

At last through the roseate visions loomed something green.

Shoes! Tiny shoes, trim and immaculate; above them a glimpse of thin, green stockings on trimmer ankles.

There was a tinkle of laughter, and Garvey came to himself, red and perspiring, and raised his eyes past the slim, green-clad body to the eyes of the Peacock.

It was she beyond question. Her hair was terribly red, even in the darkness, and it gleamed a full eight inches above her forehead, piled higher than any hair Garvey had ever seen. The moon shone through it like butter through mosquito netting.

Her neck was long and white, her lipes were redder than her hair, and her green eyes, with the close-fitting, silken dress, that undulated like troubled, weed-filled water as she moved, completed the whole daring creation. The powers that be had gone in for poster effects when they made the Peacock.

She was handsome beyond belief, and she was amused at Garvey. Her silvery laugh tinkled out again as he stared at her, his pulse a hundred in the shade.

He tried to convince himself that this physiological effect was due to his newspaper instinct, but it is to be conjectured that Lilac Jane would have had her opinion of the Peacock had she been present.

"Well, young man?" she demanded, the wonderful eyes getting in their deadly work.

"I—I'm sorry—I didn't mean—" Garvey floundered hopelessly, but he did not try to escape.

"You were handing me bouquets by staring like that? That what you're trying to say?"

She laughed again, glided up to him and took his arm. "I like you, young man," she said.

"My nun-name is Garvey, and I'm on the—the *Argus*."

She started at that and looked at him sharply. "A reporter!"

But her tinkly laugh rang out again, and they walked on. "Well, why not?" she said gaily.

Then, with entire unexpectedness: "Do you tango?"

Garvey nodded dumbly, struggling to find his tongue.

"I *love* it!" declared the Peacock, taking a step or two of the dance beside him. "Want to take me somewheres so we can have a turn or two?"

Garvey swallowed hard and mentioned a well-known resort.

"Mercy!" cried the green-eyed siren, turning shocked orbs upon him. "I don't drink! Let's go to a tearoom—Poiret's." She called it "Poyrett's."

Garvey suffered himself to be led to the slaughter, and as they went she chattered lightly. He drew out his handkerchief and dabbed gently at his temples.

"Gracious!" she drawled. "You smell like an epidemic of swooning women."

Garvey was hurt, but deep within himself he decided suddenly that scent was out of place on a masculine cold-assuager.

They turned into a brightly lighted establishment where there were already a few girls and fewer men.

They found a table, and she ordered some tea and cakes, pressing her escort not to be bashful as far as himself was concerned. Garvey ordered obediently and lavishly.

Presently the music struck up, and he swung her out on the floor and into the fascinating dance.

Now, Garvey was really some dancer. But the Peacock!

She was light and sinuous as a wreath of green mist, yet solid bone and muscle in his arms.

She was the very poetry of motion, the spirit of the dance, the essence of grace and beauty.

And when the music stopped, Garvey could have cried with vexation, though he was considerably winded.

But the Peacock was not troubled at all. Indeed, she had talked on through all the dance.

Garvey had capitulated long ago. Lilac Jane? Bah! What were a thousand Lilac Janes to this glorious creature, this Venus Anadyomene— Aphrodite of the Sea-Foam?

In the bright light of the tearoom her green eyes were greener, her red hair redder, her white throat whiter. He would have given a Texas ranch for her, with the cattle thrown in.

He tried to tell her something of this, and she laughed delightfully.

"What is it about me that makes men go mad over me?" she demanded, dreamily sipping her tea.

"Do they?" He winced.

"Oh, shamelessly. They drop their jaws, propriety, and any bundles they may be carrying. Why?"

"It's the most natural thing in the world. You have hair and eyes that few women have, and a man desires the rare." He was getting eloquent.

"But—I'm not at all pretty—thinness isn't attractive, is it?"

"It is, in you," he said simply. The fact that he could say it simply was very bad indeed for Lilac Jane.

She dimpled at him and arose abruptly. "Now I've got to vanish. Oh, Lily!"

A girl, undeniably pretty, but just an ordinary girl, crossed over.

"This is Mr.—er—Garvey, Miss Jones. Keep him amused, will you? He dances very nicely." And as he struggled to his feet, attempting a protest: "Oh, I'm coming back again," and she was gone.

Garvey tried to think of some excuse to escape from the partner thus unceremoniously thrust upon him, but the girl blocked his feeble efforts by rising expectantly as the strains of "Too Much Mustard" floated on the ambient atmosphere.

There was nothing for it but to make good. And, after all, she was a nice dancer. He found himself asking what she would have at the end of the dance.

Anyhow, he reflected, he had still his assignment to cover. The Peacock was still as great a mystery as ever—more of a mystery. But she had said that she would return. So he waited and danced and ate and treated.

Half an hour later the Peacock *did* return—with another man.

To Garvey everything turned suddenly light purple. That was the result of his being green with jealousy and seeing red at the same time.

The newest victim of her lures (for such even Garvey recognized him to be) was an elderly business man, inclined to corpulency, with a free and roving eye. Garvey hated him with a bitter hatred.

The Peacock danced once with him, then abandoned him, gasping fishily, to another girl's tender mercies.

She stopped briefly at Garvey's table, gave him a smile and a whispered: "Here, tomorrow night," and vanished in a swirl of green silk—probably in search of more captives.

Garvey put in a bad night and a worse next day. Who was she? What was her little game? What would happen tomorrow night?

He didn't care. Lilac Jane was definitely deposed in favor of a green goddess whose lure quite possibly spelled destruction.

But he didn't care.

He told the city editor that the Peacock story would be available next day, and added the mental reservation, "if I haven't resigned." And he mooned through the work in a trance that made for serious errors in his "copy."

Yet he had no illusions about it, save an undefined and noble impulse to "rescue the Peacock from her degrading surroundings."

Somehow the phrase didn't quite apply, though.

Once he thought of Lilac Jane, with her warm, normal, womanly arms stretched out to him. He took her picture from his pocket and compared it with the mental picture he carried of the Peacock, then put the photograph back, face outward.

Thus Lilac Jane's flags were struck.

Directly afterward the brazen office-boy communicated to him in strident tones that a "skoit" wanted him on the phone.

For a second he thought of the Peacock; but no, Lilac Jane was due to call. Whereupon he fled ignominiously.

It may be deduced that he had not forgotten Lilac Jane after all, merely misplaced her.

Garvey fell into the elevator, the cosmic tail of the Peacock filling his existence. He threw quoits with the god of a greater wisdom, and came out of his reverie and the elevator with a pair of jet earrings dancing before him. They were the earrings of Lilac Jane.

But beneath them, as the periods beneath double exclamation points, floated a pair of green boots.

Moodily he ate, moodily he went to his room—apartment, I beg his pardon. And at six o'clock he was ready for eight.

He took out his watch and wound it until the hands quivered and it made noises inside as though it were in pain.

He stood before the mirror and motioned at his Adam's apple, prodding the lyric tie into shape and stretching his neck the while until it seemed about to snap and leave a blank space between his chin and his collar button.

A man in love ceases mentally. All his energy is devoted to his outward appearance.

If Napoleon had been in love while on the field of Austerlitz, he would not have rejoiced in his heart, but in his surtout and small clothes.

If Wellington had been so afflicted during the battle of Waterloo, the result might have been different.

Therefore, when Garvey was finally attired, he was like unto the lilies of the field that toil not, neither do they spin. He glanced at his watch when all was at last perfect, and all but sat down suddenly. It was midnight!

But then he saw that the poor watch was travelling at the rate of a mile a minute, trying to make up for that last winding. The alarm clock said seven–thirty.

Whereupon Garvey achieved the somewhat difficult feat of descending the stairs without bending his knees. Spoil the crease in his trousers? Never!

And shortly thereafter he was at the tango tearoom, looking around eagerly for the Peacock, his heart pounding harder than his watch.

The place was crowded, and the dancers were already busy to the sprightly strains of "Stop at Chattanooga."

For a space he looked in vain. Then his cardiac engine missed a stroke.

There she was—seated at a table in the far corner.

As fast as he reasonably could without danger to his immaculateness, Garvey headed Her-ward.

Yes, it was undoubtedly the Peacock. She was leaning her elbows on the table and talking earnestly—talking to—Karl!

Garvey was abreast of the table by now. He must have made some sort of a noise, for they both looked up.

The Peacock smiled sweetly, with a touch of defiance. Karl grinned amiably, with a touch of sheepishness. And both said: "Hello!"

Then said Karl: "Old man, allow me to present you to—my wife."

Garvey choked and sat down speechless.

"Might as well 'fess it," said Karl. "Only please remember that the idea was solely mine."

"It was *not!*" said the Peacock sharply. "You wouldn't *hear* of it when I suggested it."

"Well, anyhow, I have all my money invested in this tearoom. But business has been mighty dull; it looked like bankruptcy.

"Then Mrs. Karl here—she was La Dancerita before she fell for me, you see, and—well, she's been drumming up patronage."

"It was fun!" declared La Dancerita-that-was. "I nearly got pinched once, though."

"I wrote that squib at the office that got you the assignment, thinking to help the game along a little." He smiled a deep, mahogany, wrinkled smile that disarmed when it reached the blue of his eyes. "So now you know all about the Peacock."

Garvey swallowed twice and sighed once. Then he took something from his breast pocket and put it back again.

"I—er know somebody that likes to tango," he said irrelevantly.

THE VALET

THE FIELDS ABOUT Louis-Georges house grew green in early spring, leaving the surrounding country in melancholy gray, for Louis-Georges was the only man who sowed his ground to rye

Louis-Georges was of small stature. His face was oblong, too pale. A dry mouth lay crookedly beneath a nose ending in a slight bulb. His long animal-like arms swung half a rhythm ahead of his legs.

He prided himself on his farming, though he knew nothing about it. He surveyed the tender coming green with kindly good nature, his acres were always a month ahead of his neighbors in their debut.

Sometimes standing in the doorway, breathing through the thick hair in his nostrils, stretching his gloves, he would look at the low-lying sheds and the stables and the dull brown patches of ploughed earth, and mutter "Splendid, splendid!"

Finally he would stroll in among the cattle where, in dizzy circles, large colored flies swayed, emitting a soft insistent drone like taffeta rubbed against taffeta.

He liked to think that he knew a great deal about horses. He would look solemnly at the trainer and discuss length of neck, thinness and shape of flank by the hour, stroking the hocks of his pet racer. Sometimes he would say to Vera Sovna: "There's more real breeding in the rump of a mare than in all the crowned heads of England."

Sometimes he and Vera Sovna would play in the hay, and about the grain bins. She in her long flounces, leaping in and out, screaming and laughing, stamping her high heels, setting up a great commotion among her ruffles.

Once Louis-Georges caught a rat, bare handed, and with such skill that it could not bite. He disguised his pride in showing it to her by

149

pretending that he had done so to inform her of the rodent menace to winter grain.

Vera Sovna was a tall creature with thin shoulders; she was always shrugging them as if her shoulder-blades were heavy. She dressed in black and laughed a good deal in a very high key.

She had been a great friend of Louis-Georges' mother, but since her death she had fallen into disrepute. It was hinted that she was "something" to Louis-Georges; and when the townsfolk and neighboring landholders saw her enter the house they would not content themselves until they saw her leave it.

If she came out holding her skirts crookedly above her thin ankles, they would find the roofs of their mouths in sudden disapproval, while if she walked slowly, dragging her dress, they would say: "See what a dust Vera Sovna brings up in the driveway; she stamps as if she were a mare."

If she knew anything of this feeling, she never showed it. She would drive through the town and turn neither to right or left until she passed the markets with their bright yellow gourds and squashes, their rosy apples and their splendid tomatoes, exhaling an odor of decaying sunlight. On the rare occasions when Louis-Georges accompanied her she would cross her legs at the knee, leaning forward pointing a finger at him, shaking her head, laughing.

Sometimes she would go into the maids' quarters to play with Leah's child, a little creature with weak legs and neck, who always thrust out his stomach for her to pat.

The maids, Berthe and Leah, were well-built complacent women with serene blue eyes, quite far apart, and good mouths in which fine teeth grew gratefully and upon whom round ample busts flourished like plants. They went about their work singing or chewing long green salad leaves.

In her youth Leah had done something for which she prayed at intervals. Her memory was always taking her hastily away to kneel before the gaudy wax Christ that hung on a beam in the barn. Resting her head against the boards she would lift her work-worn hands, bosom high, sighing, praying, murmuring.

Or she would help Berthe with the milking, throwing her thick ankles under the cow's udders, bringing down a sudden fury of milk, shining and splashing over her big clean knuckles, saying quietly, evenly:

"I think we will have rain before dawn."

And her sister would answer: "Yes, before dawn."

Leah would spend hours in the garden, her little one crawling after her, leaving childish smears on the dusty leaves of the growing corn, digging his hands into the vegetable tops, falling and pretending to have fallen on purpose; grinning up at the sun foolishly until his eyes watered.

These two women and Louis-Georges' valet, Vanka, made up the household, saving occasional visits from Louis-Georges' aunts, Myra and Ella.

This man Vanka was a mixture of Russian and Jew. He bit his nails, talked of the revolution, moved clumsily.

His clothes fitted him badly, he pomaded his hair, which was reddish yellow, pulled out the short hairs that tormented his throat, and from beneath his white brows distributed a kindly intelligent look. The most painful thing about him was his attempt to seem alert, his effort to keep pace with his master.

Louis-Georges would say "Well, now Vanka, what did they do to you in Russia when you were a boy?"

"They shot my brother for a red." Vanka would answer, pulling the hairs. "They threw him into prison, and my sister took him his food. One day our father was also arrested, then she took two dinner pails instead of one. And once she heard a noise, it sounded like a shot, and our father returned her one of the pails. They say he looked up at her like a man who is gazed at over the shoulder." He had told the tale often, adding: "My sister became almost bald later on, yet she was a handsome woman; the students used to come to her chambers to hear her talk."

At such times Louis-George would excuse himself and shut himself up to write, in a large and scrawling hand, letters to his aunts with some of Vanka's phrases in them.

Sometimes Vera Sovna would come in to watch him, lifting her ruffles, raising her brows. Too, she would turn and look for a long time at Vanka who returned her look with cold persistence, the way of a man who is afraid, who does not approve, and yet who likes.

She would stand with her back to the fireplace, her high heels a little apart, tapping the stretched silk of her skirt, saying:

"You will ruin your eyes," adding: "Vanka, won't you stop him."

She seldom got answers to her remarks. Louis-Georges would continue, grunting at her, to be sure, and smiling, but never lifting his eyes: and as for Vanka he would stand there, catching the sheets of paper as they were finished.

Finally Louis-Georges would push back his chair, saying: "Come, we will have tea."

In the end he fell into a slow illness. It attacked his limbs, he was forced to walk with a cane. He complaned of his heart, but he persisted in going out to look at the horses, to the barn to amuse Vera Sovna, swaying a little as he watched the slow circling flies, sniffing the pleasant odors of cow's milk and dung.

He still had plans for the haying season, for his crops, but he gave them over to his farm hands, who, left to themselves, wandered aimlessly home at odd hours.

About six months later he took to his bed.

His aunts came, testing with their withered noses the smell of decaying wood and paragoric, whispering that "he never used to get like this."

Raising their ample shoulders to ease the little black velvet straps that sunk into their flesh, they sat on either side of his bed.

They looked at each other in a pitifully surprised way. They had never seen illness, and death but once—a suicide, and this they understood: one has impulses, but not maladies.

They were afraid of meeting Vera Sovna. Their position was a difficult one: having been on friendly terms while Louis-Georges' mother lived, they had nevertheless to maintain a certain dignity and reserve when the very towns folk had turned against her. Therefore they left her an hour in the evening to herself. She would come creeping in saying:

"Oh my dear," telling him long unheard stories about a week she had spent in London. A curious week full of near adventure, with amusing tales of hotel keepers, nobility. And sometimes leaning close to him, that he might hear, he saw that she was weeping.

But in spite of this and of his illness and the new quality in the air, Vera Sovna was strangely gay.

During this illness the two girls served as nurses, changing the sheets, turning him over, rubbing him with alcohol, bringing him his soup, crossing themselves.

Vanka stool long hours by the beside coughing. Sometimes he would fall off into sleep, at others he would try to talk of the revolution.

Vera Sovna had taken to dining in the kitchen, a long bare room that pleased her. From the window one could see the orchards and the pump and the long slope down to the edge of the meadow. And the room was pleasant to look upon. The table, like the earth itself, was simple and abundant. It might have been a meadow that Leah and Berthe browsed in, red-cheeked, gaining health, strength.

Great hams, smoked fowl with oddly taut legs hung from the beams, and under these the girls moved as if there were some bond between them.

They accepted Vera Sovna's company cheerfully uncomplainingly, and when she went away they cleared up her crumbs, thinking and talking of other things, forgetting.

Nothing suffered on account of his illness. The household matters went smoothly, the crops ripened, the haying season passed, and the sod in the orchards sounded with the thud of ripe falling fruit. Louis-Georges suffered alone, detached, as if he had never been. Even about Vera Sovna there was a strange quiet brilliancy, the brilliancy of one who is about to receive something. She caressed the medicine bottles, tended the flowers.

Leah and Berthe were unperturbed, except from overwork; the face of Vanka alone changed.

He bore the expression at once of a man in pain and of a man who is about to come into peace. The flickering light in Louis-Georges' face cast its shadow on that of his valet.

Myra and Ella became gradually excited. They kept brushing imaginary specks of dust from their shoulders and bodices, sending each other in to observe him. They comforted themselves looking at him, pretending each to the other that he was quite improved. It was not so much that they were sorry to have him die, as it was that they were not prepared to have him die.

When the doctor arrived they shifted their burden of worry. They bought medicine with great relish, hurriedly. Finally to lessen the torment they closed their eyes as they sat on either side of his bed, picturing him already dead, laid out, hands crossed, that they might gain comfort upon opening them, to find him still alive.

When they knew that he was really dying they could not keep from touching him. They tried to cover him up in those parts that exposed too plainly his illness: the thin throat, the damp pulsing spot in the neck. They fondled his hands, driving doctor and nurse into a passion.

At last, in desperation, Myra knelt by his bed, touched his face, stroked his cheeks, trying to break the monotonous calm of approaching death.

Death did not seem to be anywhere in him saving in his face, it seemed to Myra that to drive it from his eyes would mean life. And it was then that she and her sister were locked out, to wander up and down the hall, afraid to speak, afraid to weep, unless by that much they might hasten his death.

When he finally died, they had the problem of Vera Sovna.

But they soon forgot her trying to follow the orders left by the dead man. Louis-Georges had been very careful to see to it that things should go on growing, he had given many orders, planned new seasons, talked of "next year," knowing that he would not be there.

The hens cackled with splendid performances, the stables resounded with the good spirits of the horses, the fields were all but shedding their very life on the earth as Vanka moved noiselessly about, folding the dead man's clothes.

When the undertaker arrived Vanka would not let them touch the body. He washed and dressed it to suit himself. It was he who laid Louis-Georges in the shiny coffin, it was he who arranged the flowers, and he finally left the room on the flat of his whole noisy feet for the first time in years. He went to his own room overlooking the garden.

He paced the room. It seemed to him that he had left something undone, He had loved service and order; he did not know that he also loved Louis-Georges, who made service necessary and order desirable.

This distressed him, he rubbed his hands, holding them close to his mouth, as if by the sound of one hand passing over the other he might learn some secret in the stoppage of sound.

Leah had made a scene, he thought of that. A small enough scene, considering. She had brought her baby in, dropping him beside the body, giving the flat voiced: "Now you can play with him a minute."

He had not interfered, the child had been too frightened to disturb the cold excellence of Louis-Georges' arrangement, and Leah had gone out soon enough in stolid silence. He could hear them descending the steps, her heavy slow tread followed by the quick uneven movements of the child.

Vanka could hear the rustling of the trees in the garden, the call of an owl from the barn; one of the mares whinnied and, stamping, fell off into silence again.

He opened the window. He thought he caught the sound of feet on the pebbles that bordered the hydrangea bushes; a faint perfume such as the flounces of Vera Sovna exhaled came to him. Irritated he turned away when he heard her calling.

"Vanka, come, my foot is caught in the vine."

Her face, with wide hanging lips, came above the sill, and the same moment she jumped into the room.

They stood looking at each other. They had never been alone together before. He did not know what to do.

She was a little disheveled, twigs from the shrubbery clung to the black flounces of her gown. She raised her thin shoulders once, twice, and sighed.

She reached out her arm, whispering:

"Vanka."

He moved away from her, staring at her.

"Vanka," she repeated and came close, leaning a little on him.

In a voice of command, she said simply. "You must tell me something."

"I will tell you" he answered automatically.

"See, look at your hands—" she kissed them suddenly, dropping her wet lips into the middle of the palms, making him start and shiver.

"Look at these eyes—ah fortunate man," she continued, "most fortunate Vanka; he would let you touch him, close, near the heart, the skin. You could know what he looked like, how he stood, how his ankle went into his foot." He ceased to hear her.

"And his shoulders, how they set. You dressed and undressed him, knew him, all of him, for many years,—you see, you understand? Tell me, tell me what he was like!"

He turned to her. "I will tell you," he said, "if you are still, if you will sit down, if you are quiet."

She sat down with another sigh, with a touch of her old gaiety; she raised her eyes, watching him.

"His arms were too long, you could tell that—but beautiful, and his back was thin, tapering—full of breeding—"

SMOKE

THERE WAS SWART with his bushy head and Fenken with the half shut eyes and the grayish beard, and there also was Zelka with her big earrings and her closely bound inky hair, who had often been told that "she was very beautiful in a black way."

Ah, what a fine strong creature she had been, and what a fine strong creature her father, Fenken, had been before her, and what a specimen was her husband, Swart, with his gentle melancholy mouth and his strange strong eyes and his brown neck.

Fenken in his youth had loaded the cattle boats, and in his twilight of age he would sit in the round-backed chair by the open fireplace, his two trembling hands folded, and would talk of what he had been.

"A bony man I was, Zelka—my two knees as hard as a pavement, so that I clapped them with great discomfort to my own hands. Sometimes," he would add, with a twinkle in his old eyes, "I'd put you between them and my hand. It hurt less."

Zelka would turn her eyes on him slowly—they moved around into sight from under her eyebrows like the barrel of a well-kept gun; they were hard like metal and strong, and she was always conscious of them even in sleep. When she would close her eyes before saying her prayers, she would remark to Swart, "I draw the hood over the artillery." And Swart would smile, nodding his large head.

In the town these three were called the "Bullets"—when they came down the street, little children sprang aside, not because they were afraid, but because they came so fast and brought with them something so healthy, something so potent, something unconquerable. Fenken could make his fingers snap against his palm like the crack of a cabby's whip just by shutting his hand abruptly, and he did this often, watching the gamin and smiling.

Swart, too, had his power, but there was a hint at something softer in him, something that made the lips kind when they were sternest, something that gave him a sad expression when he was thinking—something that had drawn Zelka to him in their first days of courting. "We Fenkens," she would say, "have iron in our veins—in yours I fear there's a little blood."

Zelka was cleanly. She washed her linen clean as though she were punishing the dirt. Had the linen been less durable there would have been holes in it from her knuckles in six months. Everything Zelka cooked was tender—she had bruised it with her preparations.

And then Zelka's baby had come. A healthy, fat, little crying thing, with eyes like its father's and with its father's mouth. In vain did Zelka look for something about it that would give it away as one of the Fenken blood—it had a maddeningly tender way of stroking her face; its hair was finer than blown gold; and it squinted up its pale blue eyes when it fell over its nose. Sometimes Zelka would turn the baby around in bed, placing its little feet against her side, waiting for it to kick. And when it finally did, it was gently and without great strength and with much good humor. "Swart," Zelka would say, "your child is entirely human. I'm afraid all his veins run blood." And she would add to her father, "Sonny will never load the cattle ships."

When it was old enough to crawl, Zelka would get down on hands and knees and chase it about the little ash-littered room. The baby would crawl ahead of her, giggling and driving Zelka mad with a desire to stop and hug him. But when she roared behind him like a lion to make him hurry, the baby would roll over slowly, struggle into a sitting posture, and, putting his hand up, would sit staring at her as though he would like to study out something that made this difference between them.

When it was seven, it would escape from the house and wander down to the shore, and stand for hours watching the boats coming in, being loaded and unloaded. Once one of the men put the cattle belt about him and lowered him into the boat. He went down sadly, his little golden head drooping and his feet hanging down. When they brought him back on shore again and dusted him off they were puzzled at him—he had neither cried nor laughed. They said, "Didn't you like that?" And he had only answered by looking at them fixedly.

And when he grew up he was very tender to his mother, who had taken to shaking her head over him. Fenken had died the Summer of his grandchild's thirtieth year, so that after the funeral Swart had taken the round-backed chair for his own. And now he sat there with folded hands, but he never said what a strong lad he had been. Sometimes he would say, "Do you remember how Fenken used to snap his fingers together like a whip?" And Zelka would answer, "I do."

And finally, when her son married, Zelka was seen at the feast dressed in a short blue skirt, leaning upon Swart's arm, both of them still strong and handsome and capable of lifting the buckets of cider.

Zelka's son had chosen a strange woman for a wife: a little thin thing, with a tiny waistline and a narrow chest and a small, very lovely throat. She was the daughter of a ship owner and had a good deal of money in her name. When she married Zelka's son, she brought him some ten thousand a year. And so he stopped the shipping of cattle and went in for exports and imports of Oriental silks and perfumes.

When his mother and father died, he moved a little inland away from the sea and hired clerks to do his bidding. Still, he never forgot what his mother had said to him: "There must always be a little iron in the blood, sonny."

He reflected on this when he looked at Lief, his wife. He was a silent, taciturn man as he grew older, and Lief had grown afraid of him, because of his very kindness and his melancholy.

There was only one person to whom he was a bit stern, and this was his daughter, "Little Lief." Toward her he showed a strange hostility, a touch even of that fierceness that had been his mother's. Once she had rushed shrieking from his room because he had suddenly roared behind her as his mother had done behind him. When she was gone, he sat for a long time by his table, his hands stretched out in front of him, thinking.

He had succeeded well. He had multiplied his wife's money now into the many thousands—they had a house in the country and servants. They were spoken of in the town as a couple who had an existence that might be termed as "pretty soft"; and when the carriage drove by of a Sunday with baby Lief up front on her mother's lap and Lief's husband beside her in his gray cloth coat, they stood aside not be be trampled on by the swift legged, slender ankled "pacer" that Lief had bought that day when she had visited the "old home"—the beach that had known her and her husband when they were children. This horse was the very one that she had asked for when she saw how beautiful it was as they fastened the belt to it preparatory to lowering it over the side. It was then that she remembered how, when her husband had been a little boy, they had lowered him over into the boat with this same belting.

During the Winter that followed, which was a very hard one, Lief took cold and resorted to hot water bottles and thin tea. She became very fretful and annoyed at her husband's constant questionings as to her health. Even Little Lief was a nuisance because she was so noisy. She would steal into the room, and, crawling under her mother's bed, would begin to sing in a high, thin treble, pushing the ticking with her patent leather boots to see them crinkle. Then the mother would cry out, the nurse would run in and take her away, and Lief would spend a half hour in tears. Finally they would not allow Little Lief in the room, so she would steal by the door many times, walking noiselessly up and down the hall. But finally, her youth overcoming her, she would stretch her legs out into a straight goose step, and for this she was whipped because on the day that she had been caught, her mother had died.

And so the time passed and the years rolled on, taking their toll. It was now many Summers since that day that Zelka had walked into town with Swart—now many years since Fenken had snapped his fingers like a cabby's whip. Little Lief had never even heard that her grandmother had been called a "beautiful woman in a black sort of way," and she had only vaguely heard of the nickname that had once been given the family, the "Bullets." She came to know that great strength had once been in the family, to such an extent, indeed, that somehow a phrase was known to her, "Remember always to keep a little iron in the blood." And one night she had pricked her arm to see if there were iron in it, and she had cried because it hurt. And so she knew that there was none.

With her this phrase ended. She never repeated it because of that night when she had made that discovery.

Her father had taken to solitude and the study of sociology. Sometimes he would turn her about by the shoulder and look at her, breathing in a thick way he had with him of late. And once he told her she was a good girl but foolish, and left her alone.

They had begun to lose money, and some of Little Lief's tapestries, given her by her mother, were sold. Her heart broke, but she opened the windows oftener because she needed some kind of beauty. She made the mistake of loving tapestries best and nature second best. Somehow she had gotten the two things mixed—of course, it was due to her bringing up. "If you are poor, you live out-of-doors; but if you are rich, you live in a lovely house." So to her the greatest of calamities had befallen the house. It was beginning to go away by those imperceptible means that at first leave a house looking unfamiliar and then bare.

Finally she could stand it no longer and she married a thin, wiry man with a long, thin nose and a nasty trick of rubbing it with a finger equally long and thin—a man with a fair income and very refined sisters.

This man, Misha, wanted to be a lawyer. He studied half the night and never seemed happy unless his head was in his palm. His sisters were like this also, only for another reason: they enjoyed weeping. If they could find nothing to cry about, they cried for the annoyance of this dearth of destitution and worry. They held daily councils for future domestic trouble—one the gesture of emotional and one of mental desire.

Sometimes Little Lief's father would come to the big iron gate and ask to see her. He would never come in—why? He never explained. So Little Lief and he would talk over the gate top, and sometimes he was gentle and sometimes he was not. When he was harsh to her, Little Lief wept, and when she wept, he would look at her steadily from under his eyebrows and say nothing. Sometimes he asked her to take a walk with him. This would set Little Lief into a terrible flutter; the corners of her mouth would twitch and her nostrils tremble. But she always went.

Misha worried little about his wife. He was a very selfish man, with that greatest capacity of a selfish nature, the ability to labor untiringly for some one thing that he wanted and that nature had placed beyond his reach. Some people called this quality excellent, pointing out what a great scholar Misha was, holding him up as an example in their own households, looking after him when he went hurriedly down the street with that show of nervous expectancy that a man always betrays when he knows within himself that he is deficient—a sort of peering in the face of life to see if it has discovered the flaw.

Little Lief felt that her father was trying to be something that was not natural to him. What was it? As she grew older, she tried to puzzle it out. Now it happened more often that she would catch him looking at her in a strange way, and once she asked him half playfully if he wished she had been a boy. And he had answered abruptly, "Yes, I do."

Little Lief would stand for hours at the casement and, leaning her head against the glass, try to solve this thing about her father. And then she discovered it when he had said, "Yes, I do." He was trying to be strong—what was it that was in the family?—oh, yes—iron in the blood. He feared there was no longer any iron left. Well, perhaps there wasn't—was that the reason he looked at her like this? No, he was worried about himself. Why?—wasn't he satisfied with his own strength? He had been cruel enough very often. This shouldn't have worried him.

She asked him, and he answered, "Yes, but cruelty isn't strength." That was an admission. She was less afraid of him since that day when he had made that answer, but now she kept peering into his face as he had done into hers, and he seemed not to notice it. Well, he was getting to be a very old man.

Then one day her two sisters-in-law pounced upon her so that her golden head shook on its thin, delicate neck.

"Your father has come into the garden," cried one.

"Yes, yes," pursued the elder. "He's even sat himself upon the bench."

She hurried out to him. "What's the matter, father?" Her head was aching.

"Nothing." He did not look up.

She sat down beside him, stroking his hand, at first timidly, then with more courage.

"Have you looked at the garden?"

He nodded.

She burst into tears.

He took his hand away from her and began to laugh.

"What's the matter, child? A good dose of hog-killing would do you good."

"You have no right to speak to me in this way—take yourself off!" she cried sharply, holding her side. And her father rocked with laughter.

She stretched her long, thin arms out, clenching her thin fingers together. The lace on her short sleeves trembled, her knuckles grew white.

"A good pig-killing," he repeated, watching her. And she grew sullen.

"Eh?" He pinched her flesh a little and dropped it. She was passive; she made no murmur. He got up, walked to the gate, opened it and went out, closing it after him. He turned back a step and waved to her. She did not answer for a moment, then she waved back slowly with one of her thin, white hands.

She would have liked to refuse to see him again, but she lacked courage. She would say to herself, "If I am unkind to him now, perhaps later I shall regret it." In this way she tried to excuse herself. The very next time he had sent word that he wished speech with her, she had come.

"Little fool!" he said, in a terrible rage, and walked off. She was quite sure that he was slowly losing his mind—a second childhood, she called, it, still trying to make things as pleasant as possible.

She had been ill a good deal that Spring, and in the Fall she had terrible headaches. In the Winter months she took to her bed, and early in May the doctor was summoned.

Misha talked to the physician in the drawing-room before he sent him up to his wife.

"You must be gentle with her. She is nervous and frail." The doctor laughed outright. Misha's sisters were weeping, of course, and perfectly happy.

"It will be such a splendid thing for her," they said, meaning the beef, iron and wine that they expected the doctor to prescribe.

Toward evening Little Lief closed her eyes.

Her child was still-born.

The physician came downstairs and entered the parlor where Misha's sisters stood together, still shedding tears.

He rubbed his hands.

"Send Misha upstairs."

"He has gone."

"Isn't it dreadful? I never could bear corpses, especially little ones."

"A baby isn't a corpse," answered the physician, smiling at his own impending humor. "It's an interrupted plan."

He felt that the baby, not having drawn a breath in this would, could not feel hurt at such a remark, because it had gathered no feminine pride and, also, as it had passed out quicker than the time it took to make the observation, it really could be called nothing more than the background for medical jocularity.

Misha came into the room with red eyes.

"Out like a puff of smoke," he said.

One of the sisters remarked: "Well, the Fenkens lived themselves thin."

The next Summer Misha married into a healthy Swedish family. His second wife had a broad face, with eyes set wide apart, and with broad, flat, healthy, yellow teeth. And she played the piano surprisingly well, though she looked a little heavy as she sat upon the piano stool.

KATRINA SILVERSTAFF

"WE HAVE EATEN a great deal, my friend, against the day of God."

She was a fine woman, hard, magnificent, cold, Russian, married to a Jew, a doctor on the East Side.

You know that kind of woman, pale, large, with a heavy oval face.

A woman of 'material'—a lasting personality, in other words, a 'fashionable' woman, a woman who, had she lived to the age of forty odd, would have sat for long fine hours by some window, overlooking some desolate park, thinking of a beautiful but lazy means to an end.

She always wore large and stylish hats, and beneath them her mouth took on a look of pain at once proud, aristocratic and lonely.

She had studied medicine—but medicine in the interest of animals, she was a good horse doctor—an excellent surgeon on the major injuries to birds and dogs.

In fact she and her husband had met in a medical college in Russia—she had been the only woman in the class, the only one of the lot of them who smiled in a strange, hurt and sarcastic way when dissecting.

The men in the class treated her like one of them, that is, they had no cringing mannerliness about their approach, they lost no poise before her, and tried no tricks as one might say.

The Silverstaffs had come to America, they had settled on the East Side, among 'their own people' as he would say; she never said anything when he talked like this, she sat passive, her hands in her lap, but her nostrils quivered, and somewhere under the skin of her cheek something trembled.

Her husband was the typical Jewish intellectual, a man with stiff short graying hair, prominent intelligent and kindly eyes, rather short, rather round, always smelling of Greek salad and carbolic acid, and always intensely interested in new medical journals, theories, discoveries.

He was a little dusty, a little careless, a little timid, but always gentle.

They had been in America scarcely eight months before the first child was born, a girl, and then following on her heels a boy, and then no more children.

Katrina Silverstaff stopped having her children as abruptly as she had begun having them; something complicated had entered her mind, and where there are definite complications of the kind that she suffered, there are no more children.

"We have eaten a great deal, my friend, against the day of God," she had said that.

She had said that one night, sitting in the dusk of their office. There was something inexpressibly funny in their sitting together in this office, with its globe of the world, its lung charts, its weighing machine, its surgical chair, and its bowl of ineffectual gold fish. Something inexpressibly funny and inexpressibly fecund, a fecundity suppressed by coldness, and a terrible determination—more terrible in that her husband Otto felt nothing of it.

He was very fond of her, and had he been a little more sensitive he would have been very glad to be proud of her. She never became confidential with him, and he never tried to overstep this, partly because he was unaware of it, and partly because he felt little need of a closer companionship.

She was a fine woman, he knew that; he never thought to question anything she did, because it was little, nor what she said, because it was less: there was an economy about her existence that simply forbade questioning. He felt in some dim way, that to criticise at all would be to stop everything.

Their life was typical of the East Side doctor's life. Patients all day for him, and the children for her with an occasional call from someone who had a sick bird. In the evening they would sit around a table with just sufficient food, with just sufficient silver and linen, and one luxury; Katrina's glass of white wine.

Or sometimes they would go out to dine, to some kosher place, where everyone was too friendly and too ugly and too warm, and here he would talk of the day's diseases while she listened to the music and tried not to hear what her daughter was crying for.

He had always been a 'liberal,' from the first turn of the cradle. In the freedom of the people, in the betterment of conditions, he took the interest a doctor takes in seeing a wound heal.

As for Katerina Silverstaff, she never said anything about it. He never knew what she really thought, if she thought at all; it did not seem necessary for her to do or say anything, she was fine as she was, where she was. On the other hand it never occurred to him that she would not hear, with calmness at least, his long dissertations on capital.

At the opening of this story, Katerina's daughter was a little girl of ten, who was devoted to dancing, and who lay awake at nights worrying about the shape of her legs, which had already begun to swell with a dancer's muscles.

The boy was nine, thin, and wore spectacles.

And of course what happened was quite unaccountable.

A man, calling himself Castillion Rodkin, passed through one summer, selling Carlyle's "French Revolution." Among the houses where he had left a copy was the house of Otto Silverstaff.

Katerina had opened the door, the maid was down with the measles, and the doctor was busy with a patient, a Jew much revered for his poetry.

She never bought anything of peddlers, and she seldom said more than "no thank you." In this case she neither said "thank you," nor closed the door—instead she held it open, standing a little aside for him to pass, and, utterly astonished, he did pass, waiting behind her in the hall for orders.

"We will go into the study," she said, "my husband is busy."

"I was selling Bibles last year," he remarked, "but they do not go down in this section."

"Yes," she answered, "I see," and she moved before him into the heavy damp parlor which was never unshuttered and which was never used. She reached up and turned on one solitary electric light.

Castillion Rodkin might have been any nationality in the world; this was partly from having travelled in all countries, and also from a fluid temperament—little was fixed or firm in him, a necessary quality in a salesman.

Castillion Rodkin was below medium height, thin and bearded with a pale, almost white growth of hair. He was peculiarly colourless, his eyes were only a shade darker than his temples, a vague color, and very restless.

She said simply. "We must talk about religion."

And with an awkwardness unusual to him he asked "Why?"

"Because," she said in a strained voice, making a hurt gesture, "it is so far from me."

He did not know what to say of course, and lifting one thin leg in its white trousers he placed it carefully over the other.

She was sitting opposite him, her head turned a little to one side, not looking at anything. "You see," she said presently, "I want religion to become out of the reach of the few."

"Become's a queer word," he said.

"It is the only word." she answered, and there was a slight irritation in her voice, "because it is so irrevocably for the many."

"Yes," he said mechanically, and reached up to his beard and left his hand there under a few strands of hair.

"You see," she went on simply, "I can come to the point. For me, everything is a he—I am not telling this to you because I need your help, I shall never need help," she said, turning her eyes on his. "Understand that from the beginning—"

"Beginning," he said in a loud voice suddenly.

"From the beginning," she repeated calmly, "right from the very start, not help but hindrance, I need enough hindrance, a total obstacle, otherwise I cannot accomplish it."

"Accomplish what, madame?" he asked and took his hand from under his beard.

"That is my affair, mine alone, that you must not question, it has nothing to do with you, you are only a means to an end."

And he said, "What can I do for you?"

She smiled, a sudden smile, and under her cheek something flickered. "You can do nothing," she said and stood up. "I must always do it all—yes, I shall be your mistress—wait," she said raising her hand, and there was anger and pride in her. "Do not intrude now by word or sign, but tomorrow you will come to me—that is enough—that is all you can do," and in this word 'all' he felt a limit on himself that he had never known before, and he was frightened and disquieted and unhappy.

And he came the next day, cringing a little, fawning, uneasy, and she would not see him—she sent word "I do not need you yet," and he called again the next day and learned that she was out of town, and then one Sunday she was in to him.

She said quietly to him, as if she were preparing him for a great disappointment, "I have deliberately, very deliberately, removed remorse from the forbidden fruit," and he was abject suddenly and trembling.

"There will be no thorns for you," she went on in a cold abrupt voice. "You will miss that, but do not presume to show it in my presence."

"Also my floor is not the floor on which you may crawl," she continued, "and I do not permit you to suffer while I am in the room—and," she added unfastening her brooch slowly and precisely, "I dislike all spiritual odours."

"Are we all strange?" he whispered.

"It takes more than will to attain to madness."

"Yes."

Then she was silent for a while, thinking.

"I want to suffer," he murmured, and trembled again.

"We are all gross at times, but this is not your time."

"I could follow you into the wilderness."

"I would not miss you."

And it was said in a terrible forbidding voice.

"I suffer as a birthright—I want it to be something more my own than that."

"What are you going to do?" he said.

"Does one ever destroy oneself who is utterly disinterested?"

"I don't know."

Presently she said, "I love my husband—I want you to know that, it doesn't matter, but I want you to know that, and that I am content with him, and quite happy———"

"Yes," Castillion Rodkin answered and began trembling again. holding on to the sides of the bed.

"But there is something in me," she continued, "that is very mournful because it is being."

He could not answer and tears came to his eyes.

"There is another thing," she said with abrupt roughness, "that I must insist on, that is that you will not insult me by your presence while you are in this room."

He tried to stop his weeping now, and his body grew tense, abject.

"You see," she continued, "some people drink poison, and some take a knife, and others drown, I take you."

In the very early dawn, she sat up with a strange smile. "Will you smoke?" she said, and lit him a cigarette. Then she withdrew into herself, sitting on the edge of the mahogany boards, her hands in her lap.

And there was a little ease, and a little comfort in Castillion Rodkin, and he turned, drawing up one foot, thrusting his hand beneath his beard, slowly smoking his cigarette.

"Does one regret?" he asked, and the figure of Katrina never moved, nor did she seem to hear.

"You know, you frightened me—last night." he went on, lying on his back now and looking at the ceiling. "I almost became something—something."

There was a long silence.

"Shall the beasts of the field and the birds of the air forsake thee?" he said gloomily, then brightly. "Shall any man forsake thee?"

Katrina Silverstaff remained as she was, but under her cheek something quivered.

The dawn was very near and the street lamps had gone out, a milk cart rattled across the square, and passed up a side street.

"One out of many, or only one?"

He put his cigarette out, he was beginning to breathe with difficulty, he was beginning to shiver.

"Well—"

He turned over, got up, stood on the floor.

"Is there nothing I can say?" he began, and went a little away and put his things on.

"When shall I see you again?"

And now a cold sweat broke out on him, and his chin trembled. "Tomorrow?"

He tried to come toward her, but he found himself near the door instead.

"I'm nothing," he said, and turned toward her, bent slightly; he wanted to kiss her feet—but nothing helped him.

"You've taken everything now, now I cannot feel, I do not suffer—" he tried to look at her—and succeeded finally after a long time.

He could see that she did not know he was in the room.

Then something like horror entered him. and with a soft swift running gait he reached the door, turned the handle and was gone.

A few days later, at dusk, for his heart was the heart of a dog, he came into Katrina's street, and looked at the house.

A single length of crepe, bowed, hung at the door.

From that day he began to drink heavily, he got to be quite a nuisance in the cafés, he seldom had money to pay, he was a fearless beggar, almost insolent, and once when he saw Otto Silverstaff sitting alone in a corner, with his two children, he laughed a loud laugh and burst into tears.

PRIZE TICKET 177

CLOCHETTE BRIN FELT pretty sure that no minister would the awakening gravel to her window, because Clochette had to admit that she was no longer young and alluring, that her voice had lost its color as a fading tulip loses its beauty, and her eyes were not so soft as they had once been, as the steel of strife had entered rather largely of late.

Therefore all that Clochette saw in her future was a good old age and a possible set of six rose-cluster, silver-plated after-dinner coffee spoons—if she could attain them.

Clochette Brin was a ticket seller. Into the hurry of five o'clock South Ferry workers and the breakfast-regretting uptowners she wedged her way in the morning and hoisted all of a passing fair form upon the high stool at the back of the wired opening of the ticket window. Perched there like a great god on a human scale, between the cracker box and the old roped-in chair, sagging and falling in like the knees of an ancient woman.

In the very beginning, when Clochette had been young, she knew that love and lottery went together, as do heaven and harp. Also she reckoned that no matter what number your lot was set on, premiums were not worth much anyhow.

Incidentally, Clochette was nearly right.

Now at the age of thirty she knew that life was altogether a lottery of a baser sort. Therfore, she passed out the change with a heroism that goes with a woman who has become a little overheavy.

Whistling a popular air between bites of a ham sandwich and trips to the stove to stir coffee with a tarnished spoon, Clochette spent her life.

Her only family tie was a hard and uncompromising knot, a crippled mother, who hooped out the under side of a rose strewn coverlet, a living trellis.

Some women, as they grow old, lose faith and avoirdupois and, sitting on hard lean cane, go down life's pages an exclamation point, to slip at last like a splinter into the River Styx. But not so Clochette, for, having lived in the shadow of many heavy dinners, she gloried in the fact that she would make some considerable splash when she went in over the side.

Clochette did not mind passing on with the fraternity of the Silent Cold, but she would continue to object until she had as many silver spoons to call her own as had a certain very small roomer on the floor below.

Du Berry was her name, this certain small roomer, and she was delicately pink and fresh, and had hair that curled above bewitching pale ears, and she smiled so that she maddened men. She painted porcelain or something, and spent most of her time hanging out of the window.

She knew nothing of the world that had made Clochette's eyes hard. She had a gentle, generous heart, and she would have given Clochette anything she wanted if Clochette had asked. As it was, Du Berry knew Clochette only as an animated roll of "l" tickets that got unreamed by six of an evening, and then came home to be fed.

Du Berry was young and clean and wholesome, and pretty without powder, but having merely a back sink knowledge of Clochette, which lasted only through the washing of two potatoes, she never proffered her friendship.

There had come to the street a young man. He might have been twenty-five—a lean, dark, handsome, black-haired youth with a dilatory lilt.

He had no parents, nor relations, little money and apparently no occupation, at least this is the set of conclusions that most of the street came to in regard to him. A man who has an occupation does not lie in bed until ten or eleven o'clock of a morning, and yet a man without one seldom comes in by seven at night to do Indian club and dumbbell practice.

This much Clochette and Du Berry knew of him; the shadows in his room knew more. They knew that he was making himself a personal proposition by adjusting a face strap under his chin just before getting into bed, and by pulling much bath towel across a perfect Grecian back while he waited for the water to boil. Also the shadows knew that the weight of such authors as George Sand, Meredith, Moore and Dumas were the ones responsible for the knife-like crease in the young gentleman's trousers.

Doik was his name. Slender-handed as a pickpocket and warmhearted as an Irishman, Doik crept into the street that now sheltered Du Berry and Clochette, the ticketseller.

Of course, Du Berry fell in love at first sight, as you all expected, and she would have asked nothing better than to have ironed out the white shirts that flapped from his window.

Clochette loved him also, but Clochette was different. She wanted to cook herring for his breakfast and take the lovers out of his cup of tea.

It was Clochette who got acquainted first.

It came through Doik's determination to have some sort of social life. He desired friendship. He also aspired to a better knowledge of The Avenue and of fragile teacups and the well-waxed mustache. He had heard that on The Avenue love and life were ripe for the picking, and he had seen the bus framed in the cut running south of Twenty-third street.

In the meantime he talked to Clochette.

Clochette talked well because she had a great scorn for the rules of the seven-foot bookcase, and these things made her very human.

She knew that Doik was broke, that he was a gentleman, that he was extremely well built, that he might be called handsome, but beauty goes at naught in Baxter Street as a substitute for cash.

He was hoping silently to move uptown. It was while he hoped and waited that he heard from Clochette about the two yearly events in Baxter Street.

Event number one was the arrival of the man from the boggy parts of London, who did tricks on stilts. And event number two was the annual prize given by Loggie's moving picture house for unmarried women only.

"Ain't you never been there?" she asked, thrusting a hand back in the direction of Loggie's.

Doik shook his head.

"It's the darndest swell place," she went on. "They have regular prizes every Friday, and once a year, upon May 5, they have the lottery set aside for unmarried women only!"

She tossed her head a bit and smiled, liking to think that there was such preparation for the unattached women of the streets of the modern Babylon. It gave them a sort of dignity.

"The other prizes are about the same. Anyone can get in on them, but this isn't silver brushes and table scarfs, it's the regular thing."

"Um," assented Doik, "and what is it going to be this time?"

"You can't never tell," Clochette said, with averted eyes. "It's generally personal. Once they put up a joke on us. We women were all there, and we was all single, too, mind you, and all of us was in a flutter trying to make out of our numbers the winning one. The little painter girl, Du Berry, was there, too, when the award was given."

"And what was it?" Doik leaned closer.

"Wasn't nothing much," evaded Clochette.

"You ought to tell me, you know."

"Why?"

Doik reflected. Girls had been telling him things for a long while. He knew that he had a finely-developed capacity for absorbing. Also he knew that nothing is withheld from Adonis, therefore he smiled and showed a fine row of even teeth. "Aw, come on, be a sport and tell Doik!"

She blushed and stirred up the grounds in the coffee pot.

"One of 'em was a teething ring, 'tother was—"

"Yes?" he prompted.

"A smoking jacket."

She raised her eyes to get the full of his understanding and he laughed suddenly, without sound, his hands upon his knees; laughed and took his hat off and said he was confounded, and fully realized what it must have meant to the sisterhood of Baxter Street. "Who got the coat?"

"Mrs. Penell's daughter, Daisy."

"Who got the teething ring?"

"I did."

He said he was confounded again, and stood staring in the direction of Loggie's.

"What is it going to be this time?"

"I don't know," Clochette answered. "Nobody knows until the last film."

"Seems rather hard on the married women," he hazarded.

"They should worry," retorted Clochette, off guard. "Don't they get all there is in life without wanting all of the prizes? Why, it's almost an incentive to stay single, and the Lord knows," she added, "we do need an incentive."

"Yes," he said, "I suppose so—say!—" he halted, and suddenly darted off and down the stairs.

An hour later the boy was seen striding in the direction of Sam's lunch room, and three passengers in the street said they saw him bolting beef stew and a large wedge of apple pie, "and," they observed, "eating it as though he had almost forgotten how." Which he nearly had.

Clochette saw him again about two and asked him, from the tired depths of her, where he had been.

"You see," he said, "I had a dinner coming to me. So I went to it."

"I see," remarked Clochette, and added: "Say, when was you home last?"

"I haven't got any home."

"No home. Say, Doik—kid—you—ain't an orphan?"

He nodded.

"No relatives?"

"None. Last of my family, last of my name."

"No friends?"

"Only you."

"My Gawd, what are you going to do?"

"I'll stick it out," he said bravely.

"Look here," she said abruptly. "You can come up to see me any evening you like, and me and my mother will try to make up for relations lost."

"You're awfully good," he said, and a film of tears passed across his eyes and sent into twisted lines the walls of the cage wherein sat his only friend.

"You can come up tonight," she added, and turned away.

The little painter girl, sitting with her feet up on the sofa and a drawing board in her lap, sang softly in the coming glow of evening. The odor of second-hand clothes and the labor of warm multitudes came to her. There had been such an evening as this once in Babylon. And now the wondrous incense was Pete's dray of onions and the wondrous flowing garments were Mrs. O'Shay's as she sipped lemonade upon the roof of her tenement. The soft sounds of an old world were just the ordinary high-pitched tones of Mrs. Skindisky calling her kids home.

The red lights gleamed down by Loggie's—the heart's blood to a never dead desire. The postbox had grown into the dim proportions of tomorrow's possibilities, and the gold and purple bottles in the apothecary's window took on a highlight as Danny, the druggist, turned the gas on.

Presently Du Berry put down the board and leaned out the window. The police station was waking into a flurry of lights, and a uniform or two stood upon the steps. The sharp shattered laughter of a girl reached Du Berry's ears, and she slowly turned her head and was sorry and somewhat sad. And then, returning to the lights of Loggie's, she smiled and passed indifferently on to the interminable ranges of tenement upon tenement stretching away into the unlimited reaches of the evening sun, and she started and drew in her head.

There was a step upon the stairs.

No one came up after Clochette, and she had closed her door a whole hour past. The step was a man's too, and it was light and almost hopeful, yet hesitant.

Du Berry's heart swung in great sweeps as she leaned weakly against the wall. Was it—could it be?

It paused, and then it went up and on, and she stood still and grasped the knob in her hand, and then as the step died out, she opened the door swiftly and leaned out. For one second she saw the blue of Doik's trousers, and the next, the blue had passed into Clochette's apartment.

But the thing that had stopped her heart was the look the owner of them had shot at her.

Remembering this same evening, it gave Clochette much to regret.

"No, thank you," said Doik, shaking the crumbs off his knees. "I don't think I will have any more."

"Can't I read to you, ma'am, or do something to have made this an evening for you as well as me?" He said it so simply, and in such good faith, and he held his hands so tight, and looked so kind and funny, that the woman beneath the counterpane suddenly found anguish in her dumbness, and regretted, with full eyes, the fact that her limbs had been taken into the ample palm of rheumatism.

"She can't understand you," Clochette said, but she turned around and stirred something in a pitcher.

The boy wandered aimlessly about, and said presently: "Can't she hear, don't you think?"

"Yes, she can hear," said Clochette.

Sitting beside her, he read to her, and Clochette, watching, wondered sometimes at the things that Baxter Street gets in its net.

She helped him on with his coat. "You're a good boy," she said, and something in her voice made him nod a little as he reached the door.

"You wouldn't be proud, or glad, to see me sell myself, would you?" he questioned, and not waiting for an answer, thanked her and told her he would come again, and shut the door.

Now Du Berry never stayed up this late, but she heard the door of Clochette's room open and she heard it shut, and swiftly coming out into the hall, because she wanted to see him, she found herself looking into his face without an excuse, so she took his hands, and they stood so for a minute. The life of the street died down, and the horses in the stable by Pete's sagged against their stalls and stamped at the length of a Baxter Street night. But this did not affect the lives of the boy who swung dumbbells and the girl who painted porcelain.

And then he blurted out: "Are you going, too?" and she answered "Yes," and he disappeared in the night, which held also the colored bottles in Danny's apothecary shop.

Was she going? Well, she certainly guessed she was. The very next day she proved it to the whole street by buying the ticket two hours before opening time. You see, Tommy Thrupp, who sold the tickets, knew the winning number (sometimes they do, you know), and he, being fond of a certain lady who painted china, slipped it to her and told her, in a whisper that 54 was the rope around the neck of six rose cluster, silver-plated after-dinner coffee spoons.

After supper, while she was rinsing out the teapot, Du Berry told Clochette about it, out by the back sink, and Clochette's eyes hardened. "Six silver after-dinner spoons?" she said, and pondered. She looked this little frail girl over, and in her heart of hearts she knew that Du Berry was capable of giving up her life for the asking. But Clochette hated the asking of favors. And yet six rose cluster, silver-plated after-dinner coffee spoons just needed to make up the set.

"Say!" She turned so suddenly that Du Berry jumped. "Be a sport, will you? Take a chance. Let's swap tickets, mine is number 177. Let's see what will happen."

"But the spoons?" cried Du Berry, and opened her eyes, and then understood, and offered it immediately, and would have kissed Clochette besides. Therefore they swapped, and Du Berry went back into her room and closed the door, and said over and over: "Poor, poor old thing, poor dear, poor dear. I'm so glad I had it to give her. Oh! I hope Tommy was right."

The boy who played the piano at Loggie's grabbed the last handful of ragtime and sprinkled it over the audience in a closing crash of Spring sentiment, threw his knuckles into the back of the hardwood piano's trademark, threw his pompadour out of his eyes, and whirled around on his stool, accomplishing the death of the electric light over the sheets of music as he did so.

All of the sisterhood of the single waited in the dark along with Du Berry, who had come in late, and Clochette Brin, who had come in early.

One, two, three, of the sickly little lights blinked out of the dark at the side wings of the stage. Three, four, five, six, and Tommy stepped into view, whirling his great bag of numbers, and dashed to the middle of the stage, where (he hardly gave the numbers time) he proclaimed the winning number of the silver spoons to be 54, and waited.

There was a rustle as the whole of the maiden portion of Baxter Street focused their eyes upon their cards, the long disappointed sigh, as in full sight, Clochette Brin, the ticket seller, stood up, and with heroic Babylonian voice, told the residents of the unclaimed set of Baxter Street, that the rose cluster, silver-plated after-dinner spoons were hers.

Tommy's eyes roved a moment, and knowing Du Berry, smiled as he passed the prize over.

There was a stretching of necks as the sisterhood took in fully the person of the woman who had carried off their hopes.

And then all eyes went back to Tommy, who held up his hand. There was an awful silence. "The other winning number is 177," he said, and added, as Du Berry, breathless, half started from her chair: "Somebody is forfeiting her right to compete next year with this one. Allow me to present number 177."

Into the dim glow of the six lights upon the stage stepped—Doik. A little pale, his head thrust back, his chest unsteady. A splendid man in a moment when hard luck had brought him to this pass, and slowly his head came down level and he looked into the eyes of his fate.

"My Gawd!" breathed Clochette Brin, "I sold you, Doik, for a set of silver-plated spoons," and her voice broke, but Doik did not hear.

"Dear, the Lord has been merciful," said Doik, as he took the painter girl into his arms. "I got a hundred for this—and—you."

There was silence after that until one of them said: "I can't go again next year and compete for the prizes offered to"—a small catch in her voice—"unmarried ladies only—now," and something stopped the speech right there.

"No," said Clochette's voice out of the dark. "I ain't going to bother you, only I thought? (her voice rambled off in a strained and pathetic way), "I thought this might come in handy next year, when— you can't compete," and she was gone.

They struck a match, and, standing close together in its blur, they saw a little red india rubber teething ring.

RENUNCIATION

SKIRL PAVET LEANED forward, resting his head against the back of the pew; he wanted to look up but he dared not.

His prayer had been said long ago before he had slid to his knees; now he kept his head bowed not to be in the way of other people's prayers.

He fumbled in the dark for his hymn book and could not find it. He contented himself by feeling of the sole of his boot where a hole was coming.

The dim church and the odor of incense seemed to him to be quite wonderful, a sort of darkened sachet for pain. Here one shook out the garments of sin and if they could not be cleansed at least they could be perfumed. He'd heard that chorus girls did something like this—used cologne water when they hadn't time for the next curtain.

The high ceiling looked like an inverted mould to Skirl, a place where formless, terrible and ugly things were made beautiful. He crossed himself thinking about this and his trouble, looking around a little furtively with his yellow eyes set in pale firm wrinkles, like new flowers.

He could see the altar far away at the end of his supplication, its two incense burners sending up slow thin threads of scented smoke on either side of the scarlet figure of the priest.

Skirl Pavet looked into this distance, thinking how much this altar resembled a dressing-table—a dressing table for the soul—and that scarlet priest like a lovely red autumn leaf blown up against that polished thing of wood, with its great open Bible. He moved like a leaf too, here, there, as if he were trying to play a song and couldn't find the tune.

He raised his face toward the picture of the Virgin. He liked her look of dawning innocence. There was the figure on the cross, that too was beautiful, like a splendid pathetic fruit—some super-effort of nature—yet somehow too sorrowful to pluck.

The sun beating upon the stained glass of the windows threw colored lights face down upon the floor, and this was like sunlight in a forest. Everything seemed like a forest to Skirl, a great dense wood; a place where everything was in bloom—sorrow was in bloom, and repentance and hope and virtue and sin.

He thought how sweet a thing sin was. It was so fine and strong and universal. All the bowed heads with their moving mouths were impelled by sin. Sin rushed by his neck in two fine acrid streams. It was like the odor of a tanning factory where leather is made. He moved his lips also now, but only because he was troubled into nervousness about the gap left by a tooth that had loosened that morning.

He saw figures moving about; people were leaving, some of them came out of their pews on one leg, bent on it and, went away quickly. He smiled a little and got up also. Two men and a woman were dipping their hands in the holy water and, waiting until they were within the shadow of the pillar, they crossed themselves.

He dipped in his own thick hand and touched himself four times, looking about slowly at the frightened people; he splashed himself comfortably, as a bird bathes in a public puddle, throwing up myriad drops of water.

He was not ashamed, and he dried his short fingers as he descended the steps.

He remembered, now that he was in the sunlight, that he had been praying for strength, for a terrible kind of enduring strength, a fulfillment of a possible power that might have been his had he wished it, long ago.

His acknowledgment that sin was beautiful and strong was only another way of saying farewell intelligently and gratefully to what he had been, toward what he had done, giving way to what he must now do, must now be, with a sort of superb charm, a subtle and philosophic bow.

Skirl Pavet was returning after twenty-five years of absence to his wife and to his home. He pictured to himself the old house, the familiar street, the former acquaintances. Most of those people who had known him would have forgotten his name by now, even his nickname, even his pet name. They would fumble in obscure and forgotten corners for it, searching his face for a clue to the peculiarity that had given him names of any kind. He was returning with a sharp desire and a sharp dread. He knew how many windows there were to the kitchen, but he could not remember just how his wife's hands felt.

He looked away into the tall intricacies of New York's roofs. He thought back to a day when the first robin called him from the city and the quick hard life of competition. He, dreamed slowly as he turned downtown.

Strange, that he, a Pole, should be here. He looked at the sky through sudden tears. Strange too that he should be setting his face toward home and those things that had broken him, driving him like a leaf in a forest, shaken loose from its branch, stumbling in among the trunks of alien trees, beating its way toward the open, finding the fields at last, only, to creep among strong growing green things, to flutter helplessly over full round stretches of earth, slowly dying, becoming brittle, growing brown and melancholy and still more agile, till finally —

Strange that he, Skirl Pavet, whose lips had touched every holy image in Poland, had spread themselves on many an ikon's glass, had settled about many a cross, should come to this at last. To this dry renouncing of all his youth's sap and its sweetness, of all his wander-love, of his freedom. How wonderful it had been. What throats the Finnish girls had, what hands the English!

He stumbled over an unevenness in the pavement, and turned looking into the face of the crowd. Dark faces and pale, some stupid, some gay. An officer passed swinging his cane, jangling the little spur-chains that passed under his boots.

Skirl dropped his hands at his sides swinging them slowly; he always did this when he was perplexed, it gave him a feeling of such hopelessness that something would have to happen to him, something would have to come to relieve him of this awful stupidity, this idle dreaming weariness.

He thought of Polly, his wife, a middle-sized woman, with stout knees and full lips too colorless and amiable. He remembered that her nose set in well at the corners, and he reflected that this type always grow stout. She had always been a good natured woman, but mundane, jocose.

She was the daughter of a western hotel keeper. He went back over his first meeting with her. She was a favorite in the family and would have been quite spoiled, had she been quick, apprehensive or sharp. As it was she smiled at those who petted her, flourishing under kindness like a kitten, and like a kitten missed it not at all when it ceased. He had gone out there because he had heard of the opportunities the West afforded; he had come back empty-handed with this buxom, fresh-faced Polly—daughter of a hotel-keeper. She soon fell into the old business, opened a restaurant in the early Thirties, near Seventh avenue, and from that time he began to grow restless.

That was long ago. He thought of it now, moving his nose in quick successive shivers of savory memories, closing his eyes, trying to recall the pattern in the carpet one had to cross before they came to the table. Two crouching dragons, a square and two crouching dragons reversed—was that it, or had he made a mistake about the whole design. He puzzled his mind about the way she used her English; she had strange tricks with little words, a manner with her lips; he could not recall what words, what manner.

She used to sit at a long table with their oldest patrons, stout, middle-aged, stupid men. Some were dry goods merchants, some were tailors, one was a banker, another a broker.

Later when the lunch crowd had gone, the cooks and the waiters would sit at another long table in the rear, in white caps and aprons, talking slowly, softly about the making of butter sauce, of tripe *sauté*.

He smiled suddenly recalling the name of the chef, Bradley, that was a strange name. He had no teeth and his ample jowl swung in great satisfied rhythms, while a small moustache rose and fell on the sunken upper lip.

And there was Sammie, who always peered into the syrup and milk jugs, sighing and shaking his head at the manner in which they both emptied, hurrying with his food, moving his body, his arms never still, in a passion to be at the remainder of the meal before it should be lost in the stomachs that surrounded him.

Skirl had called this sordid, dirty. He had always loved the country, the open fields, the smell of spring, like the breath of a dear one after months of dreary death. The sense of buds breaking and the early rains that took liberties with the newly-sown flower beds, chasing small particles of loam into hurrying rivulets, making an effort to drag something back with them info the bowels of the earth. The sound of animals running through bramble and swamp, the crackling of little hoofs in the twigs, and the odor of new calves with moist hair. And this had been the argument he had used against her, excusing himself for going away, to have his fill of life, love, the earth.

He had a child of his own, but he had forgotten that too, laid it aside, put it back in his memory to bring out when it should please him, with the tranquillity of one who takes what he desires, never quite relinquishing what he does not, holding it to make it serve in time of need. Polly had brought it up to its fourth year with comfortable and hearty slaps on its plump, glowing cheeks, with many an apprehensive face as she picked it up, fondling it, pinching it on either side of its little wet mouth, squealing at it, becoming intoxicated with the excitement and energy of mothers who like their own; kissing its tiny white teeth, and finally, standing hands on hips, would watch it as it crawled away saying: "Isn't he a beggar?" making those animal noises that save the child from too early terror of civilization.

He had pretended to be jealous of the fat comfortable men with whom Polly sat, cracking nuts, laughing, though he knew well enough that it was part of the business of a restaurant keeper to be amiable with the guests. But somehow he didn't like the way she got their histories out of them. This he really resented. He felt that he was the only person that Polly should know all about, that where other men bought their clothes, met their brides or took their sorrows, were things about which Polly should not be curious. He resented the way these well-fed gentlemen would move back from the table, puffing out their cheeks, snapping bands from cigars, sprawling as if to say "This is an excellent place to dine, but a better place to rest."

He resented their comfortable sighs, their after-dinner circular movement of the closed mouth, their persistent heavy smoking. He hated their laughter, he hated their satisfaction with the city, the dirty streets, their tiring, dull trades. This wasn't life. He felt then that they had been swamping him, drawing in on him, killing him with gross layers of flesh, moving over and around him like a boat full of restlessly dying fish.

And because of these things, he had prayed for strength, strength to keep away from all he loved, strength to go back to all that hurt and smothered him, to renounce all, that he might end his days at last with this woman who had always been kindly, stupid, amused. To leave those others who were young and bright and who understood.

There was Ollie, tall splendid Ollie with her strange large eyes and her way of saying, "You'll not forget me, my little man."

She had been the one real passion of his life, he thought, but he had not stayed long with her. There were others, sweet women, warm, gentle creatures—all but one who had slapped his face one night in Java.

He didn't mind now, he was glad that his face would tingle with any memory, such things were seasoning to that great seasonless mass that is a man before he has loved.

He knew that he had not always been happy, perhaps he would admit that to Polly when he returned, she might be glad to know that there were times when he had missed her, had even compared her with others. He liked admitting things to Polly, she always looked cheerful and nodded, seeming to say, "That's right, keep alive."

That was the strange thing about Polly, she never resented, never rebuked, did not even seem to think what he did strange: a sort of philosophy that had its culminating belief in just that "Keep alive,"— sensing that any way people kept alive was a sort of excuse in itself.

This was a lower way of looking at it, perhaps, but it had often comforted him. Even in those days when lying awake in the four-posted bed of yellow wood, in the garret whose roofs nearly touched his head, he had decided that he wanted no other shelter than the sky.

How he felt again the soft blankets of that bed against his unshaven chin, the cool edge of the sharp sheets that he could never bear against his throat, a feeling as if he were going to be strangled, beheaded!

He had written to Polly after these twenty-five years of absence and she had written him to come. Would she really be glad to see him? It must be that, for she had no real curiosity, no comparative valuation, no desire to put one and one together to make up the whole of the fabric of life, portions, edges were enough for her. She had no other reason than just that, to let him return when he wanted to.

And suddenly there came over him a hot flush because he knew how good she was, had always been.

And the boy he would be far along in the twenties, grown up. Yet he could not visualize him. He held his hand up in the air on a level with his shoulder. People stopped, turned around, smiled. He colored and lowered it. There was where his boy would stand. Of course the people could not know what he was thinking. It was just a gesture that he had to make to feel in some way the passage of time.

He must be good to him now, must devote the rest of his life to him and to her. No more turning aside, no more running after nature, no more appreciation of lovely throats, hands, faces.

He knew how weak he was, what his passions were, great over-whelming passions, and Ollie lived here, very near his own house—and he had cared —

Well, that was the reason why he had prayed—prayed for strength to keep him straight, for wisdom to shut his eyes on everything but the inner self, on everything but those things of home that were his.

He was a Pole and he loved his God, and he recalled again the picture of the Virgin and the image of Christ taking that downward course of all things that sorrow—tears, flesh and he thought of all the holy images in other countries that had become stained with the mark of his great caressing mouth.

He was very tired, he did not know that he could be so tired. He had walked these few blocks so many times in the past, and they had not tired him, and he remembered that he had been tired when he knelt to pray.

And then he was in their street, at their door, turning the knob, walking in, and he seemed to have been away only yesterday, and the geranium flowering in the pots were those he had planted there a sun before, and the table full of stout gentlemen were those he had hated but a dawn away. And there was Polly, rising, scattering crumbs, smiling, a little stouter, gay, mundane, jocose.

And the table at the far end was surrounded by a pack of white-capped, white-aproned cooks and waiters. Only Bradley was not there, someone with a small and narrow chin had the place of honor, and no one jumped up to look into the syrup and milk pitchers.

He asked questions hurriedly to keep from losing all of his past at once, for what he had been but yesterday seemed suddenly to be less than a dream. And less than a mist were the splendid days he had spent with Ollie in Huntington, a little town through whose streets gray-faced clerks hurried, gathering at lunch time about the low ivy-covered stone wall that skirted the cemetery. Birds were in the grass then and there the lovers dodged the eyes of acquaintances behind the decaying symbol on some old stone, that had expressed a person's love for a person long gone.

And she, Ollie had thrown back her naked arms into the grass behind her head talking of a new gingham gown, of the colored post cards that were being sold to the country side, little pictures of the mill, of the church, of the library—well—

He asked about old acquaintances too and Polly answered him smiling whimsically, telling of her life; how the son of one of their

customers had taken a commission and was already at sea, and how
Tessie had taken ill and passed away in the Fall.

★ ★ ★

FINALLY he sat on the edge of his bed. Coming back had been so
easy, he remembered now how her hand felt. The way she twisted
her mouth, he had always known somehow, was toward the left,
and her western accent was quite a thing of his life.

And the boy?

The boy was married.

He hadn't thought of that.

He fumbled in his pocket for his pipe, found it and looking around
at the old rafters and the four-posted bed, sighed. Polly was stouter,
much, and yet only by a double chin was she strange to him.

He closed his eyes. He had prayed for strength—Polly was getting
his slippers, and an inertia seemed to leave him powerless to get them
for himself. Then he reached for them hurriedly.

"And Ollie?"

"Her granddaughter was christened last June."

He looked away into the street from the dirty little oblong pane.

"Let me put them on, you can't bend so easily as once, Skirl."

"I prayed today—down on my knees—" still he reached out a
stockinged foot. He was almost nodding, he laughed a little, con-
tenedly.

But later, turning his face to the wall, crossing himself with one
finger, his eyes shed tears. He could hear Polly talking downstairs to
the help, clattering with the pans, but he was tired and he dozed.

FINALE

IN THE CENTRE of the room lay the corpse. The proper number of candles burned at head and feet.

The body had been duly attended to. The undertaker had pared the nails, put the tongue back in the mouth, shut the eyes, and with a cloth dusted with bismuth had touched the edges of the nostrils.

It had been washed and dressed and made to assume the conventional death pose—the hands crossed palm over knuckles. Everything else in the room seemed willing to go on changing—being. He alone remained cold and unwilling, like a stoppage in the atmosphere.

His wife, his mother, and his children knelt about him. His wife cried heavily, resting the middle of her breasts on the hard side of the coffin boards. His mother wept also, but with that comfort of one who has seen both the beginning and the end; with that touch of restfulness that comes to those who like the round, the complete, the final.

His children knelt and did not weep. The little girl's closed palms were damp, and she wanted to look at them but dared not. The boy had that very morning discovered the pleasure of rubbing his head under his nurse's arm when she said "Come, put your shirt on," and he wanted to smile about this, but his eyes refused to grow damp, he could not permit himself the satisfaction.

On the floor, in a corner, lay what had been the dead man's dearest possession—a bright blue scarf embroidered with spots of gold. It had been given to him when passing through Italy, by a long legged Sicilian whom he had loved as one loves who must catch a train.

It was a lovely thing, but much treasuring had lined it; and the marks of his thumbs as they passed over it in pleasant satisfaction had left their tarnish on the little spots of gold.

The shadows grew and darkness fell. The room was silent save for that melancholy murmur of lips that taste tears.

A large rat put his head out of a hole, long dusty, and peered into the room.

The children were going to rise and go to bed soon. The bodies of the mourners had that half-sorrowful, half-bored look of people who do something that hurts too long.

Presently the rat took hold of the scarf and trotted away with it into the darkness of the beyond.

One thing only had the undertaker forgotten to do; he had failed to remove the cotton from the ears of the dead man, who had suffered from ear-ache.

THE EARTH

UNA AND LENA were like two fine horses, horses one sees in the early dawn eating slowly, swaying from side to side, horses that plough, never in a hurry, but always accomplishing something. They were Polish women who worked a farm day in and day out, saying little, thinking little, feeling little, with eyes devoid of everything save a crafty sparkle which now and then was quite noticeable in Una, the elder. Lena dreamed more, if one can call the silences of an animal dreams. For hours she would look off into the skyline, her hairless lids fixed, a strange metallic quality in the irises themselves. She had such pale eyebrows that they were scarcely visible, and this, coupled with her wide-eyed silences, gave her a half-mad expression. Her heavy peasant face was fringed by a bang of red hair like a woolen table-spread, a color at once strange and attractive, an obstinate color, a color that seemed to make Lena feel something alien and bad-tempered had settled over her forehead; for, from time to time, she would wrinkle up her heavy white skin and shake her head.

Una never showed her hair. A figured handkerchief always covered it, though it was pretty enough, of that sullen blonde type that one sees on the heads of children who run in the sun.

Originally the farm had been their father's. When he died he left it to them in a strange manner. He feared separation or quarrel in the family, and therefore had bequeathed every other foot to Una, beginning with the first foot at the fence, and every other foot to Lena, beginning with the second. So the two girls ploughed and furrowed and transplanted and garnered a rich harvest each year, neither disputing her inheritance. They worked silently side by side, uncomplaining. Neither do orchards complain when their branches flower and fruit and become heavy. Neither does the earth complain

when wounded with the plough, healing up to give birth to flowers
and to vegetables.

After long months of saving, they had built a house, into which
they moved their furniture and an uncle, Karl, who had gone mad
while gathering the hay.

They did not evince surprise nor show regret. Madness to us means
reversion; to such people as Una and Lena it meant progression. Now
their uncle had entered into a land beyond them, the land of fancy.
For fifty years he had been as they were, silent, hard-working, unimag-
inative. Then all of a sudden, like a scholar passing his degree, he
had gone up into another form, where he spoke of things that only
people who have renounced the soil speak of—strange, fanciful,
unimportant things, things to stand in awe of, because they discuss
neither profits nor loss.

When Karl would strike suddenly into his moaning, they would
listen awhile in the field as dogs listen to a familiar cry, and presently
Lena would move off to rub him down in the same hard-palmed
way she would press the long bag that held the grapes in preserving
time.

Una had gone to school just long enough to learn to spell her
name with difficulty and to add. Lena had somehow escaped. She
neither wrote her name nor figured; she was content that Una could
do "the business." She did not see that with addition comes the
knowledge that two and two make four and that four are better than
two. That she would some day be the victim of knavery, treachery
or deceit never entered her head. For her, it was quite settled that
here they would live and here they would die. There was a family
graveyard on the land where two generations had been buried. And
here Una supposed she, too, would rest when her wick no longer
answered to the oil.

The land was hers and Una's. What they made of it was shared,
what they lost was shared, and what they took to themselves out of
it was shared also. When the pickle season went well and none of
the horses died, she and her sister would drive into town to buy new
boots and a ruffle for the Sabbath. And if everything shone upon
them and all the crops brought good prices, they added a few bits of
furniture to their small supply, or bought more silver to hide away
in the chest that would go to the sister that married first.

Which of them would come in for this chest Lena never troubled
about. She would sit for long hours after the field was cleared, saying

nothing, looking away into the horizon, perhaps tossing a pebble down the hill, listening for its echo in the ravine.

She did not even speculate on the way Una looked upon matters. Una was her sister; that was sufficient. One's right arm is always accompanied by one's left. Lena had not learned that left arms sometimes steal while right arms are vibrating under the handshake of friendship.

Sometimes Uncle Karl would get away from Lena and, striding over bog and hedge, dash into a neighboring farm, and there make trouble for the owner. At such times, Lena would lead him home, in the same unperturbed manner in which she drove the cows. Once a man had brought him back.

This man was Swedish, pale-faced, with a certain keenness of glance that gave one a suspicion that he had an occasional thought that did not run on farming. He was broad of shoulder, standing some six feet three. He had come to see Una many times after this. Standing by the door of an evening, he would turn his head and shoulders from side to side, looking first at one sister and then at the other. He had those pale, well-shaped lips that give the impression that they must be comfortable to the wearer. From time to time, he wetted them with a quick plunge of his tongue.

He always wore brown overalls, baggy at the knee, and lighter in color where he leaned on his elbows. The sisters had learned the first day that he was "help" for the owner of the adjoining farm. They grunted their approval and asked him what wages he got. When he said a dollar and a half and board all through the Winter season, Una smiled upon him.

"Good pay," she said, and offered him a glass of mulled wine.

Lena said nothing. Hands on hips, she watched him, or looked up into the sky. Lena was still young and the night yet appealed to her. She liked the Swede too. He was compact and big and "well bred." By this she meant what is meant when she said the same thing of a horse. He had quality—which meant the same thing through her fingers. And he was "all right" in the same way soil is all right for securing profits. In other words, he was healthy and was making a living.

At first he had looked oftenest at Lena. Hers was the softer face of two faces as hard as stone. About her chin was a pointed excellence that might have meant that at times she could look kindly, might at times attain sweetness in her slow smile, a smile that drew lips reluctantly across very large fine teeth. It was a smile that in time might make one think more of these lips than of the teeth, instead of more of the teeth than the lips, as was as yet the case.

In Una's chin lurked a devil. It turned in under the lower lip secretively. Una's face was an unbroken block of calculation, saving where, upon her upper lip, a little down of hair fluttered.

Yet it gave one an uncanny feeling. It made one think of a tassel on a hammer.

Una had marked this Swede for her own. She went to all the trouble that was in her to give him the equivalent of the society girl's most fetching glances. Una let him sit where she stood, let him lounge when there was work to be done. Where she would have set anyone else to peeling potatoes, to him she offered wine or flat beer, black bread and sour cakes.

Lena did none of these things. She seemed to scorn him, she pretended to be indifferent to him, she looked past him. If she had been intelligent enough, she would have looked through him.

For him her indifference was scorn, for him her quietness was disapproval, for him her unconcern was insult. Finally he left her alone, devoting his time to Una, calling for her often of a Sunday to take a long walk. Where to and why, it did not matter. To a festival at the church, to a pig killing, if one was going on a Sunday. Lena did not seem to mind. This was her purpose; she was by no means generous, she was by no means self-sacrificing. It simply never occurred to her that she could marry before her sister, who was the elder. In reality it was an impatience to be married that made her avoid Una's lover. As soon as Una was off her hands, then she, too, could think of marrying.

Una could not make her out at all. Sometimes she would call her to her and, standing arms akimbo, would stare at her for a good many minutes, so long that Lena would forget her and look off into the sky.

One day Una called Lena to her and asked her to make her mark at the bottom of a sheet of paper covered with hard cramped writing, Una's own.

"What is it?" asked Lena, taking the pen.

"Just saying that every other foot of this land is yours."

"That you know already, eh?" Lena announced, putting the pen down. Una gave it back to her.

"I know it, but I want you to write it—that every other foot of land is mine, beginning with the second foot from the fence."

Lena shrugged her shoulders. "What for?"

"The lawyers want it."

Lena signed her mark and laid down the pen. Presently she began to shell peas. All of a sudden she shook her head.

"I thought," she said, "that second foot was mine—what?" She thrust the pan down toward her knees and sat staring at Una with wide, suspicious eyes.

"Yah," affirmed Una, who had just locked the paper up in a box.

Lena wrinkled her forehead, thereby bringing the red fringe a little nearer her eyes.

"But you made me sign it that it was you, hey?"

"Yah," Una assented, setting the water on to boil for tea.

"Why?" inquired Una.

"To make more land," Una replied, and grinned.

"More land?" queried Lena, putting the pan of peas upon the table and standing up. "What do you mean?"

"More land for me," Una answered complacently.

Lena could not understand and began to rub her hands. She picked up a pod and snapped it in her teeth.

"But I was satisfied," she said, "with the land as it was. I don't want more."

"I do," answered Una.

"Does it make me more?" Lena asked suspiciously, leaning a little forward.

"It makes you," Una answered, "nothing. Now you stay by me as helper—"

Then Lena understood. She stood stock still for a second. Suddenly she picked up the breadknife and, lurching forward, cried out: "You take my land from me—"

Una dodged, grasped the hand with the knife, brought it down, took it away placidly, pushed Lena off and repeated: "Now you work just the same, but for me—why you so angry?"

No tears came to Lena's help. And had they done so, they would have hissed against the flaming steel of her eyeballs. In a level tone thick with a terrible and sudden hate, she said: "You know what you have done—eh? Yes, you have taken away the fruit trees from me, you have taken away the place where I worked for years, you have robbed me of my crops, you have stolen the harvest—that is

well—but you have taken away from me the grave, too. The place
where I live you have robbed me of and the place where I go when
I die. I would have worked for you perhaps—but," she struck her
breast, "when I die I die for myself." Then she turned and left the
house.

She went directly to the barn. Taking the two stallions out, she
harnessed them to the carriage. With as little noise as possible she
got them into the driveway. Then climbing in and securing the whip
in one hand and the reins fast in the other, she cried aloud in a hoarse
voice: "Ahya you little dog. Watch me ride!" Then as Una came
running to the door, Lena shouted back, turning in the trap: "I take
from you too." And flinging the whip across the horses, she disappeared in a whirl of dust.

Una stood there shading her eyes with her hand. She had never
seen Lena angry, therefore she thought she had gone mad as her
uncle before her. That she had played Lena a dirty trick, she fully
realized, but that Lena should realize it also, she had not counted on.

She wondered when Lena would come back with the horses. She
even prepared a meal for two.

Lena did not come back. Una waited up till dawn. She was more
frightened about the horses than she was about her sister; the horses
represented six hundred dollars, while Lena only represented a relative. In the morning, she scolded Karl for giving mad blood to the
family. Then toward the second evening, she waited for the Swede.

The evening passed as the others. The Swedish working man did
not come.

Una was distracted. She called in a neighbor and set the matter
before him. He gave her some legal advice and left her bewildered.

Finally, at the end of that week, because neither horses nor Lena
had appeared, and also because of the strange absence of the man
who had been making love to her for some weeks, Una reported the
matter to the local police. And ten days later they located the horses.
The man driving them said that they had been sold to him by a young
Polish woman who passed through his farm with a tall Swedish man
late at night. She said that she had tried to sell them that day at a fair
and had been unable to part with them, and finally let them go to
him at a low price. He added that he had paid three hundred dollars
for them. Una bought them back at the figure, from hard earned
savings, both of her own and Lena's

Then she waited. A sour hatred grew up within her and she moved
about from acre to acre with her hired help like some great thing
made of wood.

But she changed in her heart as the months passed. At times she almost regretted what she had done. After all, Lena had been quiet and hard working and her kin. It had been Lena, too, who had best quieted Karl. Without her he stormed and stamped about the house, and of late had begun to accuse her of having killed her sister.

Then one day Lena appeared carrying something on her arms, swaying it from side to side while the Swede hitched a fine mare to the barn door. Up the walk came Lena, singing, and behind her came her man.

Una stood still, impassible, quiet. As Lena reached her, she uncovered the bundle and held the baby up to her.

"Kiss it," she said. Without a word, Una bent at the waist and kissed it.

"Thank you," Lena said as she replaced the shawl. "Now you have left your mark. Now you have signed." She smiled.

The Swedish fellow was a little browned from the sun. He took his cap off, and stood there grinning awkwardly.

Lena pushed in at the door and sat down.

Una followed her. Behind Una came the father.

Karl was heard singing and stamping overhead. "Give her some molasses water and little cakes," he shouted, putting his head down through the trap door, and burst out laughing.

Una brought three glasses of wine. Leaning forward, she poked her finger into the baby's cheek to make it smile. "Tell me about it," she said.

Lena began: "Well, then I got him," she pointed to the awkward father. "And I put him in behind me and I took him to town and I marry him. And I explain to him. I say: 'She took my land from me, the flowers and the fruit and the green things. And she took the grave from me where I should lie—' "

* * *

And in the end they looked like fine horses, but one of them was a bit spirited.

THE COWARD

Varra Kolveed had led too long that life of unending sameness that has its end either in hysteria or melancholy. Twice a day the bodies of her little sisters were pushed and patted and shoved by her into and out of their shabby clothing. At six o'clock precisely the day found her laying the table for her sister's husband, her sister herself, and for those same smaller ones that had come into their care with the death of her mother. Every afternoon and every evening saw her shaking out the red tablespread also, and at nine o'clock exactly, Varra descended the first two steps leading into the streed and waited for Karl.

Varra had been engaged to Karl going on three years now, and the three years were threatening to stretch into a fourth for lack of money. Romance had died there on that second step above the pavement and had given away to habit.

Varra had never been called pretty. She had even been termed rather plain. She had never admitted this judgment to be correct. She even thought, quite frankly, that she was a little more than passable. She had lived so long among dull things that anything with a bit of color in it seemed to her beautiful, and Varra had the red round spots high up on her cheeks that one sees occasionally in Breton peasants, and Varra had very splendid curling hair, which she had never allowed to grow long since it had been cropped the year of the fever—and this hair stood up on her head in a red flaming wedge which seemed to Varra very good.

One thing only had Varra that put her above those with whom she came in contact: she had what was called a reputation.

Just when this reputation began no one could remember; even Varra had forgotten. The incident that must have led to it was a thing of the past. Sometimes Varra tried to remember what it was that had given her this reputation for courage, as she plaited her hair before she went to bed. Was it that day that she had climbed across the roof and down into the gutter and saved the new Spring robin when all the boys were timid? Or was it when she had used a knife to take out a splinter one evening as she sat on the steps? She remembered this knife, a long thin polished blade that seemed to demand bravery. And then the girl across the way had been watching, so Varra had cut herself quite a deep gash, dabbing the blood off with her handkerchief, but taking care to fold the scarlet spots out, so that they would be conspicuous all that evening when she rubbed her nose or wiped her forehead.

Anyway there the reputation was. It had become very precious to Varra because it was someone else's opinion and not her own. But gradually it became her own, and she could not always recollect whether people had said she was beautiful or courageous until she stopped to consider which of these two qualities she had given herself involuntarily.

As Varra grew up she became very proud of this reputation. She nursed it, and at the same time it kept her in a great deal of anxiety. She had to keep thinking up little things that would remind the neighbors that she was this year what she had been last—the courage that had picked her out for attention then was still one of her qualities. In the end she thought herself a little braver than she really was. Sincerely and honestly, she held to this opinion and would have raged had she been denied this little grain of personal elations.

For Varra there had been little youth, just a few hours in the sun, just a moment snatched from romanticism with some novel of the time, one short little moment of an appreciation that Spring had come and Spring would go, one lilac bloom that had meant something to her, one moment when, lying face down in the June grass, she had waited silently for her chance, had finally caught the one bird that she could remember as having had freedom, one acknowledgment that night was mysterious and frightful and something to lie under as one would lie under a guillotine waiting for the moment when the knife should descend, the knife that must inevitably be there high up in the dark against the ceiling, the something portentous that gave her this feeling of impending doom, this tightening of the feet, this thanksgiving for the heavy weave of the sheet sensed against her nose and mouth and her closed lids.

And then Varra had gone past it, without memory when it stopped and without regrets for its ending because it had no definite boundary. And she only felt a sense that within her somewhere was an island surrounded by what she now was, that was, that had been her childhood.

Many times in the years that went to the making of Varra, she had silently regretted this name she bore for bravery. When a spider was seen about the place, it was she now who had to catch and kill it. The rest of the family had grown frankly timid as Varra had grown, to all appearances, more bold. When the frying pan handle was red hot, it was Varra who came up and took it off the stove in her bare hands, smiling. It was Varra also who had to part the pair of bull pups that had flown at one another's throats. It was she who put the ropes about their necks and she it was who finally parted them.

Once or twice in the beginning she had said timidly, "I am not so brave, you know," and they had all answered, "See, true courage. She is a brave child, yes, a modest one."

And then she had become engaged, and Karl flattered her and told her that he loved her for her bravery more than anything else. Karl's chum, Monk, had also flattered Varra. Indeed, toward the end of this third year of engagement, Varra had become so accustomed to this title that she no longer lay awake trying to remember where it had its begining.

She read fairy tales where damsels with wands ruled over a world of the timid. She was always finding herself in love with the hero and the heroine of some novel. She came out of them into her own life with a little gasp of sorrow, and she went back into them again with a sigh of content.

Yet Varra had still a certain kind of acuteness. There were things that she liked and there were things that she did not like at all. The only trouble was that she failed to keep her sense of values separate. She had been called brave, so now she thought it was brave to like people that her instinct bade her to distrust. Monk was a man that instinctively bred dislike. His ill-shaped head gave her physical pain, and the wide low set ears, set on at an angle seen commonly in monkeys, made her feel a repulsion for looking at him at all, and his jaunty, quick slang with its touch of false bravado made her unhappy because she sensed in this same bravado her own bravery;

only in him there was something vulgar. The difference lay in this: he was trying to produce an illusion and Varra was trying not to disillusion.

And then had come that terrible hour when a little crowd collected about their door, overflowing into their parlor, talking all at once.

Karl and Monk had been arrested. Leaning with her forehead against the door, Varra tried to make out what they were saying. She put her hands to her throat and found it was not the spot that troubled her. Her hands slipped to her heart, and this was also lacking in appropriateness. She began untying her apron, and this was the gesture that seemed at last to be the right one. What was she doing? What were they saying? Robbery? Where? She pushed forward, still pulling at the knot in her apron.

"What is this?" she cried in a sharp voice.

"Karl and Monk have been arrested."

"What for?"

"They were under suspicion for some time—petty robberies, they said—jewelry—and then last night quite a haul from the Barnaby place."

She wasn't listening any more. Jewelry? Karl? She brought her two hands around with the apron in them, feeling for the little cheap ring on her third finger. Tears slowly rose to the borders of her pale eyes. Then she heard her sister saying, "You must be brave, dear."

Varra turned away and went upstairs.

She lay face up on the bed. This was another concession made to her reputation. She wanted to bury her eyes in the pillow, but she mustn't. What must she do? Get up, walk about? Yes, that was it—get up and walk about. Why? Where?

She went to the table and picked up a brooch Karl had given her. Stolen, too, eh? She rummaged through her bureau; a necklace of beads and a broad bracelet were all the things that she could remember as having come from Karl in their three years of courtship. She put these all together. She never stopped to question herself about her feeling in reaction to this change. She did not deny it to herself because in doing this she thought she would be a coward; and now she must show what she was really made of, if, indeed, she were a brave woman after all, or only a sham.

Toward eight o'clock, her sister knocked at her door.

"He is to be tried tomorrow," she whispered along the crack, and stole away again.

Suddenly Varra's courage gave out in one terrible storm of weeping, and she turned over on her bed heavily, pressing the bedding up around her as if she wanted to bury herself, to dig herself into oblivion. This reputation of hers had been built of the things the house was built of, the daily household sayings. It was in the atmosphere; it was a household quality, a something that had been given life to by all these things that surrounded her, and she abruptly realized that it was with the household that she was trying to bury herself. She sat up, throwing the blankets away with a quick, frightened gesture. She felt dizzy and tried to weep again and could not. She stood up before her little cracked mirror. Was she really ugly? The color had left her cheeks, but it was in her lips.

She knew now what it was that had really brought on this great fit of weeping—it was because she knew what she had before her and what she must do for Karl. What was it they had said? Oh yes, of course, she was courageous; she must begin now. Tomorrow, her little sister had said. She would have to find out where the court was.

The mid-day session was in full swing. Petty lawyers in frock coats promenaded the wide corridors like dogs on the track of game. Misery, despair, justice, injustice—all these things were their meal. They circled about this hall, their fat, small hands hidden in the tails of these sleek, shiny coats, and their bright, alert eyes darting here and there. One of these lawyers had been following a woman with his eyes for the last ten seconds as the woman stood in the shadow of the winding staircase, her hands clasped in front of her, holding a faded yellow box. She stood very still, seemed to impart something like importance to a case. Only after he had finished his pleading and retired behind the railings did the case again drop into its poverty and ugly despair once more.

He approached Varra now, his oiled black hair shining as he stepped across the bar of light falling in at the wide entrance.

"Are you represented?" he spoke softly, pleasantly, and he dropped his hands to his side, his coat tails swinging. He was very proud of this coat; it had been nicknamed the "Case coat," or the "Coat of appeals."

Varra turned toward him slowly and looked at him a minute. Then she said, "What?" fearing that perhaps this man had something to do with the whole system of judicial ruling.

He repeated his question, adding that she really should have a lawyer. She shook her head and moved off. What she had to do must be done alone; therein lay the impetus. She did not need help to be courageous. She could save Karl alone. She could tell the lie that would set him free. She was strong enough to go straight up to the judge and pronounce the words that would throw suspicion on to herself. And besides, she had the necklace, the ring, the brooch and the bracelet, all together in this little yellow box. If they did not believe her, they would believe their eyes. How would she come by this plunder unless she herself had stolen it?

She moved toward the doors. She could see the benches filled with sleepy looking people. She felt herself rudely pushed aside by a German woman who was speaking in a shrill voice to the court attendant who would not let her pass. Varra felt very lonely. After all, what was the use; no one was here to help her; no one was here to know what she was doing. She should have told them at home. No, Karl would be the only one to know.

A feeling of tenderness swept over her for Karl. After, she loved him; and her own impending sacrifice made him seem newborn in all the splendor of the deed. She looked up into the face of the court attendant and smiled. "May I sit down and watch awhile?" she asked cunningly, hoping that he would be pleased with her and treat her as some one with a really superior nature, so it would give her confidence in herself.

He did like her frank smile, and the red-rimmed eyes looking up into his, coquettishly, made him stand aside for her, and made him watch her as she moved to a seat.

She leaned forward a little, looking straight ahead of her. There was the raised platform with the judicial desk. There were the clerks, the court stenographer, the petty lawyers, the police—the relatives weeping, the dry-eyed curiosity seekers. The man in black sitting with slightly bowed head behind the desk must be the judge. She looked around, but could not see either Karl or Monk. Some dreary prisoners were sitting back to her on a bench within the railing, and a reporter stood beside the clerks' desk, pad in hand. Why were all these people sitting here? What did they want to see? What they themselves had escaped, what they themselves would have some day to go through, perhaps?

The dirty black curtains, with their heavy tassels at the windows, took her attention. They were like the smaller curtains at the windows of a hearse, only the tassels were too terrible and too heavy. They seemed like judges that had grown sulky beneath their wigs of dust, like something that would finally fall into the cup of life and lie there, black and horrible and menacing, spoiling it at the lips, as mother spoils the beauty of wine, the malignity of vinegar.

Varra looked at the judge. She wondered why people neglect to make friends with judges, as it would help so if they were on a calling basis. If this judge had said to her once, "Please pass the tea, Miss Kolveed," she would now be able to go right up to him and whisper into his ear to be kind to Karl, and all would be over. But she had neglected to do this, and so it was going to make a difference.

Some mean case of some sort had just come up. Two men, one an officer and the other a Pole, stood before this bar of justice, holding up a strip of lace. She could not hear a word that was said, and she was glad. It would not spoil this great thing she had come to do. Yet she looked at this length of lace, stretching away and coiling into a senseless mass in a roll of silks in a box, as though it were very strange. What had lace to do with prison? With good and bad? Couldn't lace even escape this defiling exposition? Hereafter Varra knew that lace would be something that she could no longer wear. She had thought dully that inanimate objects could not be contaminated, could have nothing in common with human beings; that was neither here nor there. She closed her eyes.

She could hear a steady droning, the shuffling of feet, a half-suppressed sob. She opened her eyes. The Pole was being led away by an officer, and on this side near her, a woman had arisen weeping. Something rose in Varra's throat—it was her grief. Something dropped down into her throat—it was her tears. She must not cry. If she had wept, she would have been a coward. At that moment, she heard the names of Karl and Monk.

She half-started to her feet! Several heads turned toward her, and someone whispered: "A relative, probably."

Yes, that was Karl; that black, curly hair was Karl's, but why did he hang his head? She did not even look toward Monk. She was angry because they must be hurting Karl where they gripped his arms on either side. Yes, she must get up now. She got up, holding the box in her hand. She heard someone saying: "Is your name Karl Handmann?" And she saw Karl move, but she could not hear his answer. Then again the same voice: "And you, Monk Price?" And she heard Monk answering, loud and with his usual bravado: "That's me."

She was down by the railing now. Her heart was pounding terribly. God! was bravery as cruel as this? She held the yellow box out in front of her as though this were her first duty. Someone laid a hand on her. She heard her own voice, "I am coming, Karl." She saw him turn around. She saw the judge's astonished eyes. The clerks paused, the stenographer, without raising his head, waited for the next remark.

Now, now she must be brave. She was going to show Karl and all the world what she was made of—the stuff—what was it—iron—oh, yes, she was made of iron. Everything went black. She began again: "I—your Honor—I." She shook her head, laughed a little and turned abruptly, holding the box. "I can't," she said, and slid to her knees.

She heard the noise subsiding, the fluttering of paper cease. The footsteps no longer moved around her. She heard only the clock striking, but she could not move. Perhaps she was dying.

She came to. Several men were plying her with water. The court attendant was back at his place. She heard the people walking again. She got to her feet.

"How do you feel now?" someone asked her, and someone else said softly: "Poor girl, was he your sweetheart or a brother?"

Varra opened her mouth. "Did—did he get off?" They seemed afraid to tell her something, and she demanded sharply in that voice she used to the children: "Come, come! Tell me."

"No. The little one with black, curly hair got—got several years."

"But," someone else chimed in, thinking it might comfort her, "the other one's case, Monk, has been suspended for a further hearing. He made a very good plea for himself—lively, rather impudent, but he made some laugh. That always helps."

Varra turned slowly to the steps and stood there staring out into the day. She was not thinking about Monk nor about Karl. She was thinking about herself. After all, she was a coward. She could kill spiders and hold hot frying pans and save birds, but she was nothing more, a small town brave—a woman without real courage, something to despise, something to hate. God, how she hated herself—how she hated those people who had begun this defeat, those people who had started it all by praising her—oh, she was horrible.

She was hungry and turned in at one of the dirty coffee stalls. She looked in the mirror—yes, she thought herself still beautiful, but now that was all.

She knew that Karl was innocent—she had seen it in his eyes. And she knew that Monk was all that was low and base and mean. She felt that he had drawn Karl into this to save his own skin. What an ugly beast he was, how red the tips of his ears had been that moment in court when she had looked at him.

She began to justify herself. Could she have confessed to something she had not done to save Karl, who wasn't guilty? No, a thousand times no. Why? Because it would have placed her below him. It would have made her something vicious and criminal. She would have allied herself to save him (it's true) with all the dirt and filth that was in that corrupt body of Monk. How could she have done this? Would he still have loved her? Perhaps the sacrifice would have been too splendid, and besides he would have known that she wasn't really guilty. Perhaps, too, he would have denied her, refused her sacrifice. Then, what a beautiful thing it would have been. Perhaps he would have gotten off altogether and she also. How wonderful that would have been! And then he would have said to her again, "I love you because you are brave more than for anything else."

And now he had got several years, and Monk was as yet unsentenced.

When she reached home, she trembled, as though the street must already know her for what she was. She crept to her room, fearing that she would waken the family, and opened the door carefully, hardly daring to breathe. She undressed slowly, standing in the middle of the room. She got into bed as she had never gotten into it since she was a child, furtively, with a crouching movement, and drew the sheets over her throat.

She lay there, staring into the darkness—yes, that was it, that was the reason that she had failed, because she could not make herself seem so low, so mean, so petty before Karl, who was really good and clean and strong.

But what hurt most was her lost pride in herself; this was terrible. All through the night she kept saying to herself, "What must I do now?"

She got up again, lighting a candle. Was she still beautiful? People had called her ugly—she grinned at herself in the mirror. No, she was really ugly. She blew the light out, then lit it again. "How can I tell if I am ugly or handsome if I make faces?" She looked. She saw her face, a rigid, set, white thing shining out of the glass at her. No, she was not so bad.

She went back to the cot and sat on it, her bare feet touching the floor. Was there anything that she could do yet? She decided that she was not really good looking at all, and now she was not even brave.

She could not cry. She said these things to herself, half aloud; still, they did not make her wince—neither beautiful nor brave—ugly, a coward. Yet she loved Karl—she hated Monk. She was more like Monk after all—quite a lot like Monk.

She fell asleep.

The next afternoon when Monk's case came up, a woman holding a yellow box walked briskly into the court and down the aisle. The attendant went after her. This time he did not like something in her step.

She spoke in a loud, resolute, almost coarse voice, directly at the judge, paying no attention whatsoever to Monk.

And this time she went through with it.

When, with extreme reluctance, Monk was released, she did not even look at him. Instead, she smiled and asked for a mirror. People moved aside to let the slimy, ugly body of Monk pass, but Varra was paying no attention to them. She put down the pocket glass and said hurriedly, softly, "No, I am really quite ugly."

She had forgotten Karl, she had forgotten Monk. She looked at the black curtains with their heavy tassels.

THE DIARY OF A DANGEROUS CHILD

WHICH SHOULD BE of Interest to All Those Who Want to Know
How Women Get the Way They Are

SEPTEMBER first:

Today I am fourteen; time flies; women must grow old.

Today I have done my hair in a different way and asked myself a
question: "What shall be my destiny?"

Because today I have placed my childhood behind me, and have
faced the realities.

My uncle from Glasgow, with the square whiskers and the dull
voice is bringing pheasants for my mother. I shall sit in silence during the meal and think. Perhaps someone, sensitive to growth, will
ask in a tense voice, "What makes you look thoughtful, Olga?"

If this should be the case, I shall tell.

Yes, I shall break the silence.

For sooner or later they must know that I am become furtive.

By this I mean that I am debating with myself whether I shall
place myself in some good man's hands and become a mother, or
if I shall become wanton and go out in the world and make a place
for myself.

Somehow I think I shall became a wanton.

It is more to my taste. At least I think it is.

I have tried to curb this inner knowledge by fighting down that
bright look in my eyes as I stand before the mirror, but not ten
minutes later I have been cutting into lemons for my freckles.

"Ah woman, thy name, etc."—

SEPTEMBER third:

I could not write in my diary yesterday, my hands trembled and I started at every little thing. I think this shows that I am going to be anaemic just as soon as I'm old enough to afford it.

This is a good thing; I shall get what I want. Yes, I am glad that I tremble early. Perhaps I am getting introspective. One must not look inward too much, while the inside is yet tender. I do not wish to frighten myself until I can stand it.

I shall think more about this tonight when mother puts the light out and I can eat a cream slowly. Some of my best thoughts have come to me this way.

Ah! What ideas have I not had eating creams slowly, luxuriously.

September tenth:

Many days have passed; I have written nothing. Can it be that I have changed? I will hold this thought solitary for a day.

September eleventh:

Yes, I have changed. I found that I owed it to the family.

I will explain myself. Father is a lawyer; mother is in society.

Imagine how it might look to the outer world if I should go around looking as if I held a secret.

If the human eye were to fall upon this page, I might be so easily misunderstood.

What shame I might bring down upon my father's head—on my mother's too; if you want to take the whole matter in a large sweeping way—just by my tendency to precocity.

I should be an idiot for their sakes.

I will be!

October fourth:

I have succeeded. No one guesses that my mind teems. No one suspects that I have come into my own, as they say.

But I have. I came into it this afternoon when the diplomat from Brazil called.

My childhood is but a memory.

His name is Don Pasos Dilemma. He has great intelligence in one eye; the other is preoccupied with a monocle. He has comfortable spaces between his front teeth, and he talks in a soft drawl that makes one want to wear satin dresses.

He is courting my sister.

My sister is an extremely ordinary girl, older than I, it is true, but her spirit has no access to those things that I almost stumble over. She is not bad looking, but it is a vulgar beauty compared to mine.

There is something timeless about me, whereas my sister is utterly ephemeral.

I was sitting behind the victrola when he came in. I was reading Three Lives. Of course, he did not see me.

Alas for him, poor fellow!

My sister was there too; she kept walking up and down in the smallest sort of space, twisting her fan. He must have kissed her because she said, "Oh," and then he must have kissed her more intensely, because she said, "Oh," again, and drew her breath in, and in a moment she said softly, "You are a dangerous man!"

With that I sprang up and said in a loud and firm voice: "Hurrah, I love danger!"

But nobody understood me.

I am to be put to bed on bread and milk.

Never mind, my room in which I sleep overlooks the garden.

OCTOBER seventh:

I have been too excited to make any entry in my diary for a few days. Everything has been going splendidly.

I have succeeded in becoming subterranean. I have done something delightfully underhand. I bribed the butler to give a note to Don Pasos Dilemma, and I've frightened the groom into placing at my disposal a saddled horse. And I have a silver handled whip under my bed.

God help all men!

This is what I intend to do. I am going to meet Don Pasos Dilemma at midnight at the end of the arbour, and give him a whipping. For two reasons: one, because he deserves it, second, because it is Russian. After this I shall wash my hands of him, but the psychology of the family will have been raised one whole tone.

I'm sure of this.

Yes, at the full of the moon, Don Pasos Dilemma will be expecting me. His evil mind has already pictured me falling into his arms, a melting bit of tender and green youth.

Instead he will have a virago on his hands! How that word makes me shiver. There's only one other word that affects me as strongly—Vixen! These are my words!

Oh to be a virago at fourteen! What other woman has accomplished it? No woman.

OCTOBER eighth:

Last night arrived. But let me tell it as it happened.

The moon rose at a very early hour and hung, a great cycle in the heavens. Its light fell upon the laburnum bushes and lemon trees and gave me a sense of ice up and down my spine. I thought thoughts of Duse and how she had suffered on balconies a good deal; at least I gathered that she did from most of her pictures.

I too stood on the balcony and suffered sideface. The silver light glided over the smooth balustrade and swam in the pool of gold fishes.

In one hand I held the silver mounted whip. On my head was a modish, glazed riding hat with a single loose feather, falling sideways.

I could hear the tiny enamel clock on my ivory mantle ticking away the minutes. I began striking the welt of my riding boot softly. A high-strung woman must remember her duties to the malicious. I bit my under lip and thought of what I had yet to do. I leaned over the balcony and looked into the garden. There stood the stable boy in his red flannel shirt and beside him the fiery mare.

I tried to become agitated, my bosom refused to heave. Perhaps I am too young.

I SHALL leap from the balcony onto the horse's back. I whistled to the boy, he looked up, nodding. In a moment the mare was beneath my window. I looked at my wrist watch, it lacked two minutes to twelve. I jumped.

I must have miscalcuated the shortness of the distance, or the horse must have moved. I landed in the stable boy's arms.

Oh well, from stable boy to prince, such has been the route of all fascinating women. I struck my heels into the horse's side and was gone like the wind.

I can feel it yet,—the night air on my cheeks, the straining of the great beast's muscles, the smell of autumn, the gloom, the silence. My own transcendent nature—I was coming to the man I hated—hated with a household hate. He who had kissed my sister, he who had never given me a second thought until this evening, and yet who was now all eagerness,—yes counting the minutes with thick, wicked, middle-aged poundings of a Southern heart.

When one is standing between life and death (any moment might have been my last), they say one reviews one's whole childhood. One's mind is said to go back over every little detail.

Anyway mine went back. The distance being so short it went back and forth.

I thought of the many happy hours I had spent with my youngest sister putting spiders down her back, pulling her hair, and making her eat my crusts. I thought of the hours I had lain in the dust beneath the sofa reading Petronius and Rousseau and Glyn. I thought of my father, a great, grim fellow standing six feet two in his socks, but mostly sitting in the Morris chair. Then I remembered the day I was fourteen, only a little over a month ago.

How old one becomes, and how suddenly!

I grew old on horseback, between twelve and twelve one. I drew rein on the full four strokes of my horse's hoofs; I raised my silver mounted whip. I threw back my head. A laugh rang out in the stillness of midnight. It was my laugh, high, drenched with the scorn of life and love and men. It was a good laugh. I brought the whip down—

Octop' twenty-seventh:

I have changed my mind.

Yes, I have quite changed my mind. I am neither going to give myself into the hands of some good man, and become a mother, nor am I going to go out into the world and become a wanton. I am going to run away and become a boy.

For this Spaniard, this Brazilian, this Don Pasos Dilemma scorned my challenge, the fine haughty challenge of a girl of youth and vigor, he scorned it, and cringing behind my mother, as it were, left me to face disillusion and chagrin at a late hour at night, when no nice girl should be out, much less facing anything.

For as you may have guessed, it was not Don Pasos who rode to meet me, it was my mother, wearing his long Spanish cloak.

November third:

In another year I shall be fifteen, a woman must grow young again. I have cut off my hair and I am asking myself nothing. Absolutely nothing.

Poetry

THE DREAMER

The night comes down, in ever-darkening shapes that seem—
To grope, with eerie fingers for the window—then—
To rest, to sleep, enfolding me, as in a dream.
   Faith—might I waken!

And drips the rain with seeming sad, insistent beat.
Shivering across the pane, drooping tear-wise,
And softly patters by, like little fearing feet.
   Faith—'tis weather!

The feathery ash is fluttered: there upon the pane,—
The dying fire casts a flickering ghostly beam,—
Then closes in the night and gently falling rain.
   Faith—what darkness!

CALL OF THE NIGHT

Dark, and the wind-blurred pines.
   With a glimmer of light between.
Then I, entombed for an hourless night
   With the world of things unseen.

Mist, the dust of flowers,
   Leagues, heavy with promise of snow,
And a beckoning road 'twixt vale and hill.
   With the lure that all must know.

A light, my window's gleam,
   Soft, flaring its squares of red—
I lose the ache of the wilderness
   And long for the fire instead.

You too know, old fellow?
   Then, lift up your head and bark.
It's just the call of the lonesome place,
   The winds and the housing dark.

JUST LATELY DRUMMER BOY

His face is set with parapet
    Of tears that come too soon.
He has no drum, and so he plays
    Upon a pallid moon.
There is no music in his heart
    Yet he makes a little tune.

The soldiers walk, the soldiers stalk
    Like terrible gray wheat.
And as they walk they make no sound,
    They move on phantom feet.
Incomplete their vestments are
    Their mission incomplete.

And so they pass, dim in the grass
    Outcome of shot and shell.
He has no music in his heart
    And yet he plays quite well.
Perhaps his music-master is
    Just lately—Israel.

SOLITUDE

I seek no solitude but this—
    This one within my little room—
Four candles set apart to watch
    With wistful eyes the coming gloom.

And this, the shrouded mantelpiece
    And sober gap of fireside-place;
And this, the darkened wonder of
    A framed picture of a face.

This is my perfect solitude
    Within my conquering abode,
The goal of haunting memories
    That walk beside a chartless road

THE PERSONAL GOD

Creeds of a kind we've always had
To crouch by our dim fireside.
And here some gossiping wench arose
And the worth of some good name died;
Yea, the whole stale world went rocking
To the sting of her poisoned heels,
As a sky-car mangles the stars
For lack of the guiding wheels.
Though all of us sin most fully
When hushed in our neighborly sweats,
Yet sometimes a man goes empty
For the urge of things, and forgets.
We stick to the same old pattern,
All daubed and kissed and marred,
But I'll use my own gray plaster
And I'll build me a personal God.
I'll breathe out his flaccid belly,
I'll cup out his sightless eyes,
I'll sob in the labor bending,
As I handle his plastic thighs.
And he shall be rash of judgment,
And slow in the use of the rod.
My God shall giggle in spite of himself,
In the way of a personal God.
He shall heed no other's message;
He shall follow no dusty path;
He'll believe in no written pity;
Nor yet in a written wrath;

He'll breed no circle of platters
Nor take root in your yearly fees;
He'll ask no patient toll of tears
Nor the terrible toll of the knees.
So, when all of you flock to your fancy,
The God that is always the same,
My God shall halt and be human
And his judgment shall halt and be lame.
Yea, the devil came down your pass,
Blown in on the strength of the breeze,
And because your Gods were duplicates
He shattered you on his knees.
I'll work my clay as I find it,
All hushed as it lies in the sod,
And he shall be built for better or worse
In the way of a Personal God.

THIS MUCH AND MORE

If my lover were a comet
    Hung in air,
I would braid my leaping body
    In his hair.

Yea, if they buried him ten leagues
    Beneath the loam,
My fingers they would learn to dig
    And I'd plunge home!

DEATH

Down the dusty highway, on the broken road,
  With curls as thin as smoke is hovering round his head,
Came the slow procession with its dreaming load:
  The man who stopped his living that he might be dead.

On the sodden plank-bridge, musing through the town,
  Thus, with hands before him, crossed like girls' who pray,
So the vivid corpse came, with his head bent down,
  In the chill of morning and through the common day.

Straight his lips, *sans* laughter, all the pain left in,
  Quiet as a chancel that breathes a morning prayer;
So the stately body, with its rigid chin
  And its startled, leaping-high, thin, damp curls of hair.

Thus does one consider, death and man debate,
  Some must leave to-morrow, but some must know to-day;
And some approach too early, but most approach too late,
  When the tang of random youth has dropped into decay.

Heavy feet, like women's hands pregnant with vast prayer,
  All his muted splendor caught upon Death's loom,
With his throat fast fettered to the branches of his hair,
  But with soul tobogganing upon the sled of doom.

Through the dark'ning city to a narrow space,
  With a song between his teeth, silence in control,
With a little humor clenched within his face
  And a little wonder wedged within his soul.

IN CONCLUSION

Not every pipe is builded for our lays,
   Some hour the echo of our feet will flee,
   For, all unenvied, high eternity
Is deep with those who leave eternal ways.

No hate, no love, and no parental prayer
   Lives in the young; old wines they do not hold,
   And hate and love are outlived by the old—
Too near to death for passion and despair.

And we who live our time alway too fast,
   Whose lips beneath the kiss fall into dust,
   Will feel on the blade of Time untimely rust,
So all of us outlive our hearts at last.

Yet I who loved, and you who loved, and all
   Who rose most steeply and were not above
   Great human pity and inhuman love,
Will not be found ignoble when we fall.

DUST

The Nation falls. And still the Hosts arise
   To walk above this hemisphere of pain,
Built by the voice of man. Indebted to those eyes
That bled the mind's deep blood of old surprise
That nothing lives, and nothing ever dies.

      ★ ★ ★

As once, this road we walk each hour above
   Was every hour prostrate before the Lord,
The leveled prayer of some too human flame—
   An Idol dropped to dust while still adored.

And so it is for every temple praised
   Some whispered penance to the dust is flung
And there to cleave, until some wo shall stir
   The cloistered ashes of that anguished tongue.

And I, who in mine own grave am a guest,
   Am stranger in myself as absolute.
   I banquet at myself in high dispute
And to myself pledge wines still unaddressed.

So all who have been flung up from the Pangs,
   And, by some Hand retossed before the fruit
Will once again be found beneath that flower
   Within the clenched fingers of its root.

And I—I, too, am falling to that height
   One with the Kneeling, emptied of their breath
For you who walk above, to call it Dust—
   For us below, the Miracle of Death.

BIRTH

Fore-loved, fore-crowned, and fore-betrayed,
      And thrice our quality been weighed,
  And thrice our hearts been spit with steel
  To prove us worthier to feel
Both love and hate creep through that blade,
      The wings of doom press tip to tip,
And all dead hands like bricks are laid
  And reach like mansions to the sky—
      The parting, weeping lip to lip,
  That all things born must alway die.
And that the seed of Nothing lies
  Yet here within this envied Much—
  So we are forecast, and of such
The child's first sobbing prophesies.

THE YELLOW JAR

White butterflies are creeping near
　　This yellow jar where rose-leaves lie,
Like simple nuns in gowns of fear,
　　Like humor and like tragedy.

And down they steal with throbbing wing
　　Across the pool of shadows, where
That other bowl of dust is king
　　With blossoms past, with tear, with prayer.

One was the rose you brought, and one
　　Was you. The symbol lied—it seemed
You were the summit of the sun;
　　Now you are less than that you dreamed.

In life we loved you, and in death
　　There is devotion for you, too;
Only the witless human breath
　　Is mourning for the death in you.

Yet what of you, I wonder, stands
　　Without the stillness of the room,
Beyond the reach of rising hands,
　　Still smiling at this china tomb!

White butterflies are creeping past
　　The jar of death, the yellow jar;
For butterflies are not the last
　　To sense things are not as they are!

THE LAST TOAST

My tears are falling one by one
Upon the silence of this bed;
Like rain they crown his quiet head,
Like moons they slip within his hair;
They came like wine and passed like prayer
Into the goblets of the dead.

TO AN IDOL

It sat with folded hands and grinned
    Upon our sky.
Each ocher lock that streaked its head
    Was curled and dry.
A little dust of aged despair
    Was in each eye.

Both somber wooden breasts seemed weighed
    With heavy tears,
Dropped and forgotten long ago
    In other years,
But waiting still to fall like fate
    Upon the ears.

Beneath its girdle and its chains
    Each carved foot stood;
Incapable of pangs or pains,
    Or sweats of blood.
Conceived in superstition
    And doomed in wood.

And yet behind abysmal leer
    And faulty frown,
Throbbing faintly out of space
    That shadows drown—
We hear God's grim machinery
    Run down.

SHADOWS

A little trellis stood beside my head,
And all the tiny fruitage of its vine
Fashioned a shadowy cover to my bed,
And I was madly drunk on shadow wine!

A lily bell hung sidewise, leaning down,
And gowned me in a robe so light and long;
And so I dreamed, and drank, and slept, and heard
The lily's song.

Lo, for a house, the shadow of the moon;
For golden money, all the daisy rings;
And for my love, the meadow at my side—
Thus tramps are kings!

LOVE SONG

I am the woman—it is I—
Through all my pain I suffer peace;
Through all my peace I suffer pain;
This insufficient agony—
This stress of wo I cannot feel—
These knees that cannot bend to kneel—
A corpse that flames and cannot die—
A candle with the wick torn through—
These are the things from which I grew
Into the woman whom you hate—
She whom you loved before you knew—
Loved, loved so much before you knew.

All I cannot weep—in tears,
All I cannot pray—in prayers;
For it is so the wild world moves,
And it is so that Tame Man loves.
It is for this books fall to ruin;
For this great houses mold and fall;
For this the infant gown, the pall;
For this the veil that eyes weep through;
For this the birds go stumbling down
Into the cycled ages where
Their squandered plumage rends the air.
For this each living thing that dies
Shakes loose a soul that will arise
Like ivory against black space—
A quiet thing, but with a face

Wherein a weeping mouth is built—
A little wound where grief is spilt.

I am the woman—even so—
Through the years I have not swerved,
Through the years I've altered not.
What changes have I yet to know?
Through what gardens must I crawl?
How many roses yet must fall?
How many flowers yet must blow?
How many blossoms yet must rot?
How many thorns must I yet bear
Within the clenched fists of despair?
To be again she whom you loved—
Loved you so much, so much did care—
Loved, loved so much, so much did care!

LINES TO A LADY

Lay her under the rusty grass,
  With her two eyes heavy and blind and done;
Her two hands crossed beneath her breast
  One on one.

Lay her out in the paling eve,
  With its sudden tears and white birch-trees;
And let her passing seem to be
  One with these.

Close her out of this hour of grief,
  And casting the earth on her, like a breath,
Sew her tenderly, that she may
  Reap her death!

And close her eyes, close, close her lips,
  For still, too still is her smitten tongue;
Her hour's over, her breath has passed,
  And her song is sung.

Lay her under the wild red grass
  In the fields death-tossed and bowed with rain;
And let her silence seem to move
  Within the grain.

THE LAMENT OF WOMEN

Ah My God!

Ah my God, what is it that we love!
This flesh laid on us like a wrinkled glove?
Bones caught in haste from out some lustful bed,
And for momentum, this a devil's shove.

What is it that hurriedly we kiss,
This mouth that seeks our own, or still more this
Small sorry eye within the cheated head,
As if it mourned the something that we miss.

This pale, this over eager listening ear
The wretched mouth its soft lament to hear,
To mark the noiseless and the anguished fall
Of still one other warm misshapen tear.

Short arms, and bruised feet long set apart
To walk with us forever from the start.
Ah God, is this the reason that we love—
Because such things are death blows to the heart?

TO THE HANDS OF A BELOVED

His hands, I love to think, have left some trace
On some white wall or dusty balustrade.
Good, eager hands, cast outward for a space
And touching things a little ere they fade
And fall and are with death anointed and dismayed.

I like to think that some day as I pass
This tall and somber mirror I shall win
The touch of his quick fingers from the glass
When, searching in his face for what had been,
He paused here utterly confounded, looking in.

On some object, unnoticed, cast aside,
Some hour he'll strike with careless palm outspread,
And there'll remain of him, though he had died,
A memory that shall lift him from the dead;
And weeping between my hands, I shall be comforted.

TO ONE IN FAVOUR

When the throne stands empty, and the king goes down,
   Down into the darkness by your high white tent,
And shall sheath his gray sword, lay aside his crown;
   Then, O tall white woman, shall you be content?

Shall you be contented, lying on his knee,
   Murmuring face downward, lips within his palm?
Then shall you remember, thus you once kissed me,
   Only wilder, madder, closer in my arm?

When he shall release you, turn his eyes to sleep;
   Will you lift a little, looking in his face,
And recall out parting, for a moment weep
   Down upon his doublet, tarnishing the lace?

And when up the sun rides, and the daylight comes,
   Loud with sudden sparrows, and their latest talk,
Will you take his face so, in your two long thumbs
   Kiss his mouth for kindness, then rise up and walk?

TO A BIRD

Up from some leafy cover hot with June
  And odorous with spicy mysteries
  Of herbs unknown, a red bird dipping flies,
Whistling a little sadly, out of tune,
    Under a slow moon.

Lifts and turns, and, like blots on a wall,
  Leaves fleeting shadows in its drowsy flight;
  The earth beneath, and all above the night,
And stealing out between the last leaf's fall
    A new bird's call.

Singing its way into the South once more,
  No more returning; and the dropping leaves
  The branches strip like arms thrust out of sleeves—
And though the wind doth through the whole world roar
    A feather only stirs upon its floor.

TO THE DEAD FAVOURITE
OF LIU CH'E

The sound of rustling silk is stilled,
With solemn dust the court is filled,
No footfalls echo on the floor;
A thousand leaves stop up her door,
Her little golden drink is spilled.

Her painted fan no more shall rise
Before her black barbaric eyes—
The scattered tea goes with the leaves.
And simply crossed her yellow sleeves;
And every day a sunset dies.

Her birds no longer coo and call,
The cherry blossoms fade and fall,
Nor ever does her shadow stir
But stares forever back at her,
And through her runs no sound at all.

And bending low, my falling tears
Drop fast against her little ears,
And yet no sound comes back, and I
Who used to play her tenderly
Have touched her not a thousand years.

I'D HAVE YOU THINK OF ME

As one who, leaning on the wall, once drew
Thick blossoms down, and harkened to the hum
Of heavy bees slow rounding the wet plum,
And heard across the fields the patient coo
Of restless birds bewildered with the dew.

As one whose thoughts were mad in painful May,
With melancholy eyes turned toward her love,
And toward the troubled earth whereunder throve
The chilly rye and coming hawthorn spray—
With one lean, pacing hound, for company.

FROM FIFTH AVENUE UP

Someday beneath some hard
Capricious star—
Spreading its light a little
Over far,
We'll know you for the woman
That you are.

For though one took you, hurled you
Out of space,
With your legs half strangled
In your lace,
You'd lip the world to madness
On your face.

We'd see your body in the grass
With cool pale eyes.
We'd strain to touch those lang'rous
Length of thighs;
And hear your short sharp modern
Babylonic cries.

It wouldn't go. We'd feel you
Coil in fear
Leaning across the fertile
Fields to leer
As you urged some bitter secret
Through the ear.

We see your arms grow humid
In the heat;
We see your damp chemise lie
Pulsing in the beat
Of the over-hearts left oozing
At your feet.

See you sagging down with bulging
Hair to sip,
The dappled damp from some vague
Under lip.
Your soft saliva, loosed
With orgy, drip.

Once we'd not have called this
Woman you—
When leaning above your mother's
Spleen you drew
Your mouth across her breast as
Trick musicians do.

Plunging grandly out to fall
Upon your face.
Naked–female–baby
In grimace.
With your belly bulging stately
Into space.

IN GENERAL

What altar cloth, what rag of worth
Unpriced?
What turn of card, with trick of game
Undiced?
And you we valued still a little
More than Christ.

FROM THIRD AVENUE ON

And now she walks on out turned feet
Beside the litter in the street
Or rolls beneath a dirty sheet
      Within the town.
She does not stir to doff her dress,
She does not kneel low to confess,
A little conscience, no distress
      And settles down.

Ah God! She settles down we say;
It means her powers slip away
It means she draws back day by day
      From good or bad.
And so she looks upon the floor
Or listens at an open door
Or lies her down, upturned to snore
      Both loud and sad.

Or sits beside the chinaware
Sits mouthing meekly in a chair,
With over-curled, hard waving hair
      Above her eyes.
Or grins too vacant into space—
A vacant space is in her face—
Where nothing came to take the place
      Of high hard cries.

Or yet we hear her on the stairs
With some few elements of prayers,
Until she breaks it off and swears
    A loved bad word.
Somewhere beneath her buried curse,
A corpse lies bounding in a hearse;
And friends and relatives disperse,
      And are not stirred.

Those living dead up in their rooms
Must note how partial are the tombs,
That take men back into the wombs
    While theirs must fast.
And those who have their blooms in jars
No longer stare into the stars,
Instead, they watch the dinky cars—
      And live aghast.

SEEN FROM THE 'L'

So she stands—nude—stretching dully
Two amber combs loll through her hair
A vague molested carpet pitches
Down the dusty length of stair.
She does not see, she does not care
       It's always there.

The frail mosaic on her window
Facing starkly towards the street
Is scribbled there by tipsy sparrows—
Etched there with their rocking feet.
Is fashioned too, by every beat
       Of shirt and sheet.

Still her clothing is less risky
Than her body in its prime,
They are chain-stitched and so is she
Chain-stitched to her soul for time.
Ravelling grandly into vice
Dropping crooked into rhyme.
Slipping through the stitch of virtue,
       Into crime.

Though her lips are vague and fancy
In her youth—
They bloom vivid and repulsive
As the truth.
Even vases in the making
       Are uncouth.

IN PARTICULAR

What loin-cloth, what rag of wrong
Unpriced?
What turn of body, what of lust
Undiced?
So we've worshipped you a little
More than Christ.

TWILIGHT OF THE ILLICIT

You, with your long blank udders
And your calms,
Your spotted linen and your
Slack'ning arms.
With satiated fingers dragging
At your palms.

Your knees set far apart like
Heavy spheres;
With discs upon your eyes like
Husks of tears;
And great ghastly loops of gold
Snared in your ears.

Your dying hair hand-beaten
'Round your head.
Lips, long lengthened by wise words
Unsaid.
And in your living all grimaces
Of the dead.

One sees you sitting in the sun
Asleep;
With the sweeter gifts you had
And didn't keep,
One grieves that the altars of
Your vice lie deep.

You, the twlight powder of
A fire-wet dawn;
You, the massive mother of
Illicit spawn;
While the others shrink in virtue
You have borne.

We'll see you staring in the sun
A few more years,
With discs upon your eyes like
Husks of tears;
And great ghastly loops of gold
Snared in your ears.

TO A CABARET DANCER

A thousand lights had smitten her
    Into this thing;
Life had taken her and given her
    One place to sing.

She came with laughter wide and calm;
    And splendid grace;
And looked between the lights and wine
    For one fine face.

And found life only passion wide
    'Twixt mouth and wine.
She ceased to search, and growing wise
    Became less fine.

Yet some wondrous thing within the mess
    Was held in check:—
Was missing as she groped and clung
    About his neck.

One master chord we couldn't sound
    For lost the keys,
Yet she hinted of it as she sang
    Between our knees.

We watched her come with subtle fire
    And learned feet,
Stumbling among the lustful drunk
    Yet somehow sweet

We saw the crimson leave her cheeks
    Flame in her eyes;
For when a woman lives in awful haste
    A woman dies.

The jests that lit out hours by night
    And made them gay,
Soiled a sweet and ignorant soul
    And fouled its play.

Barriers and heart both broken–dust
    Beneath her feet.
You've passed her forty times and sneered
    Out in the street.

A thousand jibes had driven her
    To this at last;
Till the ruined crimson of her lips
    Grew vague and vast.

Until her songless soul admits
    Time comes to kill:
You pay her price and wonder why
    You need her still.

SUICIDE

Corpse A
They brought her in, a shattered small
Cocoon,
With a little bruised body like
A startled moon;
And all the subtle symphonies of her
A twilight rune.

Corpse B
They gave her hurried shoves this way
And that.
Her body shock–abbreviated
As a city cat.
She lay out listlessly like some small mug
Of beer gone flat.